The Sunday Telegraph

GUIDE TO
LOOKING AFTER
YOUR PROPERTY

The Sunday Telegraph

GUIDE TO
LOOKING AFTER
YOUR PROPERTY

Everything you need to know about
maintaining your home

JEFF HOWELL

MACMILLAN

First published 2002 by Macmillan
an imprint of Pan Macmillan Ltd
Pan Macmillan, 20 New Wharf Road, London N1 9RR
Basingstoke and Oxford
Associated companies throughout the world
www.panmacmillan.com

In association with *The Sunday Telegraph*

ISBN 0 333 90788 4

A CIP catalogue record for this book is available from
the British Library.

Typeset by SetSystems Ltd, SaffronWalden, Essex
Printed and bound in Great Britain by
Mackays of Chatham plc, Chatham, Kent

Contents

Acknowledgements

Many building colleagues have helped me to answer these questions. My special thanks go to Tony Poole and George Bennett of Mercury Plumbing and Heating, Dave Simms of DSE Electrical, Jay Webb of Fenestration Associates, Steve Bradford, Mike O'Leary, Peter O'Shea and Eddie Bennett.

Thanks also to all the staff on *The Sunday Telegraph Review* who have helped make the Ask Jeff feature such a success, and to Jack Scott, former editor of *Building Engineer*, who encouraged me to start writing.

Introduction

Buying and maintaining a home is the greatest single item of expenditure in most peoples' lives, but the average person embarks upon home ownership with surprisingly little idea about how to look after their prize investment.

Until quite recently, most British people lived in rented accommodation, with repairs and maintenance being the responsibility of the landlord – either private or local authority. Those who did buy their own homes usually managed it only after first saving up for years with a building society, so when they did finally become homeowners, they had already rented for years, and had some idea of the dos and don'ts of property care.

But since the deregulation of the financial sector in the 1980s, it has become easier for anyone with an income to buy a home rather than find one to rent, and many people now buy houses and flats without ever having really thought about the responsibility this carries. And whilst the estate agents and mortgage lenders are keen to tell first-time buyers how much money they can borrow as a multiple of their earnings, they never seem to mention that an additional sum of between 1 and 5 per cent of the value will need to be spent every year to keep it in good order.

In an ideal world, homeowners would engage the professionals – chartered surveyors – to advise them, and to arrange and supervise building work. But most people are unwilling to pay the professional fees involved. Quite often this is because they are so unimpressed by the performance of surveyors during the first and only contact they have with them, which is during the home-buying process itself. The average surveyor doing a mortgage valuation, or home-buyer's report, gives a passable impression of someone who doesn't want to get the knees of his suit dirty, doesn't want to commit himself to saying anything about the property, and simply issues a list of things that should be looked at by other 'experts'.

Into this breach leap the companies and individuals offering 'free' surveys. Homeowners never seem to realize that this is nothing more than a crude marketing trick. And whilst people complain about the difficulty of finding a decent builder, there is never any shortage of advertisements for 'quick-fix' solutions for leaky roofs, draughty windows and damp walls. In fact, the first experience that most homeowners have of this end of the building industry is when their mortgage valuation survey report instructs them to invite estimates for 'treatment' from damp-proofing and timber treatment companies. In reality, rising damp only occurs in pre-1877 houses standing in swamps, most wood-worm holes date from before the Relief of Mafeking, and dry rot is cured by mending the gutters. But, given the green light by the surveyor's report, these companies are quick to find 'evidence' of rising damp, woodworm and dry rot, and to specify remedial chemical treatment available from them-selves.

There is a clear conflict of interests in having these so-called problems diagnosed and treated by the same com-panies, but the Royal Institution of Chartered Surveyors (RICS) will do nothing to stop its members from directing their unsuspecting clients down this route.

There are many other unnecessary, damaging or bogus building treatments and gadgets mis-sold to the public, ranging from foam roof undercoatings to external wall coverings. Many of them are sold on the promise of 'zero maintenance', by companies interested only in a quick profit. Some of these businesses are even 'phoenix' companies, who offer twenty-year guarantees for their useless products, and then liquidate every year to avoid responsibility for failed work, setting up again with slightly altered company names. Consumer protection legislation being practically non-existent in the UK, there is nothing at all illegal about any of this.

And even if you do know a trained, competent, conscientious builder, then always remember that all building problems are liable to be mis-diagnosed if you turn to the wrong tradesman. After all, a carpenter will usually seek a solution that involves timber; a plasterer will suggest plaster, and a decorator will want to cover it up and paint it.

A recurrent theme in readers' letters is, 'I have been told that my x, y or z needs replacing – what do you think?' The missing information in these questions is, told by *whom*? Because if it was by somebody who was trying to sell you the replacement, then the chances are that their opinion was not objective.

Of particular concern in this respect is the role of the privatized utilities, such as British Gas Services. Many people still refer to British Gas as the 'Gas Board', and assume that if the British Gas Three Star Service engineer tells them that their boiler needs replacing, then he is doing so out of a sense of public duty. But British Gas Services is now a private company, owned by the Centrica Corporation, who also own the Automobile Association and Goldfish Credit

Cards. British Gas Service engineers receive commission (which British Gas prefer to call 'team rewards') for persuading customers to buy new boilers and central heating systems, and for selling other chargeable services, such as a 'Powerflush'. So you should bear in mind that it is just possible the engineer's judgement might be swayed by this when he tells you that your boiler is beyond repair, and that you need to buy a new one.

The most common question that I get asked is, 'How can I find a decent builder?' But in many cases this is the wrong question. What the homeowner should really be asking is, 'What building work does my home need, and what is the best way of getting this done?' This book is for anybody seeking the answers to those questions. Over the past four years I have received over 4,000 readers' questions, and what follows is a selection of answers to the most common ones.

A Note on Measurements

The British construction industry has officially used the metric system of measurement since 1970. This puts it in line with engineering and farming, but at odds with estate agents and euro-sceptic politicians. The only comment I would make on this is that the metric system is not a fiendish plot by the European Union, but is also the official system in most Commonwealth countries and former Eastern Bloc countries, and much of the developing world. The metric system is an attempt to harmonise a world-wide system of measurement. Although it is not without its faults, it is simpler and less prone to error than the old imperial system. To avoid ambiguity, the British construction industry uses millimetres, rather than metres and centimetres, and on construction drawings you will often find that the comma after thousands, and the 'mm' after all measurements, is omitted. So a town house is 5500 wide, a door opening is 2100 high, and a kitchen worktop is 600 deep. The style used in this book is that where a reader's letter uses imperial measurements, these are left as written, and the metric equivalents are added in brackets. My answers are written using metric. Readers who feel a need to translate metric into imperial are advised to forget about complicated conversion formulae, and instead to compare the figures on either side of a steel tape measure. You'll soon get the hang of it. For easy reference, the nearest equivalents are:

                25mm =   1 inch
                50mm =   2 inches
                75mm =   3 inches
               100mm =   4 inches
               150mm =   6 inches
               300mm = 12 inches
               and 1 metre = 39 inches, or 3 feet 3 inches.

For weights, a kilogram is just over two pounds, and 50 kilograms is roughly a hundredweight. A metric tonne (1000 kilograms) is about the same as an imperial ton. For temperatures, I have been thinking in degrees Celsius (or Centigrade) for so long that I find Fahrenheit (which is not an English system, but a Prussian one) confusing. In Celsius, water freezes at 0 and boils at 100, 20 is a comfortable temperature indoors, 30 is too hot to go out in the sun without a hat, and 60 is the recommended British Standard temperature for hot water.

Who is Jeff Howell?

My first building site experience was during summer vacations from university, and I loved every minute of it. I graduated in 1975 with a degree in Nuclear Engineering and the Philosophy of Science which, naturally enough, made me fairly unemployable, so I just carried on with the building site work. I found I could do most things, but I realized that bricklaying was something that you really had to be taught how to do. So I wangled my way on to a bricklaying course at a government training centre, and then spent the next ten years, more or less, as a full-time brickie.

With my engineering and philosophy education, though, it soon became clear to me that a lot of what goes on in the construction industry is based more on witchcraft than science, and this has informed my observations and opinions throughout my building career.

In 1989 I was teaching part-time at a couple of building colleges in London, and I was in the right place at the right time when a lecturing job came up at South Bank Polytechnic. And when, shortly afterwards, the polytechnics were rebranded as universities, I was able to boast that I had gone from being a brickie to a university lecturer in two years. That's how CVs are written, isn't it? I taught Construction Technology and Building Science for eight years – mostly to undergraduate surveyors. There were always a few excellent students in each year – usually the ones who had experience of the building trades – but the majority only tagged along hoping to get the qualification. I decided to quit on the day when I organized a construction site visit and only three – out of a class of thirty – turned up. (It didn't count towards the degree, they explained.)

While I was lecturing, I wrote a few pieces about bricklaying and damp-proofing that got published in trade journals, and then in 1997 I got the chance to write a weekly column in the *Independent on Sunday*. Two years later the column moved to the *Sunday Telegraph*, and the 'Ask Jeff' readers' questions and answers section has made me aware of the many problems that householders have in getting building work done on their homes.

I have also 'done up' three homes of my own, so whilst I make every effort to defend builders from unwarranted criticism (there are plenty of cowboy customers out there as well), I am only too aware of the parlous state of the building industry, and how frustrating it can sometimes be finding a good tradesman, and getting him to turn up on time and finish the job.

BRICKWORK

Brick walls are one of the mainstays of building construction down the ages. The historical principle is simple. If you lived in a part of the world where there were a lot of trees (which included most of Britain until the sixteenth century) then you built your walls with wood. If there was no wood but you had access to broken stone, then you built your walls with stone. If you didn't have either of those, then it was probably because you lived on clay, as in most of Central and Southern England and the Low Countries. These areas have a history of building with raw earth, and many examples survive, such as the cob houses of the West Country and the clay lump buildings of East Anglia.

But it had been known since Greek and Roman times that if you fired the clay in a kiln then you got a more hard-wearing material. At first this was used only to make clay roof tiles, but as kiln techniques got more sophisticated it became possible to produce large quantities of burnt clay bricks. Following the Great Fire of 1666, the London Building Acts have always required all new buildings to have brick walls.

Brick construction reached its peak in the eighteenth and nineteenth centuries, and many of the surviving brick terraced houses that still make up around 50 per cent of our housing stock were built with a skill and attention to detail that we will never see again. The twentieth century saw the introduction of the cavity wall, first built with two leaves of brickwork connected by wrought-iron ties, and later with an inner leaf of various types of lightweight concrete blocks. These are referred to by lay-people as 'breeze blocks' but are actually made from aerated pulverized fuel ash (PFA). God knows how many banned toxic waste materials will be discovered in them in years to come.

The last twenty years has seen the introduction of insulation materials into the cavity. This has made the building of brick walls ever more difficult, and, coinciding with a drastic reduction in the availability of skilled bricklayers, means that modern brick houses are usually built very badly. So, whilst a Victorian brick-built house remains a sound investment, one built since the Second World War may be hosting many problems.

Older brick houses are often spoilt by having the surface of the mortar joints (the 'pointing') replaced with sand-and-cement. This is much harder than the original sand-and-lime mortar, and can cause many problems. If there is any movement in the brickwork then the new pointing will be unable to move with it, and this can result in cracking damage to the bricks; and because sand-and-cement is impermeable to moisture, the mortar will be unable to breathe, concentrating moisture evaporation in the bricks, which may then lose their faces through frost damage or salt crystallization. Damaging repointing is a classic example of misunderstanding the nature of traditional building materials. Our forebears understood that the pointing between the bricks was a sacrificial material, which served its purpose by being gradually worn away, and would be replaced every half century or so. But today, when surveyors or builders see weathered pointing, they see it as a defect, and

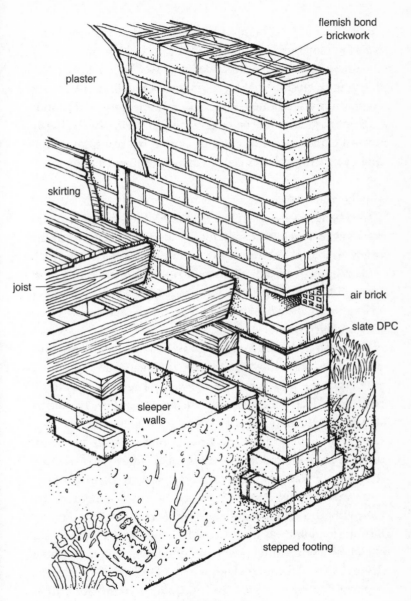

Solid brick wall

think it would be better to replace it with a more hard-wearing material.

Lime mortar is easy to make and use. The only problem is trying to find a bricklayer prepared to use it. There is a common myth amongst builders that lime-and-sand mortar will not harden unless cement is mixed into it. This is simply not true, and once you get a brickie to try using sand-and-lime, you will probably have a convert on your hands.

Cavity wall ties

I have bought a house built in 1984 and the surveyor's report recommended getting a specialist to check the condition of the cavity wall ties. The firm I got in drilled a hole in one wall, looked through an optical instrument, and announced that all the wall ties were corroded and needed replacing, at a cost of £6,000. I cannot understand how a relatively new house could need so much work.

Neither can I. Houses built with cavity walls around the turn of the century (with wrought-iron wall ties), and those built between 1964 and 1981, are those most at risk of wall-tie corrosion. The wall ties are galvanized mild-steel strips which hold the two leaves of the cavity wall together. In 1964 the British Standard for the zinc coating on mild-steel wall ties was lowered, but it was put up again after 1981 (after the first cases of wall-tie corrosion were discovered!). In any case, you cannot tell the state of wall ties by viewing them within the cavity through a boroscope; you need to expose them in the mortar joints of the brickwork – at least two on each elevation – one at high level and one lower down. Building Research Establishment Digest 401, 'Replacing Wall Ties', explains the correct procedure (available from CRC Publications see USEFUL CONTACTS, Construction literature).

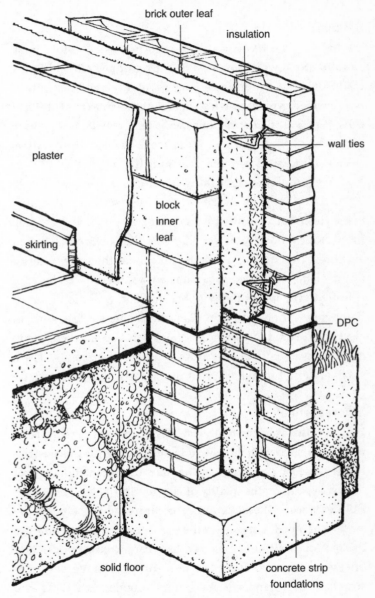

Cavity brick-and-block wall

Labels: brick outer leaf, insulation, wall ties, plaster, block inner leaf, skirting, DPC, solid floor, concrete strip foundations

Cleaning

We have a pre-1918 house with a red pressed Cheshire brick elevation from which we have recently stripped old and firmly established ivy. Unfortunately the newly exposed brickwork is now covered with thin white marks and remnants of the tendrils. We have tried numerous methods to remove them – soap and water, wire brush etc., all without success. How can we clean the brickwork without damaging it?

You have done the right thing in removing the ivy, as once it gets into the mortar joints it can cause serious damage to brickwork. But you must be as gentle as possible removing the residues, because if you damage the surface of a burnt clay brick (the 'fire skin'), then you expose the softer interior to the elements, and this can hasten weathering. So be very sparing in the use of the wire brush. Plain water is the least-damaging option, and you may have some success with an electric-powered pressure washer. If this fails then brick-cleaning acid is available from builders' merchants. Try a small area first to make sure it doesn't discolour the surface.

Efflorescence

Why is it that modern red house bricks appear to effloresce so much, compared with those used in older houses? Is this unsightliness caused by a change in the 'mix' during manufacture or does it depend on the quality of clay used?

Efflorescence – the appearance of fluffy white salts on the surface of a wall – indicates the passage of moisture through the materials. Builders used to take care to keep bricks and brickwork covered from the rain during storage and construction, but standards have now slipped, and what you are describing is probably the result of sloppy workmanship.

The efflorescence will wash off in time, and does not cause any long-term harm.

Our cottage has a cavity-walled extension built in 1976 with Celcon blocks. After about eighteen/twenty years the south-east-facing kitchen wall began to be affected by efflorescence and has been so ever since, despite periodical scraping off, sealing and repainting with emulsion. No other wall is affected. Can you recommend a remedy that will prevent this nuisance continually recurring?

Efflorescence indicates the passage of moisture through the wall – in your case towards the inner surface. If there are no obvious leaks from outside then the most likely source of the moisture will be condensation. Water vapour from cooking and washing activities in the kitchen could be condensing within the wall and then drawn to the surface where it evaporates, leaving the efflorescence. Permanent ventilation and the use of a cooker hood may help. For a more complete diagnosis of the problem try one of the specialist dampness surveyors mentioned (see USEFUL CONTACTS, Dampness and Timber Surveyors).

My bungalow is forty to fifty years old and I bought it in 1997. The first winter I noticed white patches on the brickwork under the windows. I had had cavity wall insulation put in, but the cavity insulation firm say it is nothing to do with that, and a damp-proofing firm say the damp-proof course is OK, and that the problem is only cosmetic. Do you have any suggestions?

If the efflorescence is only below the windows then it is probably caused by faulty window sills, which are failing to throw rainwater clear of the walls. The anti-capillary groove on the undersides of the sills may have been blocked with paint, and if you scrape them clean then the rain should drip off the edge, and not run back to wet the wall. The cavity insulation may have made things worse by making the brickwork colder, and interfering with the drying-out process.

Mortar: Sharp sand?

I have read your comments on the use of sharp sand in mortar. I have noticed the sharp sand in mortar in England and in the USA, but every time I ask a builder or brickie why, or when, they should use sharp sand in 'muck' they do not know the answer. As a retired engineer I find it incredible that no one (except you) seems to advocate the use of sharp sand, and no one seems to know why it was once used. Please tell me where to look for more information regarding the different types of cement, mortar or 'muck' which can be used. (Strength and elasticity etc.) The only builder who seemed clued in to the use of sharp, was a plasterer, who wanted a particular type of sharp to use when plastering/rendering a room. In metallurgy, there is lots of information regarding strength of materials which are stronger or weaker, depending on the shape of the crystalline structure of the molecules in the metal. I suspect that sharp is less likely to slip over its neighbours than soft, and thus is inherently 'stronger'.

I don't know of any particular written information on this subject to refer you to. It's just what I have picked up through experience. When working on old buildings I noticed that mortars made with the soft 'building' sands tended to shrink and crack away from the old mortar in the repair, so I started to try to match the sand with the original. It's quite easy to do, using a standard nest of sieves. What I believe likely is that following the Second World War there was a vast over-production of ordinary Portland cement, and so the manufacturers probably started to promote cement mortars in place of the traditional lime mortars. Cement is not as fatty as lime, and a mortar made with cement and sharp sand is difficult to work with, so builders started using soft sands with a high clay content, to make it more workable. In my experience this type of mortar does not perform well; even quite strong mixes will weather away in a few years if exposed to the elements, as in garden walls. Lime-and-sharp-sand mortars, on the other hand, just get stronger and stronger. I agree with you about the greater strength of sharp sands due to the slip planes. There is quite a lot of literature published regarding lime, but nobody seems interested in the sand, although there is a British Standard covering sand gradings for modern mixes. Engineers interested in masonry construction seem to be obsessed with bond strength, but my old bricklaying instructor always said the mortar was there to keep the bricks apart, not to stick them together!

Mortar for garden walls

I wonder if you are strictly correct in saying that hydrated lime and sand make a usable mortar. I had always understood that hydrated lime needed a touch of cement to set it off: it was only hydraulic lime that would work without cement. The mix we used for bedding stone was eight parts concrete sand, one-and-a-bit of hydrated lime and about one-quarter of a shovel of cement. The pointing could be done with a finer sand chosen to match any existing stone.

Hydrated lime works fine on its own, as long as it is fresh. I have been using it for mortars and plasters for ten years, and I rarely use cement. Slaked lime putty is the best, but fresh bagged hydrated lime is a good second choice, and a lot cheaper. The lime cures by reacting with CO_2 from the atmosphere. Adding cement can actually impede this process. Hydraulic lime is a different material, similar to cement; it cures by reaction with water.

Mortar: Lime or cement?

I live in a Victorian house with grounds surrounded by stone walls composed of dressed cobbles, and rough stone with mitred top stones. The walls need repairing and I have discussed with the wall man repairs using lime mortar (having noted articles by you on the use of lime mortar). In his opinion Portland cement would provide a better seal against the weather, especially when using mitred topping stones. What is the right answer?

Lime is the correct material. OPC (ordinary Portland cement) is too hard and will crack. You don't need a 'seal' against the weather; you need breathability to let the moisture escape. I don't suppose your man will believe me, though.

Lime mortar

Our house is $c.1861$, of soft brick with lime mortar and solid walls, which are rendered on the outside, finished with white masonry paint. Someone once told me that the mortar deteriorates and settles. This got me to thinking that the house might one day crack or crumble. Have I any cause to be concerned, or will the mortar be OK for a long time yet?

The Greeks and Romans used lime mortar, and some of their buildings are still looking good after thousands of years.

I'd be more worried about the masonry paint if I were you (see PAINTING AND DECORATING).

Frost damage

After a period of very wet weather followed by frost, some of the brickwork on my three-year-old house is flaking. This applies particularly to the bricks with smoother faces, those in brick-on-edge sills, and those near ground level, where the rain is splashing up off concrete paving. Is there some way of water-proofing the brickwork with a clear liquid during a warm dry spell to prevent this flaking in frost?

No. Whatever the manufacturers' claims, external water-proofing compounds are at best ineffective, and at worst can exacerbate the problem, by trapping water in the brickwork. The spalling you describe is really a design problem, because the bricks used clearly are not of suitable quality to cope with the exposure conditions. Badly damaged bricks should be cut out and replaced, and the brick-on-edge sills should be rebuilt using class 'B' semi-engineering bricks. Paving next to walls should always be at least 150mm (two brick courses) below damp-proof-course level, because of rain splash, and you may need to lower the paving if this is not the case.

Repointing

Our semi-detached bungalow is thirty-four years old. Three neighbours have had their brickwork repointed although there seemed to be nothing wrong with them. When is repointing needed, and should it be an all-over job or done in patches?

It seems unlikely that a 34-year-old property would need re-pointing, and your neighbours may have been victims of over-enthusiastic builders or surveyors, who often specify repointing in survey reports. Odd patches of brickwork may sometimes be exposed to extreme weather conditions or water leaks which erode the mortar, and these areas should be repointed, but under normal conditions a house should not need repointing for sixty to a hundred years. The pointing should be considered as a sacrificial medium which gradually erodes away, leaving the bricks intact, and over-enthusiastic repointing with strong mortars is responsible for a lot of damage.

Repointing: Old mortar mixes

I live in a barn conversion in south-east Cornwall built at least 160 years ago. It has solid 21in (530mm) random rubble walls. When it was converted ten years ago, the builder used 'ordinary' cement to repair some of the stonework which does not match the original mortar (which is a much lighter grey and appears more gritty). Do you know what mix of mortar was likely to have been used in the early nineteenth century so that I can try to match it when repointing?

The original mortar will have been made with lime, not cement, and the sand will have been a coarse local type, rather than the soft 'building' sand used in modern work. Matching your mix to the original will be a case of trial and error. Scrape out a handful and rub it between your fingers. You want to try to replicate the size of the sand grains and their distribution. With luck, you may find something close enough at a local builders' merchants; otherwise you could ask a local building college to let you borrow a nest of sieves and do a proper analysis, and then use the same sieves to reproduce the mix from a washed plastering sand. Try 4:1 sand and hydrated lime. Do a small area first and see what it looks like when it hardens. Obviously it will look cleaner and whiter than the old stuff, but it will weather-in in a few years, or you can darken it down with wood ash if you want.

Repointing: Making lime mortar

I wonder if you could tell us where to obtain lime – presumably quicklime – to make a proper lime mortar to repoint.

Lime-and-sand mortar can be made by using bagged hydrated lime, which is available from most builders' merchants. As long as it is fresh, and the mortar is mixed twenty-four hours before use, it gives good results. Use a washed coarse sharp sand rather than the finer 'building sand'. I would advise amateurs against slaking their own quicklime, as this can be a dangerous operation. Purists insist on using slaked lime putty, but this is expensive and in my experience is not essential. If you want to try it then ask your local authority building conservation officer for details of local suppliers, or send an SAE to The Building Limes Forum (see USEFUL CONTACTS, Plastering).

Repointing: Coloured mortar mix

I live in a late-Victorian mock-Tudor house, built largely with good quality Ruabon bricks. I need to do some repointing and want it to match the existing mortar for colour (it is darkish), and constitution. I spoke to an old brickie the other day, who told me that it was common in the past to mix crushed-up coke in the mix to give the colour. He said that the colours available now for colouring tend to fade with time. The mix he recommended was five parts sand, one cement, and one lime. What is your view?

I don't think you should use cement in your pointing mix. I

go for a 4:1 sharp sand–lime mix. The black colouring could be many things; wood ash was common. The carbon in ash or coke also has the effect of hardening the lime quickly. You'll have to experiment with small quantities to get a suitable colour match.

Repointing: Modern mortar

Most ready-mixed mortars sold in DIY stores dry to a grey colour. Most houses have beige mortar. Which mix (with or without cement) would match this colour? Would builders' merchants sell this mix in small amounts – of 10kg (or less) for instance?

The grey colour comes from a high proportion of cement, which is probably mixed with a washed sharp sand. This mix is intended for patch repairs to renders and floor screeds, and is not generally suitable for brickwork repairs or repointing. The colour of the 'beige' mortar used in most post-war housing comes from the impurities (mostly clay) in soft 'building' sand, which is used in a 6:1:1 sand–cement–lime mix. You are unlikely to be able to buy this ready-mixed from a builders' merchants, although you may be able to persuade a builder to give you a bucketful.

Spalled bricks

I have bought an old brick cottage. On one side of the house about a quarter of the outside bricks are spalled. I have been advised to render the house and paint it pink, which would fit into the surroundings. However, I do like the bricks. One alternative would be to render only the affected wall. What do you think?

Rendering and/or painting the outsides of old brick houses can create problems. It encloses the house in an impermeable coating, which can trap moisture within the wall. So many old country cottages have had this done to them, that surviving brick cottages are becoming increasingly rare, so yours is worth preserving. You should try to engage a bricklayer prepared to cut out and replace the spalled bricks, using lime mortar to match the original.

BUILDERS

Probably the most-asked readers' question is, How can I find a good builder? The answer is that there is no foolproof way. There is one professional body – The Chartered Institute of Building (CIOB) – that represents degree-level construction professionals who, mostly, work for reputable contractors. Unfortunately for the readers of this book, these contractors work mostly on large commercial and industrial developments, and are not interested in small domestic repair and maintenance work – even though this accounts for around 50 per cent of the total market. In the mid 1990s the CIOB did start a scheme, called the Chartered Building Company Scheme, to put householders in touch with small-to medium-sized construction companies, and they claim that this is still operating. But on the only occasion that I publicized this in the *Sunday Telegraph*, the people who answered the CIOB phones denied all knowledge of it. Try contacting them and see what they say (see USEFUL CONTACTS, Building Organizations).

From there on down we are talking about trade associations. The old adage is that trade associations exist to protect their members from the public, and I would not dissent from that. Trade associations in general may claim to check members' financial standing and professional repute, but this is often perfunctory and does not confer any legal protection upon verbal agreements entered into with its members. The best way to protect yourself against shoddy workmanship is to have a signed contract with your builder, and then you are both covered by civil law. There is a simple Joint Contracts Tribunal (JCT) document called 'Building contract for a homeowner/occupier' which can be bought from the Construction Confederation for £10.99 (and is also promoted by the National Federation of Builders – see below). But in my experience, most homeowners are too timid to suggest it to their builders, and most builders are too scared to sign it. Both sides need educating. If both client and builder became more accustomed to contractual agreements then the work would get done better, a lot faster, and builders would get paid on time.

The most influential trade association, which covers medium-sized construction companies, is the National Federation of Builders. They are keen to present their members as the reputable side of the domestic sector and they are probably right. Members offer customers a building insurance guarantee scheme (Benchmark Plan), for an extra payment, which means that most customers refuse it.

Successive governments have refused to implement a compulsory registration scheme for builders, and the latest attempt at voluntary registration, the Quality Mark, seems doomed to failure, since it asks reputable builders – who already have far more work than they can handle – to pay to join the scheme, whilst it does nothing to legislate against the cowboy operators.

How to find a good builder

We need a few simple repairs doing to our Victorian conversion flat – moving a radiator, putting up some shelves, plastering a ceiling, and extending the tiling around the bath. We have called seven separate builders, of whom only two came round to look at the work, and neither of them has ever called us back. How on earth can we find a decent builder to do this work?

There are no easy answers to this one. There are plenty of good builders around, but they are usually booked up for months, if not years, in advance and can afford to be choosy about which jobs they take on. Also, many good builders do not like the hassle of working in the domestic repair and maintenance sector (i.e. doing small jobs in peoples' houses), and prefer being employed by contractors to work on building sites.

Builders who do work in the domestic sector are there for a variety of reasons: they may prefer the relative peace and quiet away from the big sites, and the ability to choose their own hours, or they may really like the conservation aspect of restoring old houses; or it may be because they are complete cowboys who wouldn't last five minutes on a proper site, and only work for cash because they are signing on the dole, avoiding paying tax, or have been made bankrupt.

The usual advice is to use a builder recommended by friends or relatives. This may or may not work. It is likely to put you in touch with someone who is polite, turns up on time, and feeds the cat when you're away, but is absolutely no guarantee of their construction skills or knowledge.

Another suggestion is to use a builder who is a member of a trade association. This is no guarantee at all, as trade associations exist largely to protect their members from the public. The Federation of Master Builders, for example, whilst it claims to check applicants' accounts and credit worthiness, does not require any evidence of construction training or qualifications. The two major exceptions to this are CORGI (Council for Registered Gas Installers) and the NICEIC (National Inspection Council for Electrical Installation Contracting), which have rigorous checking and monitoring procedures and can initiate legal action against interlopers.

At present the best advice is to direct all your building work via a registered architect or surveyor. Get them to advise you on what needs doing, and ask them to find a building contractor and supervise the work for you. This should extend to drawing up a contract with the contractor, and handling the payments. There is no need for you to have anything to do with the builders at all, if you so wish. You will have to pay a professional fee for this service, but a good architect or surveyor will probably save you at least the amount of his or her fee, and maybe more (see USEFUL CONTACTS, Architects and Surveyors).

How to engage a builder

I've never had any building work done before so I don't know the routine involved. We've got a three-bed semi with a carport. We want the carport taken out and a two-storey extension added to the side of the house, making the kitchen bigger and adding a toilet and utility room downstairs and two further bedrooms upstairs. We have identified a local builder through recommendations. Seems like a nice bloke. He has gone ex-directory and doesn't advertise. Says he doesn't want to get too big and only takes on new customers to whom he's been recommended by word of mouth.

He came round twice. Once to see what we wanted and another time to measure up. He's provided a single page of typed estimate saying not much more than the external size of the extension ('2400mm × 8700mm comprising kitchen extension, utility area, cloakroom with shower and passageway on ground floor and two bedrooms on first floor'), that the price includes supply of plans and seeking planning approval, and allows for external rendering to match existing. No painting included in estimate. That's all it says. Estimate is £31,200 plus VAT.

Is this usual? No plan provided, no mention of windows or doors (location or quality), no mention of any extra radiators or light fittings. Nothing to say what kind of floor or ceiling finish. Are all these add-ons? I am very uneasy about commissioning any further work on such a flimsy estimate, but everybody speaks highly of the man and his work seems to be of a high standard.

How should I take things forward? Is there a standard form of contract that should be drawn up when employing builders? Also, do you know if it might be cheaper and more practical to extend the extension contract to include fitting double glazing throughout the house and having the kitchen fitted or are specialist firms better and cheaper? Grateful for any advice.

I would say that for a project of this size it would be unwise to engage a builder who you know only by word of mouth on an imprecise design-and-build contract (which is what you have described). Your builder may well be a totally trustworthy, trained, experienced etc. person/company – but it would still be as well to have an independent construction professional supervising operations and acting as your middleman (see USEFUL CONTACTS, Architects and Surveyors).

Cash job

I've recently had a lot of different building jobs done. Each time the materials were needed, the builder asked me to make out a cheque for the suppliers. When all the jobs were done, he asked if I would pay his bill (the labour) in cash. This is obviously to avoid tax, or he may even be bankrupt and can't put any money in his bank account. It doesn't bother me how I pay him, but could I be considered to be a party to him avoiding tax?

The Inland Revenue has recently tightened up the rules with regard to construction site work, and trade employers have to be careful to make due deductions or to collect exemption certificates from subcontractors. But as a private householder this is not your concern. Whether you pay by cash or cheque, it is up to your builder to declare his profits to the taxman, and nothing to do with you. However, you would be wise to get an invoice or receipt for work done, in case problems arise later. And the best thing is always to have a written contract with a builder before work starts. The JCT Building contract for a homeowner/occupier (see p. 17) costs £10.99 and carries the Crystal Mark of the Plain English Campaign (see USEFUL CONTACTS, Construction Literature).

Paying cash: A builder's story

I was warmed to read your comments about the folly of punters paying cash! This brings up the issue of 'cowboy clients' who, although one could never say that anyone deserved to get robbed, go as close to asking for it as anyone can. After all, if their builder is prepared to defraud the Inland Revenue and Customs and Excise by accepting a cash payment, then they surely won't think twice about defrauding the punter either!

I run a roofing company and we recently had a call from a punter with problems on a relatively new roof. We sent a written quotation explaining that the flashings to all the abutment walls need to be replaced and that eaves ventilation and ventilation tiles should be provided. The punter rang back and in the course of two or three calls, did his best to persuade us that the work could be carried out without scaffolding. We pointed out that both he and we had a legal responsibility to provide a safe working environment. We also pointed out that, if we didn't use a scaffold, the workmen would be concentrating more on self-preservation than on carrying out the work properly and it would also be impossible to properly check the work on completion. We stood our ground.

Then he called once more asking me 'if we would do it for cash' or whether we were going to take a high moral standpoint on this issue? We pointed out that we ran our business professionally and that we liked to do things properly. This included complying with our legal responsibilities with regard to VAT. We were now beginning to think that if this punter was prepared to try and defraud the Customs and Excise, would he exercise the same criminal intent when it came to settling our account? A week later we received a letter from him saying that he had employed another contractor. No doubt he has employed someone who he will pay cash, saving the VAT, and who is prepared to carry out the work without a scaffold – a cowboy! If it all goes wrong, who is to blame?

The government won't get rid of cowboys by forming registration schemes. The cowboys won't register. The legitimate companies will register and this will increase their overheads and costs as a result, making the attraction of cowboys even greater. Punters and the public as a whole need to be educated. Once it becomes socially unacceptable to pay cowboys cash, people will stop doing it; just as they stopped keeping slaves and drinking and driving.

I cannot add any more to this eloquent plea from a real professional.

Contracts

I am in the process of obtaining planning and building control permission to build an extension to the kitchen of my house. It's a single-storey extension of about 22m² total floor area – not a huge job. However, I do want to ensure that it is built to the correct standards, with a proper contract to protect myself against shoddy workmanship, poor materials, delays etc. I'm a civil engineer by profession so I know a little bit about the construction industry. I am not familiar though with standards, normal conditions of contract etc. for small building works of this nature.

You need the JCT Building contract for the homeowner/occupier. This was launched with a big publicity drive in late 1999, with the promise that it would soon be widely available in high street stationers and bookshops. This has not happened, but the contract is still available direct from Construction Industry Publications (see USEFUL CONTACTS, Construction Literature).

Professional supervision

I inherited my mother's property which has been standing empty for ten months. My initial plan was to modernize it and let it out. It is in a conservation area, has cracks inside, needs a new kitchen, bathroom, decorating, central heating – I don't know where to start. I contacted a builder I had used in the past and he came to see it, but I haven't heard from him since. I live over one hundred miles from the property and don't have time to visit it frequently. Where can I find a trustworthy builder who would be responsible for an empty property and who would work unsupervised? The value of the property does not justify an expensive architect.

There is a common misconception that architects' and

surveyors' fees are an expensive addition to the costs of repairing or altering a building. But if you are not in a position to specify and supervise building works yourself, then you may well end up paying builders for unnecessary or sub-standard work. A good local architect or surveyor will specify building works, employ contractors, and supervise the whole operation, and should be able to save you a sum well in excess of his fees, whatever the value of the property. If he doesn't, then you should ask for your money back (see USEFUL CONTACTS, Architects and Surveyors).

Trade associations

We have had three quotes for damp-proofing our 1920s terraced house. One for £550, one for £2,300, and one for £7,875. The last is from a member of the British Wood Preserving and Damp-proofing Association, and my husband thinks that he must know what he is talking about. But how can there be such a difference in the three prices?

In the first place, it is highly unlikely that your 1920s house needs damp-proofing. It will have been built with an integral damp-proof course, which will still be doing its job. All three damp-proofing companies will have used electrical moisture meter readings from the wall surfaces to 'diagnose' the existence of rising damp, but these meters are not meant to be used on walls; they are calibrated for use on timber, and will always give high readings on wallpaper and plaster, especially if there is any surface condensation present.

The British Wood Preserving and Damp-proofing Association is a trade association, not an officially sanctioned professional body. Its members like to boast that they are more highly trained than non-members, and use this to justify higher prices and more extensive works. But in my experience members of this association are just as likely as non-members to misdiagnose problems, and specify unnecessary treatment.

Insurance

I am about to have an extension built by a small-sized local building company. Should I tell my buildings insurer, and is there any insurance I should take out during the work for damage against the main house? Also is there an insurance that gives me legal protection should I encounter any difficulties?

Yes, you should give full details to your insurers. This is because the finished work will increase the rebuilding costs of the property, and you may find yourself under-insured in the event of making a claim. There is also the question of increased security risks while the building work is taking place (scaffolding, temporary window and door openings etc.) – your insurers are unlikely to raise your premiums for this, but again, there could be a problem if you made a claim and you hadn't told them. Damage to the main house whilst the extension is being built should be covered by your builder's public liability insurance, so make sure that he is adequately covered.

Regarding your relationship with your builder, you will be legally covered during the course of the work providing you have signed a suitable contract, and you can cover your-self against possible future defects by entering into a war-ranty scheme, which is usually available for around 1 per cent of the contract price.

Safe working platforms

I live in a three-storey Edwardian house of the type you see all over London. It is not particularly tall, yet I am told that 'the

regs' now forbid you to work on the roof unless scaffolding is erected. Can this really be true? Does it mean that you cannot hire someone to use a ladder to fix a tile? Surely houses will fall into disrepair as their owners, unwilling to pay vast sums of money for the simplest of jobs, fail to maintain their roofs?

No, none of this should be the case. Health and Safety Regulations require all reasonable steps to be taken to provide safe working platforms, but there are still occasions when it is convenient and safe to use a ladder. But in any case, scaffolding towers are now very cheap to hire, and it should be possible for builders to work at competitive prices without risking their lives.

CHIMNEYS

In these days of central heating, it may seem strange that fireplaces, flues and chimneys should cause problems for so many readers. But most weeks my postbag contains two or three chimney queries. In many cases, the problem is due to the fact that the chimney is no longer in use. Rain landing on the chimney stack or falling into the flue via the chimney pot will always percolate down and may appear as dampness further down inside the house. When fireplaces are regularly used for their original purpose, then the heat of the fire will constantly dry things out, but when there are no fires then other steps need to be taken. It is important to maintain a drying flow of air through the flue, and if the fireplace opening is bricked up in the room, then this is best achieved by venting the flue at ceiling height. This allows a flow of warm air from the top of the room to enter the flue and flow upwards by natural convection, and also helps to ventilate the room. It is also a good idea to stop excess rain from entering the flue by fitting a terracotta cowl, either into the top of the existing chimney pot, or in place of it.

Leaks at high level often manifest themselves as staining on the chimney breast within the loft space. This may look alarming but is probably not a problem as long as there is sufficient ventilation within the roof space. Regular leaks on the prevailing (windward) side of the chimney breast may be caused by inadequate flashing allowing rainwater to flow straight down the side of the brickwork, which is usually

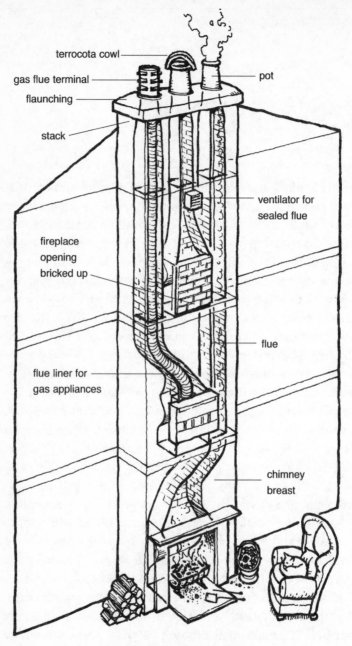

terrocota cowl

gas flue terminal

flaunching

pot

stack

ventilator for
sealed flue

fireplace
opening
bricked up

flue

flue liner for
gas appliances

chimney
breast

Chimneys/flues/fireplaces

apparent from the staining pattern. Flashing round chimney stacks has to be applied with great care and attention. It should always be in proper lead (not stick-on 'Flashband' or similar), and tucked a good 25mm into the brick joints.

Isolated damp patches that appear further down the breast, often with a brown stain, could be caused by rainwater dripping down inside the flue and hitting an obstruction or bend. If this occurs near an inside ceiling level, then the stain sometimes spreads out across the ceiling, especially if this has been repaired or replaced with plasterboard.

In neglected, unvented flues, it is not uncommon for rainwater to find its way right down to the ground floor fireplace, and over time the soot and tar can be leached out into the surrounding brickwork, where it is often misdiagnosed as 'rising damp'. The soot contains hygroscopic salts, which, apart from giving very high readings on electrical moisture meters, also absorb moisture from the atmosphere, so where a property has a condensation problem, this can concentrate moisture in the flue, and cause staining on the surface of the chimney breast, even when there are no rainwater leaks.

Another problem concerns the removal of part of a redundant chimney breast. Victorian terraced houses were built with large chimney breasts, often back-to-back on the party walls. These contain a huge number of bricks and probably weigh twice as much as the wall itself, so they provide a buttressing effect which stabilizes the building, as well as providing ventilation to the rooms. Chimney breasts are often partially removed, to provide extra space within rooms, and the brickwork above is supposed to be supported by spanning across the room to the wall opposite with steel joists (RSJs). It never is. The danger is not of the bricks falling down into the room – because they are bonded into the party wall itself. Rather, it is that the centre of gravity of the wall has been shifted, and over the long term, this may result in movement of the whole terrace.

Readers in houses whose chimney breasts have been removed also report being troubled by their neighbour's noise, and even their smells. So the removal of a chimney breast is not something to be undertaken lightly.

The other common problem with chimneys concerns using an old flue as a vent for a gas fire or boiler. This is a very dangerous thing to do unless the old flue has been prepared with a purpose-made flue liner.

Staining on chimney breast

My house was built about 1937, and two of the fireplaces (bedroom and dining room) are closed off and vented at grate level. The front-room fireplace is still in constant use during the winter with coal and log fires. There is now staining and dampness on the chimney breast in the bedroom upstairs. Is this because the vents are in the wrong place?

Closed-off fireplace openings should be ventilated to allow a draught to travel up the redundant flue and dry out the chimney stack, thus stopping rainwater from percolating downwards. The logic of venting the flue just below ceiling level is that the air in a room is warmer higher up, so this position is more likely to produce a satisfactory convection current, for venting both room and flue. But the staining you describe is more likely to be due to a build-up of tars and salts from the smoke of the downstairs fire, whose flue will pass to one side of the breast in the bedroom. These deposits are hygroscopic – i.e. they absorb moisture from the atmosphere – which gives rise to the phenomenon of 'chimney damp'. Staining on upstairs chimney breasts is especially common with log fires – these burn at a lower temperature than coal, and produce more tar. Get the flue swept regularly, and if the problem persists, then you may have to get it re-lined.

Stains on chimney breast

We had a leaking chimney in our old cottage lined with 'Thermocrete' by the bag method. This is covered by a 25-year guarantee, but after a year we are still getting brown stains coming through on the chimney breasts. What can we do?

This is a lining method where concrete is poured around an inflated rubber mould. The first thing is to check the terms of the guarantee. It is possible that water has seeped out of the concrete and leached tars through to the surface. You could try washing the area down and coating it with a sealer such as Ratcliffe's Styptic or Polycell Stain Block before redecorating.

Chimney damp

I wonder if you can help with this problem in a 37-year-old house. For the past four years we have had damp lifting plaster/ emulsion paint over a chimney breast between two first-floor bedrooms. It carries two flues, one 6in (150mm) from the gas central heating boiler and one 9in (225mm) from an open living-room fire. They are both lined. We have an excellent local builder who has improved but not solved the problem by rendering the stack above the roof and replacing lead flashing which he thought did not extend far enough. He also topped the flues with cowls. Strangely enough there does not appear to be any evidence of damp where the stack goes through the roof space. Realistically, we could not expect you to solve the problem by remote control – but would be delighted if you could! Our builder does not know what else to do and we wonder whether you can suggest whom we should approach for further advice.

It could be salts in the masonry absorbing moisture from the atmosphere (hygroscopic salts). This used to be called 'chimney damp'.The fact that the flues are now lined means that there is no flow of ventilating air to dry the brickwork (apart from in the roof space, which is presumably well ventilated). You could try replastering with a cement/lime-based renovating plaster (such as Tilcon's 'Limelite'), but if that doesn't solve it then the easiest thing would probably be to mask it with a false stud wall.

Stained ceiling next to chimney

We moved into our current property about a year ago, and whilst this problem was not obvious initially, it became apparent very soon after moving in. The offending damp patch is showing through the plasterboard ceiling which butts up against a disused chimney with two flues, both capped and vented. The bricks do not feel wet but the stain shows on the ceiling and when measured with a damp meter shows high levels. I have spent many hours in the loft to see if water is coming in elsewhere but have seen nothing short of the tiniest of occasional trickles. I may have solved the problem but in your opinion, how long should it take to dry out the plasterboard?

The problem could be caused by hygroscopic salts in the flue, left by previous fires. This used to be called 'chimney damp'. The salts absorb moisture from the atmosphere. Electrical moisture meters give high readings in the presence of salts, even when the material is acceptably dry.

Smoke in room

I have lived in my house about thirty years and have always had open fires. I never had much trouble until the last eighteen months, when I have had smoke returning down the chimney into the living room. It seems to come in puffs. I've had a cowl put on top of the chimney and had it swept, but the smoke still comes back down. The chimney sweep said the cowl might be too low. I do have some tall trees about 15ft (3m) away from that side of the house and I wonder if they are causing a down draught. Have you any suggestions?

Smoky fireplaces can be very difficult to cure, especially where the chimney is on an external wall, rather than coming up through the ridge of the roof. All sorts of environmental factors can create bursts of positive pressure, which cause the smoke to be blown back down the flue. Internal draughts and kitchen extractor fans can also sometimes draw air down the flue. But are you sure you haven't carried out any draughtproofing measures in the past eighteen months – such as having replacement windows fitted? A fire will not work in an airtight room – it needs an incoming draught to feed the flames and carry the smoke up the flue. If the doors and windows are all draught-proofed, then you may need a separate air supply for the fireplace, ducted in under the floor to a vent next to the fire.

If all these factors have been accounted for, then it may be worth trying an aerodynamic cowl, which uses the wind to create an uplift. Colt make a range of these, with different models suitable for different exposure conditions. For further information call The Loft Shop (see USEFUL CONTACTS, Loft Conversions).

Chimney won't draw

What's going on when a wood-burning fireplace, open flue, won't draw? We really smoked up the house with this problem the other night. Time for a chimney sweep? Do chimneys ice over? How can you test before you light a fire? Thanks for any help or ideas for further investigation.

Difficult to say without looking at it. Could be anything. Bird's nest? Maybe you should get your own set of rods and brushes for future emergencies. They're relatively cheap from builders' merchants, and can be used for rodding drains too. But first make sure you have a sufficient air supply to the room with the fireplace, as described in the previous question.

Smoke in other rooms

My semi-detached house (1898) has a living room with an open coal fire, a dining room with a gas fire, and a kitchen with an extractor fan. If I light the coal fire, and have the extractor fan working in the kitchen, the dining room becomes full of smoke! The chimneys have been swept and smoke pellets in each fireplace indicated that there is apparently no problem with the smoke rising out of the chimney pots. I am at a loss as to what to try next, and would be grateful if you could help.

It sounds as though there is insufficient ventilation in the kitchen, so the extractor fan is drawing air in through the nearest inlet, i.e. down the dining-room chimney, which must be in the adjoining room. Not only is this annoying, but it is potentially dangerous, as when the gas fire is lit, the fan will be sucking in carbon monoxide from the flue gases. You urgently need extra permanent ventilation in both the kitchen and the dining room – either airbricks or floor vents

– and you should keep the kitchen door closed when the extractor fan is running.

Removing chimney breast

I own a two-bedroom mid-terrace Victorian house. The bathroom, upstairs and at the back of the house, has a chimney breast; the kitchen directly below it does not. The chimney breast appears to be supported with 6in × 3in (150mm × 75mm) timber, taken to the supporting walls. Should I reinstate the chimney breast in the kitchen, or at least replace the timber with an RSJ?

For many years builders and DIYers removed fireplaces and chimney breasts in downstairs rooms without giving it a second thought, supporting the breast above by bolting a couple of steel gallows brackets to the party wall, or, as in your case, inserting some extra timbers into the floor. It is now accepted that this is not the best thing to do to an older house, and surveyors usually comment on removed chimney breasts in homebuyer's reports. This does not mean that the brickwork above is liable to come crashing down, because it will be bonded into the party wall or flank wall. But it is a warning that the equilibrium of the structure may have been altered by the removal, and that in the future some kind of movement or settlement may occur. So when chimney breasts are removed nowadays, the preferred method is to insert rolled steel joists (RSJs) to transfer the load across to the opposite wall. Unless there is obvious movement or cracking, there is no immediate need for you to do this now, but it could be part of any future building work in the kitchen. Alternatively, you could consider taking out the breast in the bathroom as well, thereby giving you more space, and putting the supporting RSJs in the roof space. You should seek advice from a structural engineer about this.

Removing part of chimney breast

You have referred to the potential damage caused by removing a chimney breast from a downstairs room. Does the same problem apply to a top-floor room? And does the same potential damage occur if only the face of the breast is removed, leaving the sides and 'a bit round the corner at the edges', so that a proposed bookcase fits within the space currently occupied by the chimney and the brick sides of the chimney form the sides of the bookcase?

Yes, the problem is one of removing any section of the breast and failing to support the remaining brickwork above it. In a top-floor bedroom this would mean the part of the breast remaining in the loft space, and the chimney stack above the roof line. This situation can be especially danger-ous, as in smaller bedrooms the bed is often situated against the wall from which the breast has been removed. There have been several instances of chimney stacks being blown over in gales and crashing through roofs. Remember, there is a very large amount of weight in a chimney stack.

Extending the fireplace opening upwards to make space for bookshelves is a reasonable compromise, as long as the redundant flue is also vented just below ceiling level.

Installing

We live in a house with no chimney. What are the options for putting in a fireplace or other means of some winter cheer or focus? One hears such horror stories of potentially lethal chim-ney/flue installations.

Constructing fireplace openings, flues and chimneys used to be a standard part of the bricklayer's craft, so if you can find a bricklayer of the old school, he should be able to sort you out. The least disruptive option is to cut a fireplace opening in an outside wall and construct an external chimney breast. If the chimney breast has to be on the inside then it will require cutting through floor and ceiling timbers, and making sure they are adequately fire-protected.

An easier option may be to install a solid-fuel stove with a cast-iron flue pipe up to ceiling height, and a twin-walled insulated flue liner through upper floors and roof space. Ask your local authority Building Control Department for guidance.

Readers in smoke-controlled areas will need to buy stoves with catalytic converters, or resort to 'coal-effect' gas fires. The regulations for these are the same as for any gas-fired appliance, and they must be installed by a CORGI-registered gas fitter (see CORGI block advert in Yellow Pages under 'Gas Installers').

Draughts

We have a dining room with a large inglenook fireplace, in which we light a fire only occasionally in winter, for dinner parties. The rest of the time the chimney creates a huge draught, and is clearly allowing valuable heat to escape, but I am loath to have it blocked up. Is there any simple device that would allow us to stop the draught when the chimney is not in use, but open it when we want a fire?

Fireplace openings should never be completely blocked off – a small flow of air up the flue is essential to ventilate the chimney breast and stack and prevent a build-up of dampness. One way of preventing excess heat loss is to use a chimney balloon. The balloon is inflated inside the flue, but is still supposed to allow a small flow of ventilating air to pass around the edges. This is achieved by having a small air bypass cut off one corner. In the ones I have tried, I found the balloon expanded and filled the whole flue, regardless of the cut-off corner, so I recommend a piece of plastic waste pipe – or even a cardboard tube – should be inserted next to the balloon as well. The balloon can be deflated and removed from the flue when you want to light a fire. Call the Chimney Balloon Company (see USEFUL CONTACTS, Fireplaces and Chimneys).

Using chimneys as gas flues 1

We are about to have gas fires installed in our 1934 house and were therefore interested and a little concerned to read your comments about the advisability of lining chimneys in older houses before doing this. Our installers have said that lining is not necessary, but I would be grateful if you could tell me whether 1934 is considered an 'older' house, and where one can go for advice about this. Is the potential danger due to age, or to the materials that were used in a particular period?

1934 is definitely 'older' in this context, since the chimneys will have been built with bricks and lime mortar, and whilst probably being structurally sound, will not be airtight enough to contain the exhaust fumes from gas fires. The problem is the carbon monoxide in these fumes, which is a deadly poison; if it leaks through the brickwork into the bedrooms above, then it can be fatal. Even houses built with purpose-made concrete flue liners in the 1960s and '70s are now thought to be inadequate for this purpose, and there-fore metal flue liners must be inserted in all older flues before they are used to vent gas fires or boilers. You should use only CORGI-registered gas fitters, as they will be up-to-date with all the necessary safety regulations.

Using chimneys as gas flues 2

Friends of mine are very proud of their recently installed living gas fire (3kW). Their house is late 1920s with a very tall stack. A stainless-steel lining has not been installed. How can I convince them that the chimney should be lined?

The most dangerous thing to do with a chimney is to vent a gas fire into it. Every year there are sad cases of people killed by carbon monoxide poisoning, often innocent victims sleeping upstairs from the source of the fumes, which can seep through brickwork and plaster. Old brick flues must be specially lined before gas-fired appliances are vented into them, and a wise second line of defence is an electronic carbon monoxide detector (a useful Christmas present for student offspring living in dodgy bedsits). Try to persuade your friends to check with CORGI, or their local authority Environmental Health Department.

Opening up fireplaces

We want to re-commission the downstairs fireplaces to use open fires. They are currently fitted with a gas fire and blocked off respectively. Are there any pointers you can offer as to the best way to do this?

As long as the flues are still open – i.e. not capped at the top or lined with gas flue liners – then you will probably just be able to open them up and use them. Get a local chimney sweep round to sweep them and give his opinion. Only problem is, if the parging (the mortar lining the flue) has broken down you may, in time, get staining on the breasts above. It wouldn't bother me, but some people get worried about it.

Smells from next door

Have you any suggestions as to how to approach the subject of the smells from an en suite bathroom next door coming into our bedroom? There is a chimney breast in the party wall. We wonder if they have used it for venting of one kind or another. The noise is bad enough, but the smell is quite another matter. Have even thought of pouring polystyrene granules down the chimney, or investigating via fibre-optic camera. Any advice would be very much appreciated.

I suggest you approach the neighbours and ask them what they're doing with their smells. If there's a bathroom vent going into a redundant flue then it should really be lined with a flexible flue liner or plastic ducting. This is not just to get the smells vented to the outside of the building, but water vapour too – otherwise there could be condensation occurring within the chimney breast. It is always better for bathrooms to be ventilated directly through to an outside wall, and this can usually be achieved by ducting through the ceiling void.

If your neighbours won't co-operate then it sounds like a job for the local authority environmental health officer, as there is clearly a health issue at stake.

Regarding noise entering via the chimney breast, you'd be better off blocking up the fireplace opening with a dense material such as brick. But you will still need to vent the closed-off flue with an airbrick just below ceiling level, or you could have problems with rain penetrating down from the chimney stack.

CONDENSATION

Condensation is one of the great banes of modern living. Energy-saving propaganda – much of it government sponsored – entreats us to insulate everywhere, draughtproof our doors and windows, fit double glazing, and turn the heating down. All these measures increase the likelihood of condensation, which, when it occurs within the fabric of walls, floors and ceilings, lowers their insulation value and, paradoxically, allows more heat to escape than before.

All the moisture that condenses out on windows and within walls is produced by the occupants. People may refer to their homes as being 'damp', but usually the property was dry until they came to live in it.

The most obvious symptom of condensation is misting on single-glazed windows, but if it is happening on the windows, then it is happening within the depth of the walls as well. And with double-glazed windows there may not *be* any misting on the glass, but there will still be condensation occurring within the walls.

An example: 55 per cent relative humidity at a room temperature of 20°C is a perfectly normal, average sort of state in an occupied house. If you look up the tables, they will tell you that the dew point temperature in these conditions is about 10.5°C. In other words, if any surface falls to 10.5°C or lower, then condensation will form on it. So if you take a cold can of beer out of the fridge, then it will soon be wet with condensation.

Now, if the outside temperature should fall to, say, 5°C, then the outside of the wall will be at 5°C, and there will be a temperature gradient through the wall, and where it falls to 10.5°C or below – just over halfway through the wall – the warm air passing through it from the room will be cooled enough to condense. If this condensed moisture is trapped in the wall by, for example, external paint or render, then it will not be able to evaporate, and will stay in the wall and feed the black mould that grows on the wallpaper.

Black mould is a prime symptom of condensation. Another is green mildew on leather goods in the wardrobe. The solution is to keep the bathroom and kitchen doors closed – to stop the moisture produced in these wet rooms from spreading through the rest of the house – and to open a few windows.

It is also important to keep the windows and walls above dew point temperature, which means keeping the heating on in cold weather. The British habit of having the central heating switched on for two hours in the morning and four hours in the evening may sound sensible, but scientific analysis shows that it is not energy efficient. During the 'off' periods, condensation can occur within the walls which will lower their thermal insulation value, and allow valuable heat to escape. In cold weather it is better to keep the heating on permanently, but to turn down the water temperature dial on the boiler, to provide a constant gentle heat.

Mildew in wardrobe

We have lived in a detached bungalow for just over twelve months. We have become concerned about low-level dampness/ moisture particularly in the main bedroom. The bungalow is double glazed and centrally heated. New wardrobe units (not ventilated) have been fitted to the north-facing wall and the corner of the west-facing wall. Over the winter months there have been signs of mildew on some of our shoes kept on shoe racks at low level in the wardrobe units. The bedroom is adjacent to the kitchen. Could you please recommend a solution?

The solution to your condensation problem is to keep the kitchen and bathroom doors closed at all times and to keep the windows open. That way the moisture produced by cooking and bathing will go outside rather than into your bedroom and living rooms.

Black mould in the wardrobe

My daughter's house, which is over a hundred years old, has severe problems with black mould creeping up the walls from skirting-board level, wherever the wall is enclosed by cupboards or wardrobes. The house has a modern central heating system and double glazing. The walls are solid brick. I am assured that there is a damp-proof course, and there is no evidence of damp on the outer wall. What is the prime cause of this and how can it be remedied?

The black mould is caused by condensation. This occurs when moisture produced by cooking, showering, drying clothes etc. meets the cold, unventilated surfaces at the back of the cupboards. The double glazing will not be helping, by cutting down on the natural ventilation, but the main problem is probably due to leaving the bathroom and kitchen doors open, and thus allowing moist air to find its way into the other rooms. Your daughter should open the bathroom and kitchen windows, and keep the doors closed at all times.

Mould in cupboard

I have recently moved into a 110-year-old stone-built house, centrally heated and double glazed. A bedroom cupboard situated in the northern corner of the house smells and feels cold and damp – in fact items that we have placed in it have grown mould. The pointing seems fine, and there is no obvious source of water. The cupboard is directly above the kitchen, so could condensation from the kitchen be the problem?

Condensation from anywhere. Try opening the windows.

Condensation in roof space

I live in a house built twenty years ago, and I have a problem with the loft in winter. The loft is well insulated, but in really cold weather, on the north-facing pitch, frost penetrates on to the black tarpaulin material stretched across the rafters. When the weather gets warmer, the frost melts and some of it drips as water on to the floor of the loft. What is the best way to cure this?

A big problem with thermal insulation is that while it keeps things warm and cosy on one side of it, it keeps things cold on the other, and the cold side needs adequate ventilation to remove moisture and prevent condensation. By the sound of it, the sarking felt may be one of the newer plastic varieties, and it has probably been installed too tight, so that it is trapping moisture within the loft space. So the frost on your sarking felt is not penetrating from outside, but is caused by the moisture produced within your household, rising up through the ceiling, and condensing and freezing on the cold felt. You have two alternatives: first – and much the preferred option – is to cut out the sarking felt from between the rafters, leaving yourself a traditional breathable roof (see ROOFING). Alternatively you could try to stop moist air rising into the loft by lifting the insulation, draping a vapour barrier (polyethylene sheet) across the plasterboard ceiling and timber joists, and then re-laying the insulation. This would have to be done very well, taking care to seal the vapour barrier at the edges and at the loft entrance hatch, and I would still recommend some extra ventilation to the loft space as well.

Condensation due to lack of ventilation

I live in a bungalow with PVCU windows, cavity wall insulation and fitted carpets, and consequently little air circulation, giving rise to smelly damp conditions, particularly in the bedrooms. I have had two solutions suggested to me: (1) A full or partial heat recovery ventilation system; (2) A system whereby a fan in the loft blows air into the living area creating a slight positive pressure within, which will force the moist stale air out. I would be very grateful to hear your comments on these two options, or any other ideas you may have.

I think you should open a few windows.

Condensation cure by ventilation

I was amused by your answer [above] because this is exactly what my dad has been telling me for the last two years, since I moved into a house with similar problems. I entirely accept the principle but what about when the rain is coming down in torrents or it is 5° below zero, both of which happen regularly in mid-Wales? I am reluctant to see my expensive, LPG-fuelled heat go sailing out of the window, even if it is taking moisture with it. In any event, I am fairly certain that the level of humidity most of the year round in Wales would let in more moisture than it allowed out. Furthermore, I am finding that there are all sorts of solutions besides opening windows to the unpleasant symptoms of damp and mould that my house exhibits. One of my bedroom walls was regularly saturated with running water. Investigations showed that: (1) The cavity was bridged by several pieces of rubble; (2) The airhole which should have been providing ventilation under the floor had no sleeve, so the cold air was going straight up the outer face of the inner wall and creating condensation on the inside, and (3) The airhole was too high and was on a level with the skirting board, rather than well below. I too have been tempted by expensive mechanical ventilation systems, having been assured that they would be the answer to all my problems but, fortunately, my father is helping me to identify and rectify the causes, rather than mask the symptoms.

If you had the instrumentation to accurately measure humidity you would find that the level inside is *always* higher than that outside, because it is the same air to start with, plus the moisture that you add to it by cooking, washing, breathing etc. This also means that the vapour pressure is higher inside, so that opening windows or other ventilation *always* results in a net outflow of moisture. Mechanical extraction systems are usually superfluous, apart from where rapid extraction is needed from kitchens and bathrooms.

Condensation caused by cavity insulation

Some six or seven years ago the cavity walls of our house were insulated. Since then, come the colder weather, condensation on the windows has got progressively worse. We do not have or want double glazing. Is there any remedy?

The cavity wall insulation will be keeping your home warmer, so the air is capable of holding more water vapour than before. But at the same time, it will be keeping the inner surfaces of your walls warmer as well, so that condensation does not occur on them. The result is to concentrate the condensation effect on the remaining cold surfaces, the window panes. The solution is better ventilation, so that the moist air is removed to the outside of the house before it has a chance to condense on the windows. It is especially important to keep your kitchen and bathroom doors closed, and use the cooker hood and extractor fans whenever these rooms are in use. You should also open a few windows and give the house a good airing at least once every day.

Condensation caused by double glazing

I am a pensioner living in a ground-floor flat. Although I had new double glazing fitted to all windows and the patio doors, I find the entire lot are constantly running with water. Every other day I am mopping up and leathering down, and along the tops of the window and door recesses it is becoming black. Financially, I have only limited resources. What can I do to overcome this problem?

This sounds like yet another case of double glazing making living conditions worse, rather than better. The streaming water and black mould growth you describe are typical of serious condensation, indicating that your flat does not have enough ventilation to expel the water vapour produced by your daily activities. The easiest and cheapest option is to keep the bathroom and kitchen doors closed, and to open the windows for a few hours each day. If you find this draughty, or are worried about security, then you will need to have permanent vents fitted in the window frames or walls.

Condensation on solid floor

In December 1998, the builders started on a single-storey brick-built extension to my property. I saw the blue plastic – or membrane – laid with a concrete screed over it. I had the floor tiled with suitable floor tiles. Right from the beginning, I found that on some days the grouting between the floor tiles was darker – as if it were damp. The area varied and I haven't been able to link it with the weather. Except that on a day when it was particularly hot, a very large portion of the grouting looked damp. Along one of the outside walls, I have cupboards under the wider than usual window sill. In these cupboards, I stored various boxed games (they were put in a few months after the building work had been completed). To my horror I found a greenish mould on the wooden chess pieces, cardboard and papers this summer.

Have you any idea whether I have a serious problem? The builder claims that there was nothing wrong with his work, but can't explain the situation. Should I get an 'expert' in to examine the room? If so, what sort of expert, and where do I find one? I would appreciate some guidance.

The dampness and mildew are caused by condensation. You didn't mention whether the builders put insulation in the solid floor, but it would seem unlikely. Nor did you explain why you have cupboards below the windows, rather than the usual central heating radiators. Walls below windows are notorious for dampness problems, and cupboards in such areas will always be difficult to keep dry. The other key factors in preventing condensation are heating and ventilation, and these obviously need improving.

Condensation on WC cistern

The WC cistern in our bathroom is situated on an outside wall and is continually wet with condensation, which drips on to the floor. This has ruined a carpet, which we have replaced with lino, but this is now getting stained. There is a small radiator on another wall, and the window is open most of the time. Is there anything else that can be done to eliminate the problem?

The worst condensation problems occur when cisterns are filling direct from the mains. If you have a cold water storage tank in the loft, then you should try re-plumbing the WC cistern so that it fills from this instead. The water will be slightly warmer, and condensation will be correspondingly less.

Another solution which readers have suggested is a plastic drip tray clipped on to the flush pipe below the cistern. Unfortunately, the British company that made these has recently ceased trading. Other readers have made DIY versions of this.

Alternatively, it may be possible to insulate the inside surface of the cistern using thin polystyrene sheet or ceiling tiles, stuck on with adhesive. Apparently kits are sold for this purpose in Canada. The idea is that the wall of the cistern is kept closer to room temperature, so lessening the incidence of condensation.

Use of dehumidifiers

Following a roof leak in the recent storms I borrowed a neighbour's dehumidifier, and was amazed at how much water it collected from the air. But how useful do you think a permanent dehumidifier would be, compared to, say, a humidistat-operated extractor fan?

Extractor fans work by expelling warm moist air, which is then replaced by dryer, colder air from the outside. Every bathroom and kitchen should have one – in the kitchen in the form of a cooker hood. Unfortunately during wet weather the air being drawn in will also be moist, meaning the fan has to work longer to achieve a result. Also, the humidistat-switched models are notoriously unreliable; the cheap ones are usually factory pre-set to 65 per cent relative humidity, but quickly drift up to 100 per cent, meaning that they don't work at all unless you turn them on manually.

Dehumidifiers are a much more efficient way of controlling moisture levels, regardless of the weather conditions, and are especially useful in homes where the windows are kept closed for security purposes, or where washing is regularly dried indoors. They work by passing air over a cooled element, where it condenses and drips into a container. The container must be emptied when it gets full, but most models can also be permanently piped to the existing drainage system. Dehumidifiers have the additional advantage of extracting latent heat from the condensed moisture, meaning that they warm the air as well as drying it.

What humidity?

I was very interested to read your comments about humidity and the use of dehumidifiers. Could you please tell me what is the optimum level of humidity in a house – I cannot find the information in the book accompanying my dehumidifier. Obviously 100 per cent is rain and 0 per cent a bit drastic – what should I aim for?

Opinions vary about this. Owners of antique furniture and musical instruments are often critical of dehumidifiers, as too dry an atmosphere can cause shrinkage and splitting, especially in thin timbers. A 'normal' relative humidity on a dry summer day in Britain will be around 55 per cent – most people will find this comfortable, and it is too low for moulds and mildew to grow. Humidistat-switched bathroom extractor fans are usually set to come on at 65 per cent. So the optimum level is probably between 55 and 65 per cent. The difficulty comes when you try to measure this, as the humidistats on dehumidifiers and extractor fans are notoriously unreliable, as are the dial-type hygrometers which some people have on their walls, and the 'sling hygrometers' used by some surveyors. A truly accurate electronic hygrometer will cost upwards of £200, and need annual recalibration.

Use of humidistat fans

Our builder has suggested that a humidistat fan will solve the condensation problem in our bathroom. Other people with experience of these say they make no difference. What is your opinion?

Condensation is caused by warm moist air meeting cold surfaces. The way to deal with it is by warming the surfaces – i.e. by having constant heating in the bathroom – and by getting rid of the moist air, and extractor fans are certainly a good way of doing this. The simplest option is to have a fan with an on/off switch and to run it during and after bathing or showering, until the walls and windows are dry. Humidistat-switched fans are supposed to switch themselves on whenever the relative humidity reaches a certain level – usually 65 per cent. The trouble is that many of them contain very cheap humidity sensors, and simply do not function as they are supposed to. I have tried several of these fans, and the only one that I would recommend is the Ferrob Sensortronic (see USEFUL CONTACTS, Extractor Fans).

Condensation reduced by permanent heating

For forty years I have had our boiler on for four hours in the morning and six hours or so in the evening. You now advise leaving the boiler on continuously (though reducing the boiler stat at night). Would this not increase the fuel bill to a great extent?

The idea is to keep the walls above dew point temperature, and so stop condensation forming either on them or inside them. The problem with the typical British 'morning and evening' heating practice is that between times the walls cool down and condensation occurs. Then when the heating is switched on again half the energy is used to evaporate the condensed moisture (known scientifically as the 'latent heat of vaporization'). If the room thermostat is left on 15°C and the boiler thermostat is turned down to '1' or 'min', rather than turning the heating off completely, then this problem should be avoided. Readers who have followed this advice usually report that their fuel bills go down, not up.

I note you recommend that to prevent condensation you should run the boiler all the time at a low temperature rather than turn it on and off. Surely running the boiler at a low temperature will cool the water in the hot water cylinder and eventually you will end up with tepid water?

No. Turning the boiler temperature down to its lowest setting will still be around 60°C, which is far from 'tepid', and is actually the recommended British Standard temperature for domestic hot water. Once the hot water cylinder has reached this temperature, the cylinder thermostat would have shut down that part of the system anyway. And I am suggesting that this is done at night and when the house is unoccupied, when most people have the hot water circuit turned off.

In order to follow your advice on permanent low-level heating, in my case this would mean turning the boiler thermostat well down from its usual setting. Would this not mean that the boiler would switch on and off far more often in an attempt to achieve the temperature required by the room thermostat? I would have thought this would mean uneconomic use of the boiler.

No. The boiler does not run continuously anyway, whatever the water temperature. Once the water has reached the temperature set by the boiler thermostat, then the boiler modulates, firing up and running for a few minutes at a time to keep the temperature at that level. Running it at a lower temperature will not alter this pattern.

Following your advice on central heating, you may be interested to know that in our offices we kept the heating on all through last winter, turning the thermostatic radiator valves (TRVs) down slightly at night and over the weekends. The ambient temperature never dropped below 16°C. The result was an office that was warm in the mornings and only took about half an hour to bring up to a comfortable working temperature, showing a slight saving on previous gas bills. In previous years, the place has been freezing on a Monday morning and the boiler has had to run flat out for most of the day to bring the structure back up to temperature. The walls,

including many of the internal, are over 2ft thick and act as giant storage heaters. They work well in reverse in the summer and help keep the building cool.

Thanks for practical confirmation of the advantages of this method of heating. It will always save money and energy to keep the structure above dew point temperature, as once condensation has occurred within the depth of the walls, they lose their insulation value, and allow more heat to escape to the outside.

Heating on or off?

My system has thermostatic valves on every radiator instead of a central room thermostat. If I turn the boiler down at night and leave the pump on, surely as the temperature drops in a room the thermostatic valve will call for more heat from the radiator, which means more hot water from the boiler, and it will simply remain fired up all the time to meet the demand. It is impractical to turn every valve (some twenty) down individually and so 24-hour gas usage must be more expensive than say eight hours usage.

The idea is to keep a flow of warm water going round the whole system in very cold weather, so as to prevent the wall temperature falling below dew point. To this end, your TRVs should be kept open, not closed down. You should turn down the water temperature on the boiler. I should add that TRVs should not be seen as a substitute for a room thermostat, and you should consider having one of these fitted. Preventing condensation and keeping the walls dry should improve the thermal insulation of your home and so save energy.

Extractor fans – noisy vents

Can you advise me where to purchase vents for my extractor fans that do not 'chatter', but do stop the inflow of cold air (they are wall mounted, not window mounted). Both my existing vents are in rather exposed positions; one has exposed horizontal plastic flaps, the other is shielded with one vertical flap, but both 'chatter' in even light winds. I hope you can advise of a ready-made solution before I am forced to experiment with springs, Blu-tack or *Blue Peter*-type solutions.

These external covers are known as anti back-draught shutters. They are supposed to allow air to escape when extractor fans or cooker hoods are in operation, but to prevent air being blown in from outside. The ones you have rely on gravity to keep them closed and, unfortunately, the slightest difference in air pressure between the inside and outside of the house can cause them to move and make a noise. You have three options: (1) Replace your extractor fans with more expensive versions incorporating electrically operated shutters; (2) stick with the existing shutters and silence the chattering using foam insulating strip or (3) replace the shutters with Greenwood exposed site baffles (available from electrical wholesalers) – these are inexpensive but do not completely stop incoming air currents.

CONSERVATORIES

Adding a conservatory is one of the most popular of home improvements, and the off-the-shelf conservatory industry is experiencing an unprecedented boom. But, although the idea of a glass-walled 'room in the garden' is a seductive one, many readers have discovered that things can go wrong, and conservatories can often be too hot or too cold to use.

The main drawback is that of over-heating – or 'solar gain' – caused by too much sun shining on too big an area of glass. The extent of this problem can be gauged by the fact that the number of adverts for conservatories in the glossy magazines is almost equalled by those for conservatory sun blinds and air conditioning systems. I must say that building a conservatory as a suntrap, and then paying money and using energy to cool it, has always struck me as one of the greater absurdities of the home improvement game, but this is what many people end up with.

The 'too much sun' part of the equation comes about through building a conservatory in the wrong place. For most houses, there is little choice about this, and the conservatory is plonked down outside the back door, whichever direction it faces. But when there is a choice, many people assume, wrongly, that a south-facing aspect will be favourite. Researchers at Cranfield University have found that over the course of a year, a southerly orientation actually provides fewer hours of comfortable occupation than one facing north. They also found that the higher the thermal value of the glazing, the lower the number of comfortable hours. In other words, single glazing is better than double glazing.

The 'too big an area of glass' is partly a design problem, and partly due to the Building Regulations. Conservatories get hot because of the greenhouse effect, where the sun's heat is able to pass in through the glass but, after being reflected off internal objects, it has a different wavelength, and is unable to get out again. Only a small area of glass roof is required for this build-up of heat to become excessive, but in order to stop a conservatory being classed as an extension, and thus becoming liable to building control, at least 75 per cent of the roof must be glazed. So most conservatory firms, to avoid the hassle of applying for Building Regulations approval, and of having their work inspected by the building control officer, do not offer any alternative to the complete glazed roof.

Another situation where the building control officer should be involved, but often is not, is when a conservatory is connected to the house by means of a permanent opening, rather than a closeable door. This effectively makes the conservatory part of the habitable space, and therefore, for energy conservation reasons, imposes restrictions on the area of glass, which is limited to around one-quarter of the floor area of the whole house.

The best way to keep a conservatory from over-heating is ventilation. This requires vents at both low and high level, to allow a through convection current to flow. Many owners are persuaded to buy internal sun blinds, but are not told that these are ineffective without through ventilation, and in fact can sometimes make things worse, by exacerbating the greenhouse effect described above.

Anything else? Oh yes, it is rumoured that only 30 per cent of the price of a PVC-U conservatory covers the cost of the thing – the rest is profit and salesman's commission. You see, the sun always shines for someone.

Building control

I am intending knocking down a small lean-to stone building on the gable end of my cottage and building in its place a small conservatory with a roof of Hardrow slates. Having read a few relevant books and seen some TV programmes, I was of the opinion that my intended conservatory would be exempt from Building Regulations. I have a book, published in 1999, which states that under Building Regulations 1991, Schedule 2 exemptions include conservatories under 30m² floor area provided the glazing meets the requirements regarding safety glass. The definition of a conservatory issued by the Department of the Environment (formerly the DETR, now the DTLR) seems to determine they can have solid roofs instead of the usual glass. However, the building control services at my local council claim a conservatory has to have a translucent roof and therefore the building I have in mind will no longer be classed as a conservatory. They therefore class it as an extension, even though there is no access from the house, no fixed heating system, and no sleeping arrangement, and I will therefore need Building Regulations approval. I would be grateful if you could clarify the situation.

At the end of the day, they are the people who have the power. If you argue with them, they can make life difficult for you. The general rule is that to qualify as a conservatory, and therefore be exempt from building control, the roof has to be at least 75 per cent glass, and the walls have to be at least 50 per cent glass. But if you throw yourself on their mercy, you may find them open to compromise. Keep your cool. Ask them how they feel about half slates/half glass. The worst thing that can happen is that you have to pay the fee for a building notice.

Misting in polycarbonate roof

I have a problem with condensation within the layers of my five-layer polycarbonate conservatory roof. The roofer has carried out resealing, but the problem persists. Please provide suggestions for alleviating the problem.

This type of sheeting does not include a desiccant material, so it must be allowed to breathe. Sealing the edges will only trap moisture between the layers. All the interstices must be drained and ventilated at both ends.

Overheating

We have a south-facing conservatory approximately 12in × 12in (3600mm × 3600mm) which gets much too hot to use in summer despite having roof blinds and front blinds inside the glass. We can open the door, windows and rooflights but these really need to be closed if we go out for an hour or two and then re-opened on our return. Is there another way of successfully keeping a conservatory cool? Would air conditioning be a solution?

Conservatories are often too hot for comfort. Given a choice, a conservatory should be sited on a north-facing aspect, as this has been shown to provide the greatest number of comfortable hours in a year. All conservatories need through ventilation to keep cool, which means having openable vents at low and high level. Many owners are persuaded to buy internal sun blinds, but are not told that these are ineffective without through ventilation. The problem is that once the sun's rays have passed through the glass, then the heat is inside, and it makes no difference to the internal temperature whether this is absorbed and re-emitted by the blinds, or by the floor and furniture.

I suggest you try to get permanent low-level vents fitted in the walls and/or doors, and investigate the possibility of locking the rooflights in an open position, so that you can leave them open when you go out. Of course, the advisability of this would depend on whether you have a lockable door between the conservatory and the house – otherwise you could compromise your insurance cover.

The idea of building a conservatory as a sun-trap and then installing air conditioning to cool it has always struck me as slightly crazy.

CRACKS

Cracks cause householders a lot of unnecessary distress, usually because of the fear that they might signify serious problems. This is largely a result of the publicity given to subsidence damage, and stories about huge insurance claims for underpinning and other structural work. Most internal cracks are actually harmless, and their only drawbacks are cosmetic. And in reality subsidence is a hugely over-diagnosed and overrated problem.

Subsidence first hit the public consciousness following the dry summer of 1976, and a little-noticed change in the wording of buildings insurance policies that enabled owners to claim for the repair of cracking damage caused by ground movement. Once one owner down a street had had their house underpinned at the insurer's expense, everybody else wanted it too, and almost overnight a huge army of 'specialist' underpinning contractors sprang up ready to cash in on this lucrative insurance-financed work. Underpinning is hugely expensive and disruptive, and almost always unnecessary, as when the drought eases the ground swells again, and the cracks that opened up in the summer close themselves. The insurance industry belatedly realized this, and they are now more reticent about agreeing to fund underpinning work. They also started refusing to renew buildings insurance cover on houses that had been underpinned – which was a bit strange, given that these are now sitting on several cubic metres of solid concrete and unlikely to be moved by anything much short of a nuclear explosion.

What many people fear as 'subsidence' is actually just minor differential settlement. The main causes are shallow foundations below front bays – which can cause cracks to open up between the bay and the main house – and softening of the ground due to leaking drains – this often occurs where drains run along alleys between houses, and so are close to the walls. The former is often curable by tying the bay back to the house with traditional brick stitching (or resin-bonding in serious cases), and the latter by lining or replacing the damaged drain. Old houses built with lime mortar and plaster can often cope with this sort of movement quite easily, which is why you can see brickwork above windows looking decidedly lop-sided, but with no evidence of serious cracks. Modern materials are much more brittle and can withstand very little movement. So cement mortars and renders, and gypsum plasters, tend to emphasize movement by opening up into cracks. It's like the difference between icing and marzipan.

Most cracks in internal plaster occur in gypsum-plastered surfaces. On walls they are often nothing more than drying shrinkage, and on ceilings they usually follow the lines of the joints between sheets of plasterboard. It is also a surprisingly common practice by cowboy builders to plaster over wallpaper – this looks fine for a few weeks, but then lots of cracks open up, running in all directions. I know of a house in London where a structural engineer specified £30,000 worth of structural repairs based upon such cracking, and the buyer duly got that sum knocked off the price.

The situation where cracks can result in serious problems is where they occur in external rendering. Most external renders are in sand and cement and are much too strong for the wall below. So they crack, and allow rainwater to penetrate. And once the water is behind the render, it is trapped, because strong sand-and-cement plaster is impermeable.

Cracks in external render

My forty-year-old bungalow is rendered and I have several vertical cracks, mostly under the window sills. In the past I have Sandtexed the whole of the rendering after filling the cracks with Tetrion. This lasts for a couple of years and then the cracks show again. Please tell me what I should do to give a lasting and satisfactory look to the whole exterior of the bungalow.

Cracks below window sills are sometimes an indication of structural movement, rather than simply shrinkage of the surface render. You need to hack off the render in the offending areas and investigate what is happening underneath it. If there is cracking in the brickwork then this will need to be repaired by stitching-in with new bricks. The exposed area should be reinforced with expanded metal lathing and primed with a dilute PVA solution, before re-rendering with a 6:1:1 washed sharp sand–lime–cement mix. Use a mortar plasticizer to reduce the amount of water in the mix and prevent drying shrinkage.

Cracks in render on lightweight blocks

My Victorian end-of-terrace house has a two-storey back addition built of lightweight blocks and then rendered. The rendering has many fine cracks and one large one. Rain has penetrated through the cracks and the lightweight blocks act like a sponge, causing the internal plaster to crack and 'blow'.

It is a nightmare. I bought the property eight years ago and despite having a full survey, no damp problems were found!

External render on lightweight block walls often cracks, due to the differential movement between the hard cement-based render and the softer lightweight blockwork. Where the blockwork forms the outer leaf of a cavity wall this is not such a serious problem, but when, as in your case, the wall is solid, then it can present serious difficulties. Unfortunately, there are no easy answers. The fault lies with the original builders, who did not understand the need to provide movement joints in the blockwork, or to use a soft lime-based render. The only long-term solution would be to hack off the render and replace it with the correct material (a 6:1:1 washed sand–cement–lime mix), with the provision of a movement joint where the addition joins the main house.

Cracks in render on old stone

My two-storey detached house (Ayrshire, Scotland) was built around 1890. The front and rear are sandstone while the gables are of random stone construction covered with a rough cement coating. The original coating had deteriorated over the years and I had it replaced three years ago. The replacement cement work was finished by the process of 'keying' and presented a most attractive appearance, and I was happy with it at the time. I now find that the new work has a large number of hairline cracks, about half a metre in length, running vertically down the face of the building. The property is in a coastal position, exposed to the prevailing south-west winds, and my concern is that rain penetration followed by winter frosts could damage the new surface. Could you suggest a practical method of repairing or sealing the gable short of resurfacing the entire wall?

Unfortunately, this sounds like a case of inappropriate use of modern materials on an old building. The original 'rough cement' coating was most likely harling, a traditional Scottish lime-and-sand render which was thrown against rough stone walls with a trowel or shovel. Being lime, it would move in tune with the stonework beneath, and any cracks would be self-healing. Plus, any water that penetrated the harling would be able to escape again, by virtue of lime-based materials being breathable.

It sounds very much as though the replacement render is cement-based, and this will harden into a rigid, impermeable coating, unable to accommodate movement or allow drying. The hairline cracks are a symptom of this. The only long-term solution is to remove the render coat and replace it with the correct material.

Cracks in plasterboard ceiling

The plasterboard ceiling in my 1976 well-built house suffers from cracks. I have tried many types of fillers without a successful permanent cure. Apart from rejointing with scrim or Artexing, do you have any suggestions?

I am afraid there is no foolproof remedy to cracks between badly installed plasterboard sheets. The only thing you could try is to open the cracks up to around 5mm wide, fill them with a soft filler, such as universal one-coat plaster, sand the joints flat, and cover the ceilings with heavy-grade lining paper.

Cracks in Artexed ceiling

Our roof is supported by pre-formed trusses which are at about 22in (550mm) spacing, and there is a large crack 18ft (5500mm) long across the living room, along the joint in the boards, which is at right angles to the trusses. We had the ceiling professionally Artexed over ten years ago, where the workmen sealed this crack with scrim and Artex before applying the textured coating to the whole ceiling. They confidently predicted that we would have no further problems with cracking. Needless to say the crack has returned. I have considered fitting 3in × 2in (75mm × 50mm) battens between the trusses along the joint crack and nailing the plasterboard to these, but a friend suggested an alternative approach, using strips of plasterboard 4 to 6in (100 to 150mm) wide instead, and fixing these with coving adhesive. Whichever of these methods was used, I presume that I would have to get the old Artex coating removed and have the ceiling re-coated with either Artex or plaster, or is there some way of repairing a crack in Artex?

The crack is due to the large dimensions of the ceiling, and the fact that the boards were probably butted up too tight to each other, with insufficient joints to cope with movement. But plasterboard ceilings fixed to roof trusses usually crack anyway, as the ceiling joists move in response to temperature and moisture changes within the roof space. You could try opening up your ceiling crack to around 5mm and fill it with a soft filler such as one-coat plaster, reinforcing from above with plasterers' hessian scrim. Matching the original Artex pattern will be difficult, although the manufacturers suggest using flexible decorator's filler, blended into the existing pattern with a wet cloth or brush. But it may be better to plaster over the whole lot with a smooth finish, using Artex Transform – then it will be easier to repair next time the crack opens up. Better still, finish off with two layers of lining paper.

Cracks in lath and plaster ceiling

A relative is about to have her Victorian house refurbished and among the works to be undertaken is the removal of two lath-and-plaster ceilings which are cracked and sagging. Her builder proposes to remove the plaster but not the underlying laths and then to erect replacement plasterboard directly on the laths. One can see why the builder would want to do this to avoid having to denail the joists after ripping out the laths. However, will this not make it difficult to level the plasterboards and thus make for an uneven and unstable ceiling, or is this normal practice?

Fixing plasterboard on top of laths is not a very professional way of working. But then plasterboard is an inferior material to lath and plaster anyway. Why not simply repair the cracks and damaged areas, using lime/sand/hair plaster to match the original. (Or universal one-coat plaster if that's all your builders can manage.) Finish with two layers of heavy-grade lining paper. Just like it has always been done.

Cracks – subsidence

What to do if, having had what could be described as 'subsidence' in my London house once supposedly cured, some rather worrying cracks appear four or five years later: i.e. now. The original cause wasn't problems with earth or foundations – there has been no normal-style subsidence in this area – but with a badly cracked Victorian drain which serves two or three terrace houses including ours but happens to be under the bay at the front of our house. It was sorted, supposedly, with the drains repaired, cracks dealt with and a 'galvanized steel strap' on the first-floor front room, where the bay ends. Six-month monitoring in 1995 showed no significant continuing movement – yet now come these cracks, which aren't wide enough to put in a coin or anything but are quite noticeable. My wife and I are getting on and will probably need to sell this house at some stage, so we are worried – by underreacting, by overreacting and, above all, by that dread word 'subsidence', which terrifies everyone, everywhere!

It sounds as though the only 'subsidence' you have experienced is the front bay settling away from the main house. This is quite common in Victorian terraced houses, because the bays were usually built after the main front walls were finished – i.e. they were built on earth used to back-fill the foundation trenches, which was not fully compacted. Some settlement after a hundred years is only to be expected. And the leaking drain will have softened the soil and allowed further movement to occur. Now that everything has been repaired, you almost certainly have nothing to worry about, and the tiny movement cracks that have opened up at the junction between the house and the bay are probably just long-term drying shrinkage of the new plaster.

Serious subsidence is rare, and the word is only scary because of the huge (and exaggerated) insurance claims involved. Relax. There are worse things to worry about.

Cracks – subsidence caused by leaking drain

I am desperately looking for objective advice on a property we want to buy. We have just found out that the property has been underpinned due to the fact that the corner of the house dropped approximately a quarter of an inch. This was because a drain running under the property had been leaking and that in turn damaged the foundations in that area. The repair work was carried out by the insurance company. They carried out extensive research on the property and in turn concluded in a survey that the damage was caused solely by this leaking drain.

I would be happy if I can be sure that this is a one-off problem that has been fixed and that it is not ongoing. I do not know if this is the right way to think or if I should be aware of other factors concerning this.

This sounds like a fairly typical case of settlement caused by leaking drains. As long as the offending drains have been completely renewed then there is unlikely to be any further problem. My usual advice to people in cases like this is that if you like the house then buy it – there's nothing that can't be fixed later. Your main problem is likely to be getting buildings insurance on a property on which a subsidence claim has already been made. Make sure this is sorted before you incur any further expense.

DAMPNESS

Questions about dampness constitute by far the largest proportion of my weekly postbag. Some of these concern genuine stories of water penetration – through roofs, walls and chimneys – which builders have been unable to stop. Many more describe black mould growth on walls, green mildew in wardrobes, and water running down the insides of windowpanes, which are all symptoms of condensation (see CONDENSATION).

Condensation is the result of water vapour produced within the home by human activity, and which, as a result of inadequate heating and ventilation, is allowed to condense out as liquid water on and within the building structure. Condensation is easy to cure, but some people just refuse to open the windows.

But by far the largest number of queries concern a dampness problem that does not actually exist. This is the notorious 'rising damp', which surveyors and damp-proofing company salesmen say they can detect using electrical meters. Selling damp-proofing to new homeowners on the basis of electrical meter readings must go down as one of the most successful confidence tricks in history. There is simply no independent scientific evidence to support the claim that British homes suffer from endemic rising dampness, and in every case that I have investigated the property was either bone dry, or had obvious defects such as leaking gutters, raised outside ground levels, or condensation problems. But surveyors, estate agents and mortgage lenders all go along with the 'rising damp' myth, and so homeowners continue to fork out £200 million every year for this unnecessary and often damaging work.

Electrical moisture meters are calibrated for use on timber, not wallpaper or plaster. They will always give high readings on walls at low level in old houses because of condensation (warm air rises, cool air sinks, walls are colder at the bottom and so that's where the condensation is concentrated).

But if rising damp is a myth, people ask, then why are damp-proof courses built into new buildings? The history of the damp-proof course is an interesting one, and dates from the 1877 Building by-laws – themselves following the Public Health Act (1875) which was concerned mostly with drainage and sewage disposal. So the original idea seems to have been to stop sewage – which in those days was often still running down the streets – from soaking into walls. Water will not rise by capillary action in brickwork built with cement or strong lime mortars. Suffice it to say that in Holland, much of which is below sea level, DPCs are not used. Whatever, most British houses built post-1877 have DPCs built-in – usually two courses of slate – and there is no evidence that they 'fail', or become porous over time, although most surveyors seem to accept these old wives' tales without question.

In any case, clay soils will always absorb water preferentially over brick walls (because the soil expands as it gets wet, creating a 'suction' effect), so there will only be free water available to soak into the wall once the soil has become saturated – in other words, in swamp conditions. And if your house is standing in a swamp, then you need land drainage anyway.

Oh, and by the way, if anyone tells you that your damp-ness problem is due to an 'underground stream', then that's part of the myth as well.

DAMP WALLS

Rising damp?

I am in the process of selling my house. The buyer's mortgage lender insisted on a survey for rising damp, and the surveyor's report says that there is extensive damp in all walls. There is no evidence of damp, such as wallpaper lifting, and a recent TV programme concluded that treatment for rising damp is seldom justified. What is your advice about current practice?

Rising dampness is very rare. Houses constructed since 1877 have damp-proof courses built in, and so cannot suffer from it. The problem lies with the misuse of electrical moisture meters by damp-proofing 'surveyors', who are actually just salesmen for chemical damp-proofing products. Tell your buyers that they need an independent dampness survey carried out to the standards described in Building Research Establishment Digest 245, and under no circumstances allow them to deduct the cost of damp-proofing works from the asking price (see USEFUL CONTACTS, Dampness and Timber Surveyors).

Our property has what some would say was 'rising damp', or has suffered it in the past. Patches on the wallpaper on external walls (and one internal wall) up to about one metre high. This was apparently due to an old cast-iron pipe leaking rainwater on to the external brickwork over a period of time (although a specialist firm was quick to blame it on rising damp). I was

happy enough to put it down to defective guttering, but on moving in have noticed a couple of things: the walls where the patches are do feel cold/clammy to the touch and more importantly in the cellar one wall feels very damp to the touch – could this really be rising damp?

'Rising damp' has been promulgated over the last thirty years by companies in order to sell 'damp-proofing' remedies for it. Before that, people used to accept that cellars and basements usually had a degree of moisture in the walls, owing to their being below ground level. Lime plasters used to cope well in these situations, and a lot of the current problems are caused by ignorant builders using modern gypsum plasters instead. These cannot cope with moist conditions, and they get sticky and dissolve. Also, walls that have been soaked through leaking rainwater pipes can take months to dry out. Your clammy patches will probably dry out eventually, but the wet wall in the cellar could be due to rainwater flowing into a soakaway next to the wall.

Damp patches above skirtings

My detached 1926 house is built with Accrington brick. There is a damp patch above the skirting board in one of the rooms which a local builder, using a moisture meter, 'diagnosed' as rising damp. You have expressed doubts about this kind of diagnosis on several occasions, but I have seen advertisements for the 'Shrijver' damp-proofing system, which they claim is new to this country. What is your opinion of this system?

Electrical moisture meters on their own cannot be used to diagnose the existence of rising damp, and the date of your house indicates that it will have been built with a damp-proof course, and so does not require any further form of damp-proofing. The damp patch in the plaster must have some other source, such as a leaking gutter, cracked window sill or raised ground level. If your builder cannot locate the problem then you need an independent expert, such as Abbey Independent Surveys (see USEFUL CONTACTS, Dampness and Timber Surveyors). The Shrijver system is a version of the old – and discredited – Knapen tube system, which has never been shown to have any effect on the moisture contents of walls.

(Further investigation of this problem – by Abbey Independent Surveys – revealed that the house was built with cavity walls, and builders' debris had blocked the cavity, allowing ground water from outside to track across and produce a stain on the plaster. Removing a couple of bricks and cleaning the debris out of the cavity solved the problem.)

Conflicting diagnoses

I am in the process of trying to buy a basement flat. Under 'essential repairs' the valuation survey listed the following:

'You are advised to obtain a specialist rising damp report from a member of the British Wood Preserving and Damp-proofing Association, and carry out their recommendations in full. Any treatment undertaken should form part of a long-term insurance-bonded guarantee.' On the back of this the mortgage lender withheld some money and we have now had four quotes from BWPDA firms. All of them indicated different damp spots in different parts of the house, and their estimates ranged from £600 to £3,750. Is there any reputable contractor you can recommend who provides an independent report on damp, preferably one whose views are respected by mortgage lenders?

Yes. Not a contractor but an independent surveyor (see USEFUL CONTACTS, Architects and Surveyors). In my experience, there's no such thing as a reputable 'contractor'. Almost all damp-proofing/timber treatment contractors make their money by offering free surveys and then saying you need work done. Even the ones who charge for surveys are not necessarily being objective; they do it to discourage clients from calling in other companies. The unreliability of their diagnoses is underlined by the fact that, as in your case, different 'specialist' firms usually come up with different proposals.

Damp-proofing shared walls

My Victorian terraced house has just been 'diagnosed' as suffering from rising damp to all walls (including walls shared with my neighbours). My initial thoughts are to contest this very expensive diagnosis, but how? Secondly, if rising damp is present in a shared wall do my neighbours have a legal obligation to contribute, as they will surely be reaping a benefit by effectively having their walls treated at my expense?

Chemical injection of party walls is a subject about which the damp-proofing industry does not usually have any ready answers. If a party wall genuinely suffered from rising dampness, then clearly it would be pointless injecting it only on one side, and you would have to get your neighbour's agreement to treat the whole depth of the wall, which would entail double or triple drilling and injection. But if your neighbour objected, it would be hard to get them to cooperate – even with recourse to the Party Wall Acts – without proper scientific evidence of the existence of the dampness. There have also been cases where party walls have been damp-proofed on one side, and this has caused dampness problems on the other side, where none existed previously.

The fact is, though, that rising dampness is very rare, and

your 'diagnosis' has almost certainly been made by the inappropriate use of an electrical moisture meter. You would be well advised to get an independent second opinion.

Do I need a DPC?

In my spare time I am rebuilding an old house next door to my own in order to make the two into one. With the walls stripped of plaster etc. I am now not sure what to do about a DPC. I had a company look at it but they did not even look at the outside before giving me a price! The bricks are very old, rock hard in the centre but soft on the outside so if I drill them and try to inject damp-proof fluid it won't go anywhere. I have read your comments with great interest and would like to believe I don't need a DPC, but it is a lot of work if it all goes wrong. A damp-proof 'tech rep' said I should inject the fluid at low pressure into the mortar but I am not sure about this as the mortar is very soft. As far as I know there are no obvious signs of dampness apart from one wall where the ground level outside is very high, and this wall I have tanked as a cure.

I think you should relax and stop worrying about something that hasn't happened yet. If the bricks are 'rock hard', then they won't allow moisture to pass through them, so there is no point damaging them by drilling, and then trying to inject a fluid that is not needed. If the ground level is high outside one wall, then you should lower it if at all possible. Tanking is not a 'cure' – it is like putting a plaster on an open sore. It is better to remove the cause rather than treat the symptoms.

Legal DPC?

We have lived in our mid-eighteenth-century house for the past twenty-one years. Some eighteen months ago I suspected that

the DPC we had installed on moving into the house had failed
on some of the exterior walls. The house fronts on to the
pavement of our village and is of a double 2in (50mm) hand-
clamped brick construction. As the initial DPC was an aluminium silicate injection system we decided this time to go for a
'Wallguard' product which consists of drilling a course of
bricks every 2ft (600mm) or so and then inserting 2in (50mm)-
diameter porous cylinders into them. These tubes are supposed
to draw moisture away from the surrounding brickwork. Needless to say, after a year no significant improvement to the damp
problem could be seen, neither could any contact be established with the company who installed it, even after continuous
correspondence with the Office of Fair Trading and Companies
House. I now find that I am £2,000 poorer and there are still
damp patches at floor level and 2ft or so above. Could you
advise me if (a) Is there a reliable DPC available or should I be
looking for another remedy? (b) Could the holes drilled for the
ceramic tubes be repaired and given some constructional integrity as I'm concerned that in time the said holes could lead to
some form of structural failure? (c) In your opinion is the Wallguard system we had installed a waste of time and money? (d)
Is it a legal requirement for a house to have a DPC before it
can be sold?

Wallguard have a history of going into liquidation and then
restarting with a slightly different name and different direc-
tors. Believe it or not, there is nothing illegal about this, and
Trading Standards and the Department of Trade and Industry can't touch them. The ceramic tube system was shown
not to work in the 1960s, but the consumer protection laws
in the UK are so weak that there is nothing to stop anyone
marketing a useless system. Wallguard were exposed on
House of Horrors on TV in 2000.

There is no legal requirement for a DPC, and none of the remedial DPC systems I have looked at, including chemical injection, have any effect whatsoever on the moisture contents of walls. But then rising damp is really a myth, anyway. If you want to solve your dampness problems properly then get an independent survey from someone who is not going to try to sell you anything.

Damp walls caused by raised patio

We have found that the damp-proof course of our 1917 house has been bridged by the patio laid against the external walls, in some areas up to 9in (225mm). The under-floor air vents are also below the patio level and fill with water in heavy rain. This has caused problems to decorations internally. Three solutions have been suggested: (1) Lift and re-lay the entire patio below the DPC (a large and expensive job); (2) Lift the patio stones adjacent to the wall, dig a trench out to below the DPC, bitumen paint the walls and re-lay the patio stones; (3) Take an angle grinder and remove 4in (100mm) of stone around the walls, dig the trench out, bitumen paint the walls and fill the trench with pea shingle. Your recommendation please?

No. 1 is the only option worth doing. The others will be throwing good money after bad. If your sub-floor vents are channelling surface water then you could soon have a rotten floor to cope with as well. The finished patio needs to be at least 150mm below DPC level, and sloping away from the walls. And definitely no bitumen paint anywhere.

DPC bridged by step

Your comments about raising of patio levels above the DPC struck a raw nerve and I wonder if you would offer me an opinion with regard to my house? It is a new property, built in sandstone and completed last November when I took up residence. The problem is a step, almost the full width of the rear of the house, that provides egress from the dining-room sliding door and the kitchen door on to a patio. The patio is made of standard 2ft (600mm) square concrete flags laid on packed earth and sharp sand and with which I have no problem, it being well below the DPC. However the step, again made from 2ft (600mm) square flags and supported on a raised plinth made of sandstone blocks directly cemented to the patio, is well above the DPC and in direct contact with the outer wall of the house. The flags of the step also cover about half of the area of several air bricks that are presumably intended to ventilate the space under the suspended ground floor. My question is this: Would you have a problem with this construction and would you seek to have it rectified? At this stage I have no quarrel with my builder, having always found him to be a decent chap and all I am seeking from you is an opinion as to whether the matter is worth raising with him.

The problem with the type of layout you describe is that you have bridged the DPC. Whether this creates problems would depend upon the particular moisture conditions in the area. Ideally the wall should have had a damp-proof membrane applied to it before the step was built. Where a step covers airbricks it would be good practice to provide ducts through to the front of the step.

Damp walls caused by solid floors and chemical DPCs

I was interested to read your comments about replacing suspended timber floors with concrete floors in old houses, and the subsequent problems which occur with damp in the walls. I have an ongoing problem which sounds similar, in that a few years ago a damp-proof firm replaced my timber floor with a concrete one, and chemically treated the walls against damp. This has been unsuccessful, and there is damp visible in the walls which they treated. They have been trying to think of how to resolve the problem, and they feel that chemically re-treating the walls would be the best solution. With the concrete floor and associated membrane, your article would suggest this isn't a solution.

Chemical damp-proofing is very rarely successful, and if it hasn't worked once, then there is very little point in repeating the process. It sounds as though removing the suspended timber floor with its sub-floor ventilation has upset the moisture equilibrium in the house, and forced moisture up into the walls. No amount of chemical injection or replastering will deal with this; the only long-term solution would be to remove the concrete and reinstate the timber floor.

Dampness caused by solid floors and tanking

I was interested in your comments regarding treatment for damp basements. I wonder if you could explain why concreting floors and 'tanking' walls should be avoided and exactly how it can cause dampness problems in the rooms above.

Because it traps moisture below the concrete and behind the tanking, with nowhere for it to evaporate. So the only way out is up. This can cause wood rot in the ends of the ground-floor joists.

Staining on internal walls

Is there a clear explanation for why some internal wall/floor angles of old stone buildings might seem almost to wick up and release liquid when the water table is high as it currently is? These are walls that are not otherwise damp, and dry out relatively easily in between such periods. What can or should be done to rectify this?

One reason may be that both sides of the wall are internal, and so evaporation is hindered by high internal humidity, whereas external walls have one side exposed to the lower humidity and wind and sun outside, so moisture is less able to build up in them. But the actual source of the moisture is often that the plasterer has taken the plaster right down to contact with the floor – condensation forming on a cold concrete floor can be wicked up by the plaster, and investigation often reveals that the wall behind the plaster is dry. You say that the wall dries out easily, and this would seem to confirm that the dampness is only in the plaster, because if a solid wall is saturated then it would take months to dry out.

If it is a solid concrete floor then there is also often a problem with the damp-proof membrane junction with the wall, and the only place for sub-floor moisture to escape is up the wall. The situation is often a combination of all these factors.

Why are walls wet at the bottom?

I have been following your columns and your claim that rising damp does not exist. Being a young building control officer still learning his trade, I found this quite intriguing. Can you explain why some brickwork has a distinct damp appearance and mould growth below DPC level? I have seen this where the affected brickwork is clear of ground level, free of vegetation and flowing water. If indeed rising damp does not exist could this mean that the DPC could be made obsolete?

Regarding water ingress and green growth at ground level then it must be a rainwater problem, because the salts from groundwater would kill vegetative growth. It may be as simple as rain splash, leaking gutters, or blocked gulleys. Similarly, on the inside, black mould indicates condensation, because salts from groundwater would kill mould growth.

The Dutch do not use DPCs in new work – discovering this was one of the breakthroughs in my thinking about this subject.

The 1877 Building by-laws – in which damp-proof courses were made mandatory – followed the Public Health Act (1875), which was concerned mostly with drainage and sewage disposal. So the original idea seems to have been to stop sewage – which in those days was often still running down the streets – from soaking into walls. But over the years, the idea has taken root that DPCs are to stop water rising up from the subsoil.

Damp meter readings

I am buying a 300-year-old stone/flint cottage in Somerset. The property is very sound, but the surveyor says his damp meter 'went off the scale' and has advised we install a chemical damp-proof course. The ground floor is concrete laid – presumably – over some sort of membrane, but one room is original flags on bare earth. There are no visible signs of damp in the house – no patches of mould or peeling plaster; the property doesn't *smell* damp or musty and *feels* warm and dry – and we've heard that installing DPCs in properties of this type can result in more problems than it solves. Any advice?

This sounds like another case where an old house is in an acceptably dry condition, but an ignorant surveyor has misused an electrical moisture meter to invent a problem that does not exist. And you are right – trying to 'damp-proof' a historic building like this can create problems. The most serious damage is usually caused by hacking off old lime plaster and replastering with a strong sand-and-cement mix. This should be avoided at all costs.

Leaking gutters

I live in an Edwardian-built red-brick building in Dublin. I have a problem with dampness on the walls of my dining room and sitting room. There is a guttering problem which is causing overflows and moisture to penetrate – I am getting that fixed. But I have been told that there is rising damp and that I should get it fixed and replaster the walls up to a height of 3ft (900mm) for all ground-floor walls whether they are internal or external. I am reluctant to do this because it will be very disruptive and will damage the lovely skirting boards etc. Is there any alternative? Also, my windows are in need of repair or replacement but I can't bring myself to replace wood with plastic. However, it is cheaper to buy new UPVC ones than have the existing ones repaired, and I will have to have the repaired ones painted and repainted every few years. What do you recommend?

Rising damp is a myth. Get the gutters etc. fixed and the place will probably dry out. If it doesn't, then there must be a further problem. Use the money you have saved to pay for the care of those lovely original windows. There must be some retired chippy around town who will do a proper job on them.

Penetrating dampness: Cavity walls and conservatories

We have a conservatory abutting the south-south-west-facing wall of our house, and after a long spell of wet weather the brick becomes saturated and water finds its way through into the conservatory, not through the roof it seems, but from the wall cavity above the entrance. The walls have rock wool cavity insulation but that does not appear to prevent the situation. I have been advised that repointing or a tile/slate hanging over the wet wall might be the answer. What are your views?

When cavity walls are saturated, water tends to run down the inside of the outer leaf until it meets an obstruction. In your case this is the lintel above the entrance to the conservatory. When an extension or conservatory abuts a cavity wall it requires the insertion of a cavity tray above the roof line of the new addition, to throw water clear to the outside. Your best option is to have a cavity tray installed, which can be done from the outside by cutting out short sections of brickwork. If the conservatory was built recently then this should have been done anyway, and you may have a case against the builders.

Inserting cavity trays

You have described the need for cavity trays, which is exactly the problem with my 1920s house. It has had two bay windows extended, with much larger roofs. During south-westerly gales the ceiling leaks in the ground-floor rooms where the bays cut through the outside wall. But how do you retro-fit damp-proof trays in the cavity? Local builders don't know how!

Cavity trays are needed wherever a bay, or extension, or conservatory, butts up to an external cavity wall. This is because the outer leaf of the wall above the adjoining roof line becomes an internal wall below it, so rain driven against the brickwork can drip down inside the house. Solid brick walls rarely have this problem – especially older walls built with soft bricks and soft lime mortar – because they tend to absorb the water and evaporate it away later. But recent cavity walls are often built with hard bricks and hard cement mortars, and research has shown that in conditions of driving rain, the water is forced through the gaps between bricks and mortar, and can run down the back face of the outer brick leaf.

The cavity tray intercepts this water above the roof line and channels it outwards. The fitting instructions are simple: (1) Remove two or three bricks; (2) Insert section of tray; (3) Replace bricks; (4) Move along a bit and repeat steps 1 to 3. Where the extension has a pitched roof, the cavity tray has to be installed in stepped sections to follow the pitch.

Anyone who does not know how to perform this basic construction operation should not be describing themselves as a builder.

Retro-fit cavity trays are available from several manufacturers (see USEFUL CONTACTS, Dampness).

Old farm buildings

We live in an old farmhouse which was extended by the architect-owner by converting some single-storey farm buildings to provide a dining room and lounge. When we bought the property our surveyor noted an extensive damp patch on one wall, which we thought could be due to a blocked rainwater downpipe. Unfortunately, this proved not to be the case, and the damp area has continued to grow. In addition, areas of dampness have appeared on other walls; some cover many square feet whilst others appear as random isolated patches roughly circular in shape. We have sought advice from the local council, local builders and a reputable damp-proofing company. The latter advised us it was not rising damp, and that the wall is dry in depth. The external pointing is in good condition, and the roof and gutters are sound. Nobody can explain why the dampness has appeared or how to stop it. We are at our wits' end. Can you help?

The damp patches could be due to salt contamination in the walls from animal urine, which is a common problem in converted farm buildings. The salts are hygroscopic, i.e. they attract moisture from the atmosphere. This can be easily tested for using the method described in Building Research Establishment Digest 245. If this proves to be the cause of the problem, then the salts can be drawn out by repeated application of a chalk poultice. Or, if you replaster using a breathable lime plaster, then they may crystallize out on the surface as efflorescence, and you can wash them off.

Traffic splash

I have a 200-ish-year-old brick-built cottage in Norfolk that butts right up to a narrow lane. With the beet lorries in full flight the gable wall is being plastered with mud to a height of about three feet and there are signs of damp showing up on the inside. The walls are about a foot thick. Cleaning the gable end daily isn't possible. Is there anything else I can do to protect the bricks, such as painting them with something water-proof? The bricks are in pretty good nick and the wall was repointed last year.

Interesting problem. A waterproof coating is probably not a good idea, as it could trap moisture below it. You would have to construct a 'rainscreen'-type shield, such as a timber frame clad with slate, which would catch the splashing from the road, whilst allowing the wall to breathe and dry naturally behind it. Meanwhile you should hose the mud off the walls regularly, to prevent ground salts soaking into the brickwork.

Electrical damp-proofing systems

I have an old property – fifteenth century in parts. The floor level in one of the rooms is 2ft below the ground outside. At some time in its history somebody has put in a 'reverse osmosis damp course' from Rentokil. Have you heard about this method? I have tried to contact Rentokil but they haven't even given me the courtesy of a reply. Was this a con, or could it really work? I am asking because after the recent torrential rains there are now wet patches on the walls in this room. Any information would be greatly appreciated as there is a plug behind one of the doors permanently switched on with a sign on it saying 'under no circumstances to be switched off'!

Several versions of these electrical damp-proofing systems have been produced over the years, all of which consist of wires inserted into holes or buried under the plaster. There is no independent scientific proof that any of them have any effect, although some were installed with thirty-year 'guarantees'. Rentokil's was a 'passive' system, which did not use electrical power, so it sounds as though you may have two separate systems, the other being installed by Lectros. Rentokil insist that their system should work, even though this has never been independently proved.

DAMP FLOORS

Damp patch in concrete floor

I am replacing the floor covering in my kitchen, and have the floor back to the original ceramic tiles. These are very well laid, but sometime in the house's past the kitchen/dining room has been altered so that now, the floor is about 90 per cent tiles with patches of concrete screed to the same level, where presumably the alterations were done. When I removed the old vinyl floor covering, there was an area where it was wet underneath with what looked like heavy condensation. This occurred only in the concrete screed on both sides of the wall dividing kitchen and dining room. The house doesn't in any way feel damp, but I am concerned about the moisture that I found under the floor covering when I removed it. The damp appears in an area where there are central heating pipes (the floor is slightly warm there). I am pretty confident there are no leaks in the system. Could the problem be simply condensation on the concrete floor appearing under the air-tight vinyl flooring?

What makes you so confident that the central heating pipes aren't leaking? It is quite likely that the concrete was laid to cover the pipes, and unless they were sheathed beforehand, the cement will have corroded the copper. This is a common problem.

Leaking pipes under floor

I have a 25-year-old detached house and the central heating pipes and water supply pipes are all embedded in the concrete flooring. I am confident that the damp-proof course is OK. However, there is very serious 'rising damp' which I assume must be from a leaking underground water pipe. Is there an easy way of determining this, or will it be necessary to dig up the floor to try to ascertain what is causing the problem?

Concrete corrodes copper pipes. These days they have to be sheathed if they are buried, but many houses of your vintage had them just screeded over. Instead of digging them up, the easiest thing would be to cut them off, and replace with new pipe runs in skirting ducts (floor ducts where they cross doorways).

Damp cellars

We have just bought our first house and wish to use the cellar for storage. Unfortunately the room is exceptionally damp and has a drain in the floor which we think has risen, slightly flooding the cellar in the recent wet weather. Ventilation is reasonable as the cellar still has a coal chute and open fireplace but we really don't know where to start. Do you have any suggestions that do not entail us spending thousands of pounds?

The simplest course of action would be to limewash the walls and put some pallets on the floor to keep your stuff clear of the dampness. You should investigate where the floor gulley drains to. Hopefully it feeds into the main sewer, and you will be able to measure how far it is above this. But it may just lead to a soakaway, or might be blocked, or the pipe could be broken and collapsed. More importantly, check the routes taken by the rainwater down-pipes from the roof. Many older houses have only soaka-ways for rainwater disposal, so when it rains heavily the ground gets saturated and the cellars fill up. It is usually possible to install new gulleys and pipe them into the sewer.

A more sophisticated renovation scheme would involve lining the walls with a drained, ventilated membrane system such as Platon or Newlath, (see USEFUL CONTACTS, Dampness), which can be plastered or panelled over, and fitting a new suspended timber floor.

(On no account should you consider having the floor concreted and the walls 'tanked'; thousands of cellars have been treated in this way, most of them are still too damp to use, and the process can cause dampness problems in the rooms above.)

We have a similar damp cellar problem to a previous reader. The cellar is below the garage and the wall next to the earth is wet despite a new gas boiler plus medium-sized radiator newly installed. We planned to use this area as a 'drying room' – first we would paint it with PVA glue solution followed by gloss paint. Is this sensible? You have mentioned that cellars should not be 'tanked'. What does 'tanked' mean?

Tanking means sealing the inside walls with a waterproof coating. Similar to what you are proposing, only with a material that would stay on. Your PVA and gloss paint idea wouldn't last long, as it would all come blistering or flaking off very quickly. You would be better off following the advice to line the walls with a drained ventilated membrane system.

I'm currently in the process of renovating an old cellar 14ft × 12ft (4200mm × 3600mm). The house is over 200 years old and not surprisingly the cellar is damp. The cellar floor is made up of sandstone slabs. I suspect that the cellar walls may well be sandstone also. The cellar suffers from a lack of ventilation, having only two small vents on the external walls. The cellar walls are currently covered in the original plasterwork. I'm considering a number of options and need advice as to which is the most suitable course of action: (1) Dry lining the cellar – covering the cellar floor and walls with heavy-duty plastic, then battens and then a dry floor and walls; (2) Tanking the cellar – coating the cellar in an impermeable layer of a suitable material (please suggest suitable coatings); (3) Traditional damp-proof remedies – chemical injection; (4) Semi-permanent installation of a dehumidifier – the cellar has an old drain, which could be used to carry away the excess water; (5) Installing ventilation fans in place of the vents to improve the airflow in the cellar.

The cellar is immediately below our dining room and in

consideration of the above my main priority is to prevent the dampness permeating into other parts of the house.

Dry lining may work, but if you use a timber framework then the wood will always be liable to rot in the damp conditions against the wall. And if you attempt to isolate it from the wall using polythene sheeting, then you will be trapping moisture in the wall. The same problem applies with tanking, in its many forms. And chemical injection damp-proofing, which is ineffective at the best of times, is incapable of withstanding water under pressure, so will not stop ground water penetrating laterally.

The best solution is to line the walls with a drained, ventilated membrane system, and in your case you have the advantage of having a drain, to which any collected water could be piped. Either increased natural ventilation, or a dehumidifier, or both, will be helpful in keeping the finished space dry.

Can you give me some pointers on making a cellar over to habitable space? The house is a Victorian terrace. A passageway between ourselves and one set of neighbours means there is air behind one wall. There is no cellar on the other side, so earth behind that. The main route for penetrating moisture must be from the front or exterior wall.

I have friends down the road who have bitumenized the inside of their cellars but once the radiators are in it seems very warm and humid to me.

Am I doomed to have specialists in? Is a waterproofed render enough? Presumably I can't impregnate wet bricks with silicone-style solutions? Is the earth outside the front wall supporting the house at all – could I excavate it away to dry the wall out (and backfill with gravel)?

Your friends' experience of high humidity following tanking is common. The tanking may stop liquid water penetrating from outside, but by stopping the walls from breathing it ensures that they stay saturated, and high internal humidity is the usual result. The best solution is the drained, ventilated membrane system described above.

You can excavate earth away from the walls as long as you are not going below the foundation level and, having done so, why not consider leaving this area of wall exposed and build a retaining wall next to it to hold the earth back?

(NOTE: There is always a slight risk of drying shrinkage and cracking when an old wet basement wall is exposed for the first time. The newly reduced outside ground level should be paved or concreted to stop the ground below the footings from drying out too much and shrinking.)

Wall below ground level

We are buying a property that has a severe penetrating damp problem. The house was built in c.1750–1780 and is a three-storey cottage. Because it is built on a hill, in effect up to the first floor is below the ground level of the garden next door, which seems to be the root cause of the problem. We had a full structural survey done and have been recommended to have the affected wall Vandexed. Can you tell me anything about this? Is it effective? How much does it cost? Are there any other alternatives and does chemical damp-proofing work?

Vandex is an internal cement-based tanking material. It is not a sympathetic thing to do to a historic building, and you may find that it results in high internal humidity levels, and possibly pushes moisture higher up the walls. No, chemical damp-proofing does not work, but damp-proofing is not the answer anyway if you are below ground level. The only place to apply a waterproof coating would be on the outside. Inside, you would need a drained, ventilated membrane. I suggest you need an independent expert who knows more than your surveyor apparently does (see USEFUL CONTACTS, Dampness and Timber Surveyors).

Damp basement

I need advice regarding rising damp in the basement of a Georgian building in Bath. I'm given to understand the cavity is rubble filled, and that chemical injection is unnecessary and useless. What is the best method for treating rising damp in a building of this type and age? And is it possible to 'tank' a small vault oneself?

Very unlikely that the property has rising damp. Therefore it will not need any rising damp 'treatment'. I am not keen on 'tanking' in old buildings, as it can trap moisture and create dampness problems where none existed before. If you really must use the basement as habitable accommodation, and need a dry decorative surface, then the only foolproof way is to line the walls with a drained, ventilated membrane system.

Membrane systems

You recently referred to a drained, ventilated membrane system – Platon or Newlath – in reply to a query about cellar storage. Where can I get more information on these products – stockists etc.?

Drained, ventilated membrane systems are useful for lining the insides of below-ground cellar walls to provide a dry decorative surface. They can be plastered or covered with panelling. Platon is available from Triton Chemicals Ltd, Newlath from John Newton & Co. (see USEFUL CONTACTS, Dampness).

DRYING OUT AFTER LEAKS OR FLOODS

Soaked plaster

A faulty gutter next door (now fixed) overflowed with all the extra rain and has been gushing down the back wall of our house (divided into flats). My bedroom wall has now become very cold and clammy, the wallpaper peeling off. I have read your comments that certain types of plaster will not dry out properly and I am worried that when our Victorian house was converted into flats twenty years ago, the builders may have used such a modern plaster on the walls instead of the traditional lime and sand variety which you recommend. If so, is there anything I can do to dry it out myself that is not too complicated and expensive? I want to avoid having builders in to rip off and replace the plaster, which I don't think I can afford at the moment anyway. I'd be most grateful for any DIY suggestions – it doesn't have to be a perfect result!

Don't panic. Try a dehumidifier for quick drying. The plaster should stick itself back together. The problem with gypsum plasters is that they dissolve when subjected to constant moisture ingress such as in basements. Your one-off wetting will probably not cause too much damage as long as it is now fixed.

Drying out after flood

I wonder if you would give me some advice on the best way to get rid of penetrating damp? Our overflow pipe underneath the bath flooded and has caused every wall in the bedroom and parts of the lounge to absorb the water to about 1 m up. It is a ground-floor flat with one bedroom and no central heating. From what you've written, it would seem that anti-damp paint would just trap the moisture in the walls. I am concerned as I've been experiencing breathing difficulties after sleeping overnight in the bedroom, and am due to have a baby in four weeks' time, so any advice would be most appreciated.

Heating and ventilation are the accepted ways of drying things out. If you want to speed up the process then use a dehumidifier. These can be bought for around £200 or hired from a tool hire shop. I presume you've made sure that the leak will not happen again?

Dampness following flooding

I am pretty convinced that my father's house does actually suffer from rising damp. He lives in a cottage that was built over 200 years ago and was recently flooded. After three weeks of drying time the house was redecorated, and most walls replastered using lime plaster, and then finished with lime wash. There are only a few places where the damp is coming through, and where it does it peels the lime wash off the walls. Are there any DIY rising damp treatments that we can do?

Flooding can take months to dry out. The place doesn't need damp-proofing, it needs drying. Try a dehumidifier.

Mould growth

A few months ago, water penetrated the outside wall of our front bedroom. We have cured the leak but we now have mould growing on the inside wall. My wife has read that it is dangerous for your health to allow the mould to continue to grow. Is this true? If so, what is the best way of getting rid of the mould (without further endangering your health)?

Some people say mould spores are bad for health – asthma and the like. But there are millions of mould spores in every cubic metre of air anyway. And as for when you bring that pack of mushrooms home from Sainsbury's, well . . . And Stilton cheese has a few, I believe.

As long as you are sure the leak is fixed, then things should clear up of their own accord, but if you want to hasten things along then wipe with a dilute solution of bleach in water. This is also good for black mould growth on bathroom windows, and usually keeps it away for a couple of months. Safer and considerably cheaper than proprietary mould-removing chemicals.

Cob house 1

We have just moved into a damp Devon farmhouse built of stone and cob. Broken gutters and downpipes, and built-up ground levels are obvious culprits for the damp, but the local conservation officer says that the modern cement render is exacerbating the problem. Three damp-proofing firms all say that cement render is fine, and they're also unanimous about injecting silicone damp-proof courses as part of the remedy. Who's right about the render? And is silicone damp-proofing suitable for thick cob walls?

Your local authority building conservation officer is absolutely right. Cob, which is a mixture of local earth and straw, must be allowed to breathe. Plastering it internally with sand-and-cement render will cut down evaporation, and will actually make it wetter, rather than dryer. It should be plastered with a traditional lime mix, and any external decoration should be with limewash. Silicone injection damp-proofing is ineffective at the best of times, and it would be plain stupid to try to inject it into an earth building.

Cob house 2

We have recently bought a cottage in Dorset which is part-thatched and constructed with cob walls. Obviously it has no damp-course, and is believed to be situated over or very near to underground springs, which can well up in winter when the underlying chalk becomes saturated! The floor is brick, probably laid straight on to earth. The Society for the Protection of Ancient Buildings, in its leaflets, advocates leaving things alone, and that cob walls can disintegrate if dried out (we have also been told that this is nonsense), and that plenty of ventilation and airflow should control the damp. We are thinking of digging out and laying a waterproof membrane over the whole floor area, and hoping that this will be sufficient to stop rising damp, and to leave the walls alone. Do you think that this is an advisable course of action, and do you have any alternative suggestions?

I would think that SPAB have got it right. Who told you about the 'underground springs' – a damp-proofing sales-man? It is quite true that cob walls need a certain moisture content to maintain their integrity, and, again, I would be interested to know who told you that was nonsense. I cannot think of any reason to dig up a sound brick floor, and a membrane would be wholly inappropriate for a building of this type – it would upset the moisture equilibrium and possibly damage the walls by making them *too* wet. The floor needs to be allowed to breathe, and should not be covered with carpet or any other floor covering apart from loose sisal matting or similar. It sounds to me as though you may have bought this historic building without quite understanding the implications.

Cob house made damp by cement

I live in an old thatched cob cottage in Dorset. When I moved in fourteen years ago there was a damp smell in the sitting room (the oldest part of the property) and the paint was festering and eruptions were occurring on the internal walls. The wall plaster was stripped off several times and replastered with Devonite plaster, which was meant to contain a waterproofing compound, and this was supposed to help with my problem.

After several failed attempts and a recurring damp problem, last summer we finally had the whole of the outside cob wall stripped of its cement render (which had cracked in places). The cob underneath was saturated with water and there were two very large cracks running from the top to the bottom of the cottage in the cob underneath the points where the cement had cracked. The damage was repaired, though I have since been told that instead of throwing lime mortar into the cracks, cob should have been made and used to fill the damaged areas. The whole wall was then covered with lime-mix plaster and painted with six coats of limewash. What a rotten job it is, and it has to be limewashed annually with about three coats.

However, the wall now appears to be in a much better state – though some fine cracks do open up between one year and the next – but are filled when the limewash is applied as the gritty lime tends to get into the cracks. The interior of the living-room walls is now free from festering and eruption and the plastic Dulux paints have been stripped off and Farrow and Ball natural paint has been used with great success.

Limewash and a lime render certainly cured our problem, but the maintenance is a bind! One day we will get that modern, characterless house with double glazing, a slate roof and brick walls.

Congratulations on restoring your cob house with such sympathy. I hope your new house – when you buy it – lives up to your expectations and doesn't give you any problems. But I suspect you might be disappointed (see MODERN HOUSES).

DRIVES AND PATIOS

Having a drive in front of your house can be a great boon, and most motorists who live in terraced town houses would love to have the private off-street parking that a drive represents. However, a drive is like a small private road, and like a road it needs a certain amount of maintenance – cleaning and occasional resurfacing. All drive surfaces need diligent below-ground preparation if they are to last, and cracking, crumbling concrete or tarmac is often a symptom of shoddy construction.

Of the various choice of surfaces, gravel is the most luxurious, but also the most expensive, and it requires annual raking and weed-killing. Concrete is probably the hardest wearing and lowest maintenance. A good professionally laid concrete drive could easily last for fifty years. Shame it looks so ugly. Pattern-imprinted concrete needs cleaning and resealing every few years. Tarmac is the most likely to be installed by cowboys and anyway, like tarmac roads, after a few years it breaks up and has to be resurfaced. Brick and concrete block paving looks nice, and it is easy to dig up and re-lay damaged areas, but it can be slippery when wet, and weeds grow in the joints.

Moss and lichens will grow on all surfaces, especially badly drained ones (i.e. those with an insufficient slope for surface water to run off) and in shaded locations. If they bother you, then scrub them off with a stiff yard broom, or commit yourself to a lifetime of applying proprietary path and patio cleaner-type herbicidal chemicals. I don't fancy them myself.

Frost forms more easily on darker surfaces. But see the readers' comments on block paving, below.

New homes are now having to be built with smaller areas of hard paving – to limit the surface water run-off going into the main drains – and grass block paving (where grass grows in gaps in plastic or concrete pavers) looks set to be a big seller. Maintenance is as easy as mowing the lawn.

So you pay your money and take your choice. But if you're getting a new drive installed, then the most import-ant things to look out for are proper sub-surface preparation, and attention to drainage. Rather than answer a newspaper advert by a nationwide drive company (which will only pass your details on to a regional franchisee), you would be better contacting local groundwork contractors through the Yellow Pages. Get them to give you a detailed written speci-fication of what they propose to do.

Which surface?

I have been given conflicting advice regarding my drive. It is only about 55m², but it is quite a steep slope down to the garage. One contractor (who does either tarmac or blocked paving) recommended the tarmac, as it would give better grip during icy weather, but the second contractor (who only does block paving) disagreed, saying he thought the opposite was the case.

And if you asked a contractor who did gravel drives, no doubt he would recommend his product as being better. Actually, he might have a case, although from the sound of it, you might have to keep sweeping the gravel out of your garage. A fourth possibility is perforated plastic 'grass blocks', which you back-fill with soil and plant with grass seed. If icy weather conditions are really a big problem in your area, then this may be a solution. But otherwise, I think you should decide which surface you prefer, in terms of appearance and cost, and keep a bag of road salt in the garage for those few days every winter when it might be needed.

Block paving

You may be interested in my experience on the item concerning block paving on sloping drives when frost is around. I had my tarmac drive resurfaced with Marshalls block paving a few years ago, and I consider that it seems much more prone to be covered in ice when there is a radiation frost. I put this down to the fact that the blocks are laid on several inches of dry sand which must form a much better insulating layer than the solid hardcore under the old tarmac. Hence the surface ice does not get melted so quickly by warmth being conducted up from the ground underneath.

This is an interesting observation and theory. It is also possible that the difference is due to the tarmac surface being slightly porous, and so providing a better grip in icy conditions. In general, I think block paving is a superior surface for drives, as damaged or sunken areas can be easily dug up and re-laid, whereas tarmac and concrete slab surfaces have to be either patch-repaired or totally renewed.

Pattern-imprinted concrete

Our front garden is covered with compressed smooth concrete, indented to resemble cobbles. Alas, the colour (black) was not incorporated in the concrete but sprayed on afterwards. This peeled off and subsequent repainting with aggregated exterior floor paint is wearing off under traffic. As it is pointless to repaint flaky paint, could the very smooth concrete be roughened to hold paint, or is there any other suitable treatment?

This type of patterned driveway is made from fibre-reinforced aerated concrete, with an impression of bricks or cobbles being rolled into the top as it hardens. The surface colouring is usually trowelled into the top, so that two-tone effects can be achieved, but also because colouring the concrete right through would be expensive. Once the top wearing surface has been worn away, there is really nothing that can be done to patch it up. As you have discovered, paint or any other surface coating will simply wear away or flake off. Thousands of people have had these drives installed, often under the impression that they would be 'maintenance free', and were not told that they would need to have the surface resealed every three to five years (at a cost of £600 to £800) to prevent the colour wearing off. Your options are to have the damaged areas repaired by a special-ist contractor, or to cut your losses and have it dug up and replaced with a more permanent surface, such as block paving.

Raising ground level with drive
We are planning on having our crumbling driveway and soggy front lawn replaced with imprinted concrete to make a much larger drive and parking area. We live in a 1930s bungalow with a double row of blue bricks as the damp-proof course. The upper row was drilled and injected to improve damp-proofing on the recommendation of the building society's sur-veyor before we moved in. The salesman suggested that the slope on the lawn, which is towards the bungalow, could be reduced a little if the surface of the concrete was raised. This

would bring it up to the level of our porch and to the lower edge of the double blue bricks of the damp-proof course. Drainage would still be needed and this is proposed to be along the front wall (and around the bay windows). At the moment all paths, garden etc. are six inches below the blue bricks. Is having the concrete this high a good idea?

On no account should you allow anyone to raise your external ground levels. This will result in nothing but problems (see DAMPNESS). You have already been ripped off once by paying for an unnecessary DPC injection – there is no way that a double course of Staffordshire Blue engineering bricks could allow dampness to rise and, equally, they could not possibly be 'improved' by chemical injection.

Gravel drives

Have you any advice on creating a gravel drive? Gravel is all the rage round us, but my neighbours' drives seem to be just piles of shingle tipped out over their existing driveways. Every time they move their cars pebbles spill out over the road, creating a hazard to the windscreens of passing vehicles. How should one lay a gravel drive to avoid this?

A properly constructed gravel drive is like an iceberg, in that 90 per cent of it is out of sight below the surface. The top layer should be only two layers of gravel thick, stuck into bitumen, and none of it should be finding its way on to the public highway. The preparatory work should be the same as for any drive – excavate 250mm of soil, line with a geotextile, roll in 150mm of Type 1 roadstone and 75mm of Type 2 hoggin, each of which has to be carefully compacted with a vibrating roller. Then comes the hot bitumen and the final gravel surfacing.

Unfortunately, as you say, many people's idea of making

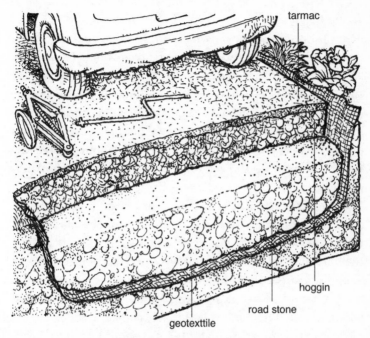

tarmac

hoggin

road stone

geotexttile

Section through a drive

a gravel drive is to order a truck-load of pea shingle and spread it over an existing drive. This might look good for a few weeks, but will quickly disintegrate as the stones are either pushed down into the soil, or scattered around the garden by spinning car wheels. Like many other construction operations, finished appearances can be deceptive, and mask a lot of preparation work. A gravel drive is not a DIY job, and specifications and quotes should be obtained from experienced groundwork contractors. The cost, for a straight single drive, will be in the region of £50 per m², so a simple straight run up to the house, twice the length of your car, could set you back around £1,000.

Tarmac

Some time ago, together with several neighbours, I had my drive surfaced with tarmac by a company no longer in business. At the time we were all happy with the result. However, the surface of the tarmac now appears to be crumbling where the edge meets the pavement. I seem to be spending ages each day removing grit from the carpets throughout the house. Is there a product available on the market that can be applied to seal the surface, or have we all been caught out and bought an inferior product?

'Tarmac' is a name that is somewhat loosely applied to a number of bituminous surfacing materials. The quality and grade vary hugely, as do the skill and diligence with which they are applied. The preparatory work should be the same as for any drive – see previous question. The tarmac finish should comprise two layers with a total thickness of at least 50mm, applied hot, and rolled in with a heavy roller.

Cowboy firms often just spread a thin layer over hardcore, or on top of the existing surface, and don't roll it hard enough. Then it can start to break up after the first winter's frosts. There is no point trying to stick it back down with anything if the foundation is inadequate.

Untidy builders

I live in a residential area of Nottingham and several of my neighbours have recently had work carried out on their driveways, mainly block paving. The contractors have all failed to clean up afterwards so that parts of the road and pavements look like Skegness beach when the tide has gone out. It is unlikely that the action of the weather alone will remove this eyesore. Apart from the fact that there seems to be little pride nowadays in leaving a site clean when the job is finished, is there any requirement by the local council to protect the road and pavement surfaces when this sort of job is done?

Most certainly. Sand and masonry on the pavement and high- way are a potential hazard to road users and pedestrians alike. You should consult your local authority Environmen- tal Health Department in the first instance. They should arrange for the waste materials to be cleaned up, and have the power to prosecute the owners and builders who have created the hazards.

Grass paving blocks

I have been trying to trace a supply of perforated blocks which have grass growing out of the holes, but which allow cars to be driven across them. The local garden centres and builders' merchants have not heard of them despite the local council using something similar on road verges. Where can I find these elusive blocks please?

There are several types of grass paving systems, which allow cars to be driven across or parked on grassy areas without damaging the turf. Councils often use perforated concrete blocks, but the new plastic versions are lighter, easier to lay, and accommodate a larger area of grass. Grass paving systems are likely to become more widely used as regula- tions require new homes to have more car parking spaces, and the environmental rules on surface drainage are tight- ened up. Two suppliers are Hoofmark Ltd and Hauraton (see USEFUL CONTACTS, Paving).

Converting front garden

I am thinking about using my front garden as a car-parking space. What are the legal requirements for doing this?

You will have to consult your local authority highways

department. On minor roads there is usually no problem, as long as traffic will not be emerging on to the road in an area of restricted visibility. However, on a 'classified' road – a principal road or bus route – planning permission may be needed. You will then have to pay the local authority to drop the kerb and rebuild the footpath as a ramp, and you will be liable for any costs incurred by the utilities companies for re-routing or ducting service pipes or cables. The total cost could reach several hundred pounds, although some local authorities offer special deals, usually when they are resurfacing the road.

Line and level

I have just done a couple of drives for my two daughters – the biggest lesson I learned from my retired builder friend was 'levels'. I kept reaching for the spirit level but of course it's being parallel with the rest that seems important but not necessarily level on the bubble as I thought. Maybe you could clarify this for us amateurs?

You are right, the lines want to be straight, not level. You need a fall of at least 1 in 40 for drainage. A level drive, path or patio (or flat roof) will always hold water.

Moss growth on patio

Two years ago I had a block paving patio laid by a builder. Since then a green algae-type growth has grown in the cracks between the blocks. I have scraped this growth out (very time consuming) and watered the patio with Jeyes Fluid. I realize this is only a temporary answer and wonder if there is a more permanent solution. When wet it can be very slippery.

Mosses and other vegetative growth will always occur in areas where rainwater is allowed to hang around, and which are shaded from sunlight and drying winds. When planning a new patio or paved area, it is important to allow for a sufficient slope and suitable drainage to a yard gulley or ditch. If neither of these is convenient then it may be best to bed the paving material on sharp sand, rather than concrete, and to have sand between the joints. Then the surface water will be able to drain away naturally. In very damp, shaded positions, a gravel surface may be more suitable than paving. If you have an existing hard-paved area which is supporting vegetative growth then you really have no alternative to either constant physical cleaning or regular chemical dosing. There are various chemical path and patio cleaners available for this purpose.

Rust marks on patio

My cast-iron patio furniture has stained the paving slabs. I've cured the source of the problem by painting the feet of the table and chairs with a bitumen-based product but the rust marks have defied all attempts to remove them.

You could try brick-cleaning acid if it really bothers you, but it seems a bit drastic and you may end up with clean patches that stand out as much as the rust stains!

ELECTRICS

'Electrics' is the name given by builders to anything in a house that is connected to the main power supply. So it covers the nests of hidden wires that run all around the house, and anything that has one or more of these wires permanently attached to it.

I have always tried not to get too closely involved in electrics, because (a) electricity is dangerous and (b) the regulations and the equipment are constantly changing. But there are basics that everyone should know, such as the position of electrical cables under wall plaster and floors.

Wall-mounted power sockets and light switches are the way in which we use and control electricity in our homes. In winter, we may use the kitchen light switch twenty times in a day, but we never stop to think about the cable route which carries the electricity from the consumer unit to the switch and then on to the light fittings. The cables are run under floors and up and down walls behind the plaster. It is useful to have an idea of where they might be, if for no other reason than to avoid drilling through them when we put shelves up.

Under timber floors, electrical cables running parallel to the joists should be clipped in place along the mid-axis of a joist. This is mostly the case with houses built since 1960. Houses older than that are likely to have been rewired since their birth, which means that new cables will have been poked or dragged into place beneath already-fixed floorboards. So the chances of the cables having been carefully clipped in place are slim. They are probably just lying on top of the ceiling plaster. Nothing wrong with that, but bear it in mind if you ever decide to drill a hole in the ceiling.

Cables which have to run perpendicular to the joists should go through holes drilled as close as possible to the vertical centre of each joist. This is the section of the joist which is in neither compression (the top half) nor tension (the bottom half), so drilling a 25mm hole through the centre of a 180mm floor joist does not, theoretically, affect its strength. Let's hope not. And make sure your electrician understands what is meant by 'centre'. (The reason these holes are usually hit-and-miss is that you can't fit an ordinary electric drill down in the space between the joists, in order to drill square, so the holes are drilled at a downward angle. Only the most dedicated electricians carry special drills with right-angle attachments.) But as long as the cables are running through holes somewhere near the centre of the joists, at least they won't be hit by nails hammered into the floor from above. Unlike copper plumbing pipes which, because of their stiffness, have to be laid into notches cut in the tops of the joists.

Behind wall plaster, cables are supposed to be run vertically to and from power sockets and light switches. This is basic good practice, in order to give other people a rough idea of where they might be. So lighting-switch cables will almost always drop down vertically from the ceiling. Power cables usually run below timber floors, and vertically up to the sockets, but in houses with solid concrete ground floors, they may drop down vertically from the ceiling above. Bear in mind, also, that unqualified electricians and DIYers may not always have been completely diligent about having vertical cable runs, and that cables can sometimes be found running at all angles around rooms. This is especially likely in kitchens or rooms that have previously been used as kitchens, where power circuits for above-worktop sockets may have been run horizontally behind tiled splashbacks.

If in doubt, or when drilling into walls close to sockets or switches, it is a good idea to trace cable routes using a metal detector or cable finder. These are inexpensive and can be bought from builders' merchants or DIY outlets.

Another common concern where electrics are involved is lighting. Is it true, as some people say, that light bulbs blow more easily in cold weather? The only logical reason for this might be that the greater temperature difference between the 'on' and 'off' states of the light causes more stress on the filament – the thin wire inside the bulb that glows white hot and gives off the light. But, since the tungsten filament of an incandescent bulb glows at around 2,500°C, the fact that it starts off at ten degrees rather than twenty, say, would appear to be neither here nor there. Neither is there any evidence that failing bulbs are a sign of faulty wiring. We must face the fact that light bulbs break more often in the winter months because there are more hours of darkness to eat up their 1,000-hour average life-spans. Since this is equivalent to only three hours per day over a year, it is hardly surprising that bulbs in heavily used rooms such as kitchens should need replacing on a fairly regular basis.

As incandescent bulbs glow white-hot, tungsten molecules evaporate from the filament and get deposited as a black residue on the inside of the glass, until the filament becomes so thin that it burns through. So a blown but thoroughly blackened bulb will be one which has served its time well; a clearer one is more likely to have failed due to impact or vibration.

A more significant factor in bulb life is which way up it goes in the fitting. Bulbs are designed to hang downwards, and if they point upwards or sideways they don't last as long. This is because, as the filament becomes thin and brittle with use, if the bulb is pointing upwards or sideways the filament can eventually collapse under its own weight. The filaments in downward-hanging bulbs are subjected to less stress and will usually only break before their time if you bash them.

Another disadvantage of upward-facing bulbs is that when they do blow, they tend to short out the whole circuit, blowing the fuse or MCB (miniature circuit breaker or 'trip switch') on the consumer unit, and plunging the whole place into darkness. This is because bits of the broken filament fall across the two bulb terminals and cause a surge in power; if the bulb is hanging downwards then the broken bits land harmlessly in the glass.

Lately, however, even downward-hanging bulbs have started to trip circuits, because of a lowering in manufacturing standards. Light bulbs used to have a little built-in fuse – a very thin strip of wire in the bayonet cap – which would burn out first, leaving the rest of the filament intact. But now, pressure on costs from overseas manufacturers has meant that most modern bulbs are unfused, and can blow at any point along the filament. So you can now buy light bulbs for 20p; but they won't last as long and they'll blow your fuses. You never, ever, get something for nothing.

Nowadays we are all supposed to be using energy-saving light bulbs, which are claimed to last for 10,000 hours. I have been a keen user of these ever since they were first introduced, but I have yet to own one which has lasted anything like that length of time. They cost at least twenty times more than incandescent bulbs, but are claimed to use only one-fifth of the electricity. This means they need to last at least 2,000 hours in order to reach break-even point, and I am suspicious about this.

Energy-saving bulbs are more accurately called 'compact fluorescents', and the latest versions consist of two or three fluorescent glass loops attached to a mounting block containing the electronics needed to keep it working. This means they cannot always be used directly in place of incandescent bulbs; the light quality is cold, as with most fluorescent tube lighting, they cannot be used with normal dimmer switches, and they are too bulky for some light fittings and shades. The packet advertising which states 'interchangeable with an ordinary bulb' does not seem to mention this. Like all fluorescent lamps, they have a high initial rate of electricity consumption until they have warmed up, so they only save energy in situations where a light would normally be left on for long periods. They lose light intensity with age, and their life is shortened by regular switching on and off. Readers have also pointed out that they may be dangerous if used on dark stairways, because of the time taken to warm up and give full illumination.

And, like all fluorescent lighting tubes, the compact fluorescents contain mercury and need to be disposed of as hazardous waste since, if crushed as landfill, the mercury may find its way into the water supply. Local authority waste sites are supposed to be equipped to deal safely with fluorescent tubes, and householders should be allowed to deposit a maximum of six tubes at a time (this being the number used in a sunbed, I am told).

Electricians are obliged to dispose of redundant fluorescent tubes via specialist contractors – a service for which they have to pay a fee. This is why so many tubes are dumped illegally in builders' skips, and why anyone driving through a city centre early in the morning will have noticed forests of fluorescent tubes apparently sprouting out of litter bins. Any government worth its green credentials would obviously provide free recycling for such a hazardous material. Ours appears keen to persuade us to use the bulbs, but doesn't want to think about the consequences.

Rewiring 1

We have lived in our semi since it was built in 1961 by a reputable builder. The whole estate is considered to be very well built and in sound condition. Over recent years a number have been rewired. As far as I am aware this has been done because the owners felt it was time to do so, rather than as the result of any specific problems. We would value your opinion on this.

It depends upon the type of cable. The 1960s saw the changeover from rubber-sheathed cable to PVC. The rubber (usually black) had a life expectancy of around twenty-five years, so it would almost certainly be needing replacement now. PVC-sheathed cable (either white or grey), though, has no known life expectancy, and should still be perfectly serviceable. However, up until about 1970, lighting circuits were usually wired in twin PVC cable with no earth wire, and whilst this is still acceptable for plastic light fittings, anything metal (such as some types of wall light) would need an earth cable running to it. Also, in the same period, it was usual for one 30 amp ring main to supply power for the whole house, whereas now, with the increased number of electrical appliances, it is normal to have one ring main for downstairs and one for upstairs. Upgrading does not necessitate a complete rewire, as the circuit can be cut in half and reconnected to provide two separate rings.

It would also be advisable to replace an old fused consumer unit with a modern one with circuit breakers (trip switches), and incorporating a residual current circuit breaker (RCCB) – sometimes also referred to as a residual current device (RCD).

You may also consider having your old light fittings replaced, as these become brittle with age and heat, and having your power points inspected and replaced if necessary. An NICEIC qualified electrical contractor (see USEFUL CONTACTS, Electrics) should be able to advise you on the best way to proceed.

(The NICEIC recommend that household electrical systems should be inspected at least every ten years.)

Rewiring 2

My house, built in 1961, has flat or monopitched roofs, with no loft space. In two rooms it has walls of unfaced brick, and all floors are concrete. An electrician who recently replaced an immersion tells me most of the house needs rewiring, and has suggested a price of around £2,000. (The kitchen is new and not included.) He says he could not 'pull through' because the wires are probably not sheathed, and he will have to fit surface ducting. Am I being conned?

Don't know. Best to get a second and third opinion. If possible pay an independent electrical engineer to do a survey; then at least you'll know he's not touting for work.

Rewiring 3

My Victorian house needs rewiring, and I read somewhere that modern regulations do not permit new electric cables to be inserted in lath-and-plaster walls, but that they must be surface mounted in plastic conduit tubes. I am worried that this will spoil the character of the house. Is there any way of getting around these regulations?

There is no regulation that replacement electric cabling in old houses must be surface mounted. It is perfectly acceptable to run cables in chases (slots) cut into old plasterwork. The new cables are normally protected by hard plastic sheathing before being plastered over, to protect them from accidental damage – when someone is nailing a picture hook into the wall, for example. But lath-and-plaster partition walls in old houses are even easier – the new cables can usually be fed down in the hollow core of the wall, and fished out into the light switches or power points. An NICEIC-qualified electrician should be able to rewire your Victorian house with minimal surface wiring.

Problem with downlighters

I have recently had a new shower room built (en suite to the top-floor master bedroom) and was dismayed to find, after only a week, water stains appearing on the plasterboard ceiling. Upon going up into the loft, I found the whole space dripping with condensation. There is white mould growing on the rafters, and water is literally dripping off the felt between the rafters. A surveyor friend says that the shower room ceiling should have incorporated a vapour barrier to stop water vapour getting into the loft, but it seems likely to me that the moisture is rising up around the bulbs of the downlighters, and it says in the instructions for these that they should never be covered.

Is there any solution to this problem, or does it mean that down-lighters are not suitable for bathrooms?

It would have been a good idea to incorporate a vapour barrier but, as you point out, this would be pretty ineffective if the water vapour was able to escape around the down-lighter bulbs. There are special sealed downlighters made specifically for wet rooms, but ordinary downlighters also come in a wide range of styles – some of them are open around the bulb, like yours, notably the 'eye ball' type with a moveable directional spot bulb. In this case, the heat of the bulb is likely to create a convection current and actually draw moist air up into the loft, like a flue. In other types of downlighter the bulb fitting is integral with the surround and these will present less of a gap for the water vapour to escape. With luck, you may be able to find some of the latter which are a similar size to the ones you have to replace, and so avoid having to make new holes. In any event, it sounds as though you need much more efficient air extraction in the shower room (see CONDENSATION), and you will also need to look at the ventilation in the roof space (see ROOFS).

Modern light fittings

We live in a modern house with loop-in lighting circuits, i.e. all wiring connections take place in ceiling roses or batten holders. We want to replace the batten holders in our kitchen with spotlights. These are available in the DIY stores as well as at electrical suppliers. However, every spotlight assembly I have looked at has only live, neutral and earth connections, but no terminals to connect the loop-in, loop-out and switch cables. What is the best way of wiring these spotlights? I have been told by some to use a terminal block, but this doesn't sound

very safe to me, as it would just be hanging in space, i.e.
connections would not be in a fireproof enclosure. I cannot
alter the cabling easily as it is not readily accessible.

Most modern homes are wired in this way – called three-
plate wiring – where all the connections are made at the
lighting point. Yet very few manufacturers consider this in
the design of their light fittings. So the new fitting comes
with connectors for the earth, neutral and switched live
conductor, to operate the light, but no provision for termi-
nating the permanent live conductors which, although they
do not connect to the light fitting, must all be connected
together to carry the supply on to the next lighting point.

Regulations and good practice require that all connections
are made in an 'appropriate enclosed accessory', which is
often not easy, given that there is very little space in the
mounting. Some fittings come with strip connectors and
instructions that clearly encourage the installer to push them
up into the ceiling void above the fitting, which is not
advisable. Strip connectors (or 'choc block', as they are
known) may be used provided they can be enclosed in the
housing or mounting of the light and that they are of good
quality – i.e. either Bakelite or self-extinguishing PVC (you
can always check this with a match). But if there is insufficient room, then you will have to fit a small four-terminal
joint box in the ceiling void. These can be as small as 50mm
in diameter, which means they can be pushed through the
hole made for a downlighter, for example. With some types
of fittings, it may be possible to adapt them by screwing
them to a circular-type pattress (like you get on a pull-cord
switch) to house the connections.

Halogen lights

What are the advantages and disadvantages of mains halogen
and low voltage halogen lamps?

Halogen lamps give a very white light and come in mains
voltage or low voltage, usually 12V. The main differences
are cost. The low voltage lamps are cheaper, but you have
the initial additional cost of a low voltage transformer. There
is a wider variety of fittings to choose from in the low
voltage range, and if the transformer is fitted remotely then
they can be used in more situations where mains voltage
would not be acceptable, such as bath/shower rooms or
saunas. As far as lamp-life and running costs are concerned,
I suspect there is little difference.

Low-energy bulbs

In the early 1980s I was responsible for a large egg production
operation. The laying stock were given a lighting programme
which simulated spring followed by long summer days of 16
hours. When the Phillips SL9 and SL18 light units were introduced there appeared to be significant potential savings and
this was monitored to confirm whether this was the case. The
lights were dated with a felt-tip pen when each was installed.
Because the lighting period each day was controlled by time
clocks in each building the life of each bulb was easily calcu-
lated. A life of 4,000–5,000 hours was commonplace with some
reaching 7,000 hours. We established however, by using a light
meter, that after 4,000 hours light intensity began to fall off
steadily. This was not evident to the naked eye. Since this was
important to the hen – a bit technical but there is a connection
between light intensity, the pituitary gland, and egg production
– it was judged better to replace the bulbs before they failed
but still after a significant saving. Thousands of bulbs were

involved in this assessment. Thorn 2D 16W light units were also monitored with similar findings. Although not significant to our application it was felt that the 2D units had a warmer tone.

This is an interesting observation, and a challenge to the manufacturers' claims of a 10,000-hour life. I put this point to Phillips for comment, but they have not replied.

Low-energy bulbs

An important point, rarely made, is that energy-saving bulbs do not save energy unless used in locations where a light source would normally be on for very long continuous periods. They have a very high initial rate of consumption until they reach steady load state. The suppliers ought to make this clear: they *increase* consumption when installed for frequent on/off lights.

Another good point, not made clear by the manufacturers.

We had assumed that our new low-energy bulbs would fit inside the shades that we had – no such luck, they were about an inch too long! So we had new shades provided which were open at the top and bottom and hung from the ceiling instead of being flush to it but which, oddly, still had a 60W limit.

Some manufacturers are now making fittings and shades compatible with low-energy bulbs, but if you have to buy them, then it makes you wonder exactly how much energy and money you are actually saving.

Emergency power supplies

My sister recently moved house to rural Kent and the day after she moved in the rains and floods swept through the area and blacked out all power supplies for a week. Since we are told that these types of weather conditions may become more common, what are the practicalities of installing some form of generator-based emergency light and power supply that would enable family life to go on – albeit in a reduced way – until proper power is restored?

Petrol-powered generators have become remarkably small and quiet in recent years, and if you live in an area prone to power cuts then it may make sense to keep one in the garage for emergency lighting using extension cables. Prices start at around £400 for a 1kW model. The other main 'essential' is to power the fridge and freezer, which may need more power (the compressor on a chest freezer may use only 500W, but it needs a higher surge of power every time it kicks in). It would also be useful to be able to power the central heating pump and boiler (without which the gas or fuel oil are of little use) but this would require wiring-in to the existing house electrical system. You should consult a qualified electrician for advice about installing the necessary switching gear. At the upper end, a 10kW diesel generator with automatic start which will power the whole house could cost between £6,000 and £10,000. The market leaders are Honda through which you can contact a local supplier (see USEFUL CONTACTS, Electrics).

Emergency supply

I live in a group of three/four households a few miles from the nearest town but within yards of each other. There is no piped gas supply available – we can use bottled. We are on the national electricity grid but in winter, suffer frequent power breakdowns. We exist well together as neighbours co-operating on many fronts. How easy/difficult would it be to install a mutual standby generator – say the small kind that powers coffee stalls on the street with light and heat – to 'cut in' or be switched on during a power cut? I understand Honda and Yamaha make these.

Another possibility would be a small wind-driven generator. Plentiful supplies of the necessary here on the coast! But I appreciate battery storage problems would arise for this.

Buying the generator is not the problem. It's installing it with all the necessary switchgear so that it cuts in and out without damaging your existing circuitry. You need to get a suitably experienced local electrician (NICEIC registered) to advise you and quote for it. Wind generators do not have to be low voltage – they can be 240V and feed back surplus power into the grid, making your meter run backwards. But you would probably need planning consent.

FLOORS

Readers' floor problems tend to fall into two main categories: solid concrete ground floors, and creaking upstairs chipboard floors. Both can be equally troublesome.

Solid concrete ground floors were introduced into Victorian houses in a big way from the 1960s onwards. The rationale was that the original suspended timber floors could be affected by rot, and many surveyors, architects, housing associations and even private owners decided that it would be a good idea to do away with the timber and replace it with a slab of good old solid concrete, poured on to a polyethylene damp-proof membrane (DPM). This may have removed the possibility of wood rot, but at the same time it deprived a house of the sub-floor ventilation which had kept it dry for decades. The perceived wisdom was that the DPM would keep the floor dry, and a chemical injection damp-proof course (DPC) would stop the ground moisture being diverted into the walls. The fatal flaw in the scenario was the blind faith in the idea that chemical injection DPCs actually worked. They don't. So tens of thousands of Victorian houses have had perfectly serviceable dry, ventilated, timber floors torn up, to be replaced with cold, hard concrete, and with the added disadvantage of damp walls. It is still being done.

Creaking chipboard blights the lives of many people who live in 'modern' homes – by which I mean mass-produced, speculatively built houses and flats of 1970s vintage onwards.

Some estate homes of this period were built with proper timber floorboards, but not many. Like concrete ground floors, chipboard upper floors were built on a misconception – that, being a man-made board material, tongue-and-groove chipboard was more stable than pesky old-fashioned real wood, and that it would therefore have none of the disadvantages of traditional floorboards (i.e. shrinking, swelling, twisting, splitting, creaking). What was not appreciated was that chipboard suffers from a phenomenon called 'creep', which means that over time, it sags between the joists, and in the process becomes distorted, so that it creaks when it rubs against the joists, and it squeaks when it binds against adjacent boards.

Both of these problems are examples of what can go wrong when builders fall for the idea that old-fashioned construction materials and methods must be inferior to new ones. It is a problem of the modern age.

Damp-proofing
You have written that the combination of a damp-proof membrane under a concrete floor with chemical injection damp-proofing in walls is ineffective. I have just bought a cottage (1820) in Cumbria with floors of flags laid on the sub-soil plus external walls 2ft thick. Please could you advise me what sort of damp-proofing would be effective? There are no obvious damp problems.

If there are no obvious dampness problems then why does your cottage need damp-proofing? Count yourself lucky to have found an old building in original condition, and restore it using traditional methods and materials. Applying modern materials to old buildings can create problems that did not exist before, and 'damp-proofing' is a prime example.

Sanded floorboards

I have been thinking about sanding and sealing the floorboards
in my dining room. However, some sections of the floor have
been ruined by successive plumbers and electricians, and need
replacing. The problem is, the modern 6in × 1in (150mm ×
25mm) floorboards from builders' merchants are narrower and
thinner than the original boards. Where can I buy suitable
matching replacement boards?

The timber sold at the builders' merchants will be PAR
(planed all round), so the 150mm × 25mm sawn size is
reduced to about 140mm × 20mm. You could try to find
second-hand boards at auctions or from architectural sal-
vage firms (or keep an eye out for boards dumped in
builders' skips). These will provide a good match in colour
and grain. But new sawn boards of the right size should be
available from specialist timber merchants, and any sawmill
will cut boards to order. Victorian floors were often laid
with rough sawn boards which were then planed and
sanded in situ. For a perfect fit buy the boards slightly over-
size and allow them to acclimatize to the room conditions
for as long as possible before fixing.

Wide floorboards

We have bought a redundant farm building to renovate as a
house. The floor is dirt at the moment and we intend having
a suspended timber floor. I would appreciate your opinion on
our using scaffold boards instead of standard floorboards. They
were used on a recent *Changing Rooms* programme on TV. We
like the idea of wider boards.

You can have floorboards any width you like. But if you
buy scaffold boards you will just be paying extra for stress-
graded timber with metal reinforcing strips fixed to each

end. Any local timber merchant or sawmill will supply you with boards cut to size, or for advice call the Enfield Timber Company (see USEFUL CONTACTS, Timber Floors).

Curling floorboards

I live in a 1930s semi with suspended wooden floorboards throughout. Over the last few months I've noticed that some of the floorboards feel through the carpet as if they are 'curling' up at the edges and coming away from the supporting joists.

This 'curling' or lifting is accompanied by the obligatory squeaky floorboard sound which is expected on a seventy-year-old house. Now I would like to pull back the carpets and secure the floorboards back to the joists but am unsure as to what means to do this is best. Should I (a) Screw the boards to the joists; (b) Hammer standard nails in; (c) Use special nails?

One concern I do have is what is causing the floorboards to curl/lift on both the ground and first floors? Is it normal to do so, or are there any other possible reasons lurking around?

The nails to use are called floor brads, which are 60mm square-cut nails with a one-sided head. These provide a good grip into the joists, the heads are easily 'lost' in the surface of the board without splitting it, and, like all cut nails, it should be relatively easy to work them loose if the boards need to be lifted for access to the sub-floor void. (Round-head, or 'wire', nails cannot be 'lost', and leave bumps on the surface of the floor. Round-heads and ovals both grip tight into the joists and cannot be worked loose, so when the boards are lifted the nail heads rip through the boards and spilt them.)

Screwing floorboards is often done to cure squeaking, but it can create difficulties. Not least that if the boards have to be lifted, it is difficult to locate all the screw heads and remove the screws. And it takes only one screw to be missed and the board will split, making it unfit for reuse.

The sudden curling of the floorboards can only be due to rapid drying shrinkage. The house in question must have just experienced a marked increase in heating and/or ventilation.

Gaps between sanded floorboards

What is the best way of sealing gaps between old floorboards? We have sanded and varnished the floors, but in some rooms wind blows cold through the gaps between the boards. We have tried doing an area with wood filler, wiped off with a damp cloth, but this takes ages, and does not always bridge the gap. Is there a better way?

The main point to note is that floorboards in Victorian/ Edwardian houses were not intended to be left exposed, and would usually have been covered with loose rugs or mats. Sanding softwood floorboards is very much a recent fashion, and is a poor substitute for tongue-and-groove hardwood boarding. Having said that, it is possible to make a good job of sanding old floorboards (although bear in mind the noise problems that bare timber floors can have, especially for downstairs neighbours (see SOUNDPROOFING)).

The gaps between the boards are due to drying shrinkage, which is accelerated in most cases by central heating, which is good, because it means that the boards are well seasoned and unlikely to shrink any further. If you want to do a really good job then you should consider lifting the boards, cleaning off the edges, and re-fitting them, wedging them up tight to each other as you go. You will probably find that tightening up all the gaps leaves you room for almost one extra complete board across the width of the room. This sounds like a major upheaval, but if it can be combined with rewiring or central heating work, or fitting insulation below ground floors, then it is probably worth it.

If you decide to leave the boards in their original state, and the gaps are large – 2 to 3mm – then you could ask a local joinery workshop to cut you tapered strips to glue into the gaps, which you then trim and sand flat. Otherwise you should save the dust from the sanding machine (collected in the vacuum bag), mix it with PVA adhesive or a proprietary resin adhesive (for suppliers see USEFUL CONTACTS, Timber Floors) and work it into the gaps with a filler knife. Sand it flat when it has dried.

Damaged teak block floor

A teak block floor, laid in 1949, is causing concern. A few of the blocks have become loose and can lift out. What would you suggest as the best substance to reseat and secure them? I really don't want to have the whole floor up and relaid.

Hardwood block floors were originally laid in hot bitumen, so you need a special solvent-based adhesive which will melt the bitumen and enable the blocks to be pushed back down into it. Lecol adhesive is available from Victorian Wood Works (see USEFUL CONTACTS, Timber Floors).

Creaky floor

My bungalow, built in 1987, has a floor of hard compressed board, so hard it is almost impossible to drive nails into it. But the problem is that the floor creaks when I walk on it. Could you suggest a remedy?

The floors are made of flooring-grade chipboard. See answers below.

Squeaking chipboard

Our 1982 Bovis house has chipboard upper floors, which creak and squeak whenever anyone walks on them. I am all for ripping out the chipboard close to the walls (made of a sort of cardboard mesh), which stand upon it, and replacing it with good solid wood floorboards. My husband is not so sure; he is afraid the inner walls will be affected. What can we do?

The problem with the lightweight plasterboard partition walls is that some of them may be bearing solely on the chipboard flooring. Those which line up with supporting walls on the ground floor, or which are spanning at right-angles across the joists would be OK, but those running parallel with the joists may be a problem. Probably best to see if you can stop the creaking by screwing the chipboard down. Avoid underfloor pipes and cables by using a metal detector, and use screws twice as long as the thickness of the boards, which are probably 18mm.

Creaky floorboards

Could I use expanding foam as a 'quick fix' for some squeaky floorboards, please?

No. You'll end up with squeaky floorboards *and* squeaky foam.

We have lived in our 1850 detached house for over twenty years, adding a two-room upstairs/downstairs extension ten years ago. During the past two to three years the upstairs floorboards have begun to creak. Is this a sign of movement or subsidence? What should we do?

Building movement or subsidence would generally have other symptoms as well, such as cracking. Although it is possible that your recent extension addition may have imposed some extra stresses on the building which have resulted in a slight distortion of one or more of the upstairs floor joists. I imagine you undertook changes to the heating system at the same time, as well, and this may have made the house dryer, and caused the timbers to dry out slightly more. But it is more than likely that the creaking is due simply to the nails working loose over time through being walked on. Try hammering the nails in tighter and see if this does the trick.

Cracked tiled floor

We bought a new flat three years ago and two of the kitchen floor tiles are cracked. I have been informed that this is due to the movement of the building. The floors are concrete and we are on the second floor. As these tiles are no longer available do we have any redress against the builder, and should this have happened after three years? We feel that spares of these tiles should have been kept if this problem was likely to arise, considering the flats were sold as luxury apartments.

The theory that your tiles have been cracked by building movement may or may not be true; this could only be confirmed if the alleged movement was measured. It is certainly common for new buildings to move, through settlement or drying shrinkage, and it is good practice to allow for this by bedding floor tiles on a flexible material such as asphalt rather than a rigid one like sand-and-cement. However, the ultimate reason for the cracking will almost certainly be that the tiles are too thin for the job. The term 'luxury' often refers only to the surface appearance of a new property, and not to the quality of the materials used. Since

the tiles are no longer available, you could justifiably claim
that the builder should re-lay the whole floor, but you may
have to take him to court to achieve this.

Brick pavers

We have recently bought an old cottage and when we took up
the carpets we found that all the downstairs floors have brick
pavers, presumably with bare earth underneath. Surprisingly,
the house didn't smell damp, and the carpets weren't damp
either; they were protected in one room by what looked like
roofing felt between carpet and floor, and in the others by a
thin layer of polythene sheeting. Although the pavers were
slightly damp, there was no sign of mould.

Presumably what we should do is take up all the bricks and
put down a damp-proof membrane before re-laying the bricks.
But what is the difference between stopping any damp below
brick level or, as had been done, above? We want to avoid the
rigmarole of taking up the bricks if we can. What do you think,
and what are the implications for the mortgageability of the
property? (We bought it for cash.)

My advice is not to mess around with it. You are lucky to
have found an old cottage with a brick floor in original
condition, and if you put in a membrane now then you'll
upset the moisture equilibrium, and could even make the
walls damp. I'm not sure why you would want to have
carpets anyway – one of the beauties of an old brick floor is
its appearance. If you must have a floor covering then use
loose sisal mats, which will still allow the floor to breathe.

Regarding mortgaging, most conventional mortgage
lenders would probably want the cottage 'modernized' (i.e.
spoilt) but there are a couple of more sensible ones, such as
the Ecology Building Society, who could be persuaded to

lend against it in its original condition (see USEFUL CON-
TACTS, Building Societies).

Repairing a solid floor

Please could you advise me with regard to resin repair of
cracked concrete floors? The company in question claims to be
able to stabilize subsidence in floors and has sent me some
literature with case histories, technical details and so forth. The
main method used seems to be the excavation of small holes
into which some form of resin is injected into the ground. I am
concerned because our neighbour intends to use this company
to underpin his small extension. My neighbour was in the
building trade almost all his life and is now in his seventies;
he is still active in doing all the necessary jobs on his home
but I am worried he has not had any experience of this
technique.

The method has been around for a few years. But before
spending thousands on patching up a solid floor, I would
sooner spend the money digging it out and reinstating with
a suspended timber floor – much warmer, dryer and less
trouble all round.

HAZARDS

The history of construction is littered with materials which, in their day, were thought to be the answer to every problem, and which later turned out to be damaging to health. The most notorious of these is asbestos, which was widely used as a fireproof lagging material and is now known to cause cancer and respiratory illness. But hot on its heels comes lead, used for water pipes and in paint, which is associated with nervous disorders, reduced intelligence, hyperactivity and behavioural problems, especially in children. Although it was banned in Australia in 1906 and the USA in 1978, lead paint continued to be used in Britain until 1992.

Formaldehyde adhesives, used to bind together the particles in many types of building board, are a known respiratory hazard, and their use is strictly controlled in a number of American states. But they continue in widespread general use in the UK.

The most toxic substances in construction are pesticides. Widespread concerns have been expressed about the safety of these chemicals for more than thirty years, but in the UK many of them continue to be licensed as 'safe' by the Health and Safety Executive (HSE), and they are routinely sprayed in thousands of homes every week – usually as a precaution against imaginary problems. Among the letters in this section are some from readers whose health has been ruined by exposure to these supposedly safe treatments.

Asbestos water tank

We bought our thirty-year-old council flat a few years ago and had central heating fitted. The council are now installing heating in the remaining tenant-occupied flats and replacing their asbestos water tanks with plastic. Our tank is tucked away on top of the airing cupboard and seems perfectly sound. In view of the asbestos scare do you think the tank is a health hazard?

The main dangers come from the brown and blue varieties of asbestos, which were used mainly for insulation and pipe lagging, and these should always be removed by specialist contractors when found. Water tanks, wall panels and corrugated roofing sheets were usually made from the less dangerous white asbestos, mixed with cement. Asbestos is only dangerous when the fibres get into the air and are inhaled, so if your asbestos-cement tank is in good condition, then it should not represent any problem, and the safest option is to leave it undisturbed.

Asbestolux garage ceiling

I am concerned about the ceiling of my garage. The house was built in 1974 and has an attached garage which backs on to the kitchen. The ceiling is covered in a type of board which I have heard called something like 'asbestoloid'. It is like asbestos and is there, I understand, for fire safety reasons. Is it asbestos? Is it dangerous? It is attached by nails and there is a broken piece at one end. Are we likely to find surveyors insisting the broken sheet, or the whole lot, should be removed or replaced if we came to sell the property?

The word you are looking for is 'Asbestolux'. It is everywhere, and yes, it contains a large amount of white asbestos, which Her Majesty's Government has recently decided might not be safe after all. Asbestolux is OK as long as you don't disturb it and inhale the fibres, so the best thing is probably to leave it alone for now. If you decide to remove it, then you should contact your local authority Environmental Health Department for advice about disposal, or for details of local approved removal contractors.

Artex 1

My lounge has an Artex ceiling with the characteristic scalloped finish. What can I do to achieve a plain surface?

Artex is a brand of textured paint used to make decorative patterns on plasterboard, or to cover up cracks in old ceilings (although this is rarely successful). Other brands are Wondertex, Suretex and Newtex, but they all tend to get referred to as 'Artex'. The big problem with these textured finishes is that they may contain asbestos. The Artex brand was still being manufactured with asbestos as recently as 1984. So textured finishes should not be drilled or dry-sanded, as the asbestos fibres could be released into the air and inhaled.

It is possible to remove Artex wet, using a steam wallpaper stripper, and taking care to bag-up the scrapings securely while still damp. The bags should be labelled 'asbestos', and disposed of specially by the local authority Refuse Department.

Textured finishes can also be covered over with plaster, so long as the surface is first primed with diluted PVA adhesive. A specialized product called Artex Transform is also available. The dilemma is that the newly plastered surfaces should really be labelled, to warn future generations that asbestos lurks beneath.

Artex 2

I read your piece about asbestos in Artex with some alarm, having lived with it for thirty-four years in one house or another. I have certainly drilled through Artex ceilings and another member of my family has recently cut out a section in order to fit a ceiling extractor fan. Having recently lost a good friend to mesothelioma, an incurable form of lung cancer caused by asbestos inhaled when he was in the building trade, I would not wish anyone else to suffer needlessly. It seems a scandal that Artex should have contained asbestos as recently as 1984 when the dangers were already well known. Surely with the popularity of DIY this is a public health issue and the public should be warned of the dangers.

It is a common danger and, as you say, a scandal. I draw attention to it whenever I can. However, the white asbestos used in Artex and Asbestolux is less dangerous than the blue and brown varieties – which is why it remained in use after the others were banned. Occasional exposure to small quantities carries a very low risk; it is regular occupational exposure which usually results in illness.

Lightning protection

I recently purchased a house with a large area of flat roof that had completely perished. I was reluctant to use traditional felt roofing and decided on copper panelling on three-quarter-inch plywood decking. It is now completed and I am very pleased with it, but I am concerned about its vulnerability in a thunderstorm, since the house is high in the Pennines and somewhat isolated. Is this type of roof more prone to being struck by lightning, and should it be 'earthed' in some way or another?

Any building can be struck by lightning, regardless of the nature of the roofing material. But most damage comes not from direct lightning hits, but from electrical discharges being conducted in via overhead telephone cables and television aerials. Protection against lightning therefore involves two processes – first, a traditional lighting conductor on the highest point of the building, to prevent lightning strikes and fire damage; and second, electronic anti-surge protectors on TV, telephone and mains electrical supplies. For details contact the National Federation of Master Steeplejacks and Lightning Conductor Engineers (see USEFUL CONTACTS, Hazards).

Radon gas

I am hoping to buy a retirement cottage in Herefordshire, but the surveyor's report states that it is in an area affected by radon gas. Is this a big problem, and how can it be dealt with? My wife is now very worried about possible harmful effects on our health, and for our visiting grandchildren.

Radon is a natural radioactive gas that seeps out of the ground in certain areas, chiefly those with underlying granite. The radioactivity is low, and usually harmless, but if it is allowed to enter a house, then it can build up to higher levels. The main health fear is an increased risk of lung cancer from breathing the gas over long periods. Surveyors are obliged to mention the risk in a given area, but this does not mean that a particular house will have a radon problem. You should be able to get a more detailed assessment from the local authority Environmental Health Department. In any case, preventative measures are easy. For a house with a suspended timber ground floor, the usual method is to fit an impermeable membrane below the floorboards, and ensure that the existing sub-floor ventilation is adequate. With a solid floor, a membrane is also applied, sometimes with the addition of a hollow polyethylene radon sump below floor level. This is attached to a vent pipe that disperses the radon gas above roof level. For more details contact Proctor Group Ltd (see USEFUL CONTACTS, Hazards).

MDF

As a life-long DIY performer I am a relative newcomer to the use of MDF board. It cuts and routs well and cleanly. But when visiting B&Q to purchase and have a large board reduced to a manageable size I am regaled with reports of how the board is banned in the USA as a hazard. There is also a warning on each board to wear a protective mask when using powered machinery, which is not always practicable for small operations. What are the true hazards associated with MDF?

The hazards of MDF (medium-density fibreboard) come from the fine nature of the dust, which can cause respiratory problems, and from the 'out-gassing' of the formaldehyde-based adhesive. It is not true that MDF has been banned, in the USA or anywhere else. There are regulations over its use in confined spaces such as woodworking shops where prolonged daily exposure is a factor, but occasional DIY use probably represents a threat no greater than that of, say, white spirit; i.e. take all reasonable precautions, and remember that some people will be more sensitive than others. When MDF has been stored for over three months, the adhesive is reckoned to have all 'out-gassed', and there are alternative, but more expensive, types using safer adhesives, which are used in hospitals and nurseries.

TIMBER TREATMENT CHEMICALS

Multiple treatments

We have just exchanged contracts on a part-barn conversion property in Norfolk. Our surveyor noted evidence of recent wood-boring beetle activity in the ridge board of the ex-barn area, where the original timbers remain and show plenty of evidence of past beetle infestation. He also commented that the timber had been treated before, probably at the time of conversion. Unfortunately, there is no record or therefore documentation/guarantee of prior treatment. We engaged a well-known timber treatment speciality firm in the area for a second opinion and estimate for complete treatment with long-term guarantees. The specialist confirmed the presence of recent activity; agreed with the surveyor that infestation was not serious; confirmed that there had been prior treatment but could not determine what with. He suggested further treatment and his quotation was reasonably priced.

As a retired industrial chemist I am aware of the dangers associated with organic insecticides and their long-lingering health hazard effects, so, upon questioning the timber man was relieved to learn that they used micro-sprays to apply an inorganic boron compound, which he said would permeate the timber over time, to a depth of approximately 2in (50mm) – the boron being poisonous to the beetle. Your comments on timber treatments have not inspired confidence. What would you treat with and how?

I am in favour of the Building Research Establishment and Health and Safety Executive advice that if timber is dry then it will not be attacked by insects or fungi. So in a normally heated and ventilated building it is not necessary to use chemical preservatives. Old flight holes are not evidence of continuing active infestation, and will generally only be in the sapwood at the surface of the timber, so they will not necessarily have weakened timbers below their design strength.

Previous treatment can be easily identified by gas chromatography. But if the property has previously been treated then you should be asking (a) how can there be continuing infestation (i.e. is there a continuing moisture problem allowing infestation to continue)? and (b) what would be the health effects of introducing an additional chemical, effectively creating a chemical 'cocktail'?

The idea that a surface-sprayed boron micro-emulsion will penetrate two inches is a rather fanciful claim. I'm afraid your 'specialist' must have got confused by the technical presentation at the chemical company's seminar. If you still think you need chemical treatment then I suggest you engage an *independent* expert who won't have the incentive of trying to sell you something.

Permethrin

I own a Victorian house which I have been renovating a room at a time myself. Where there has been evidence of woodworm I have treated the floor with a product with permethrin in it. I am suspicious of timber treatment companies and their rip-offs. However, I am faced with a living-room floor with holes from woodworm. Would you repair, replace, or treat? I have central heating. Does this help? I'm concerned for the health of my kids. Any tips?

The central heating means that the timber will dry down to a level unable to support insect activity. Obviously any boards that have been damaged very badly can be replaced, but woodworm holes in floorboards generally only occur in the sapwood at the corners or edges of the boards, and do not affect the strength sufficiently to justify their replacement. Beyond that, the holes are only a cosmetic problem. Many people claim to have been made seriously ill by permethrin, and children are usually more susceptible, since the effects are inversely proportional to body weight.

Illness

In July 1985 we moved into a house which was built at the turn of the last century. We had the timbers sprayed for woodworm (and rot protection?). A chemical called 'permethrin' was used. We moved in the day after it was done but many floorboards were still up. Shortly after our move, both my young daughter (then two and a half) and I developed myalgic encephalomyelitis (ME). Our diagnoses did not come till a few years later. As time went by and more was learned about chemical poisoning, I became increasingly convinced that the woodworm spraying was the cause of our illness. We are both still ill. I planned to return to teaching when my daughter started school (at five) but have been unable to do so. My daughter, having had quite a bit of time off school, and now almost seventeen, is struggling with part-time school to do her GCSEs.

We have been ill for fourteen years and do not now have any hope of a full recovery for either of us. The medical profession offers little or no help. I have written to you to raise awareness of this possible result of spraying with toxins. If you have any other information or letters from others confirming my thoughts, I would be grateful to hear about it.

There are many thousands of people in your position, who have become ill following exposure to permethrin. But since it is licensed as 'safe' by the Health and Safety Executive

(HSE), physicians will refuse to acknowledge that it might have injured you and your daughter. They are more likely to prescribe antibiotics, steroids and, in desperation, tranquillizers before deciding that your condition is a mental problem.

Pesticides victims support is currently being organized by the Pesticides Action Network, and you should contact Alison Craig (see USEFUL CONTACTS, Pesticides Victim Support).

In the meantime, I assume you are not still living in the sprayed house. But do you know if your current house has been sprayed? You can get it tested. You need to get into a pesticide-free environment.

Chemical dangers

I have now had ME for just over five years and have not been able to work for the last three years. I ran my own dampproofing and timber treatment business for a period of sixteen years. During the first five years or so I was actually carrying out the treatments myself. I strictly followed all health and safety procedures as detailed on the product literature and later as required by COSHH (Control of Substances Hazardous to Health Acts). The blood tests I have had show high levels of dieldrin, DDT, DDE, HCB (hexachlorobenzene), pentachlorophenol and carbaryl. I presume all of these, being persistent chemicals, will stay where they are in my blood for many years to come. During the period that I was using these products the chemical company assured me that their products were very safe. As you correctly say, people should be warned of the dangers that these chemicals represent. The chemical companies tell us that they are safe, but then they are forced into changing their formulations and moving on to different

products, permethrin being a good example. This they advertised as a safe, natural product. As I mentioned earlier these
chemicals are particularly persistent (we had to guarantee their
effectiveness for thirty years!). Some of them also tend to leach
out of timber for years, in particular the various preservative
pastes.

As you will probably have found out by now, the industry
and the Health Safety Executive (HSE) will never believe
that you followed the instructions properly. They define the
chemicals as 'safe' – so they could not possibly accept that,
even when used as directed, they can cause illness. There
are strong parallels with the tobacco industry.

INSULATION

Insulation is a good way of cutting heating costs and energy waste. Houses constructed before 1945 often had minimal insulation, and thus took a lot of energy to heat. As fuel costs rose in the 1960s, householders were encouraged to put 50mm of fluffy quilt in their lofts, and after the oil crisis of 1973 this was raised to 100mm. We are now encouraged to have at least 200mm (eight inches) of insulation above our bedroom ceilings. The 1970s also saw cavity wall insulation introduced for new buildings; first 25mm, then 50mm, and now 75mm.

The trouble with this approach is that successive thickening of insulation does not necessarily result in corresponding savings in energy. The law of diminishing returns applies. So if your uninsulated home costs £1,000 per year to heat, then wrapping it in the latest specified thickness of fluffy stuff may well reduce that outlay to £500, but doubling the thickness will not reduce the heating costs to zero. Homes in northern Europe will always need a source of internal heat, although the current government obsession with insulation encourages people to believe otherwise, and this can have unfortunate consequences.

The chief problem with a spartan fuel regime is an increased risk of condensation. Some pensioners and other low-income families have annual fuel bills of less than £150, and they achieve this by keeping their windows permanently closed, taking the fuses out of mechanical extractor fans, and blocking up air vents. The inevitable result is black mould growth on ceilings and walls, and green mildew on shoes and clothes in the wardrobe. Local authority tenants on income support are especially likely to live in such conditions, and there is usually a friendly local damp-proofing company on hand to persuade them that they are victims of 'damp', and to encourage them to sue their landlords to have their homes 'damp-proofed'. Many cash-strapped local authorities waste millions of pounds of council tax payers' money every year on this sort of nonsense.

The thermal insulation ballyhoo is set to reach new levels of absurdity shortly with a revision to the Building Regulations which will effectively end the tradition of masonry construction in Britain. The new 'Part L' document, which covers the conservation of energy in new buildings, demands yet another increase in the thickness of wall insulation. Unfortunately, another department at the Department of the Environment (formerly the DETR now the DTLR) is simultaneously outlawing the HCFC gases that have been used to manufacture the most efficient foam insulation materials. The gases, which are used to blow the bubbles in the foam, will have to be replaced with carbon dioxide, which produces a less insulating foam. So to comply with the new regulations, masonry walls will henceforth have to be around 450mm thick, an uneconomic prospect for most volume housebuilders. New homes are also to be subject to airtightness tests, which will ensure that ventilation is kept to a minimum.

This all means that from 2003, new houses will be hermetically sealed timber boxes, chock-full of chemical timber preservatives, mineral wool fibres and formaldehyde emissions from plastics and adhesives. Condensation will be a major problem, but will probably be dwarfed by the epidemic of asthma and other allergic reactions which will affect the generations of children brought up in these ghastly buildings.

If you are thinking of improving your home's insulation, then before you do anything you should get hold of a copy of the BRE booklet 'Thermal Insulation – avoiding risks', available direct from CRC Ltd. (See USEFUL CONTACTS, Construction Literature).

Cavity wall insulation 1

I am contemplating installing cavity wall insulation in our property and looking at the materials available I feel that foam would be the best on the basis that polystyrene beads would restrict any further maintenance on the wall, i.e. window frame replacement, and mineral wool could be detrimental to my health, as I suffer from emphysema. We have all heard of the advantages of cavity wall insulation, but are there any disadvantages? I have heard of damp spots appearing on the inside of walls for example.

Cavity walls were first built, in exposed coastal areas such as yours (west Wales), in order to keep out wind-driven rain. Filling the cavity with insulation will always hold the risk that moisture will be able to find its way across to the inside, whatever the insulation material. There is also the possibility that the installation will be less than perfect, leaving unfilled air pockets – these will leave 'cold spots' on the inside walls which attract condensation. Another serious problem concerns wall-tie corrosion; cavity insulation makes the outer brick leaf colder, and therefore wetter, which can accelerate rusting of the wall ties. And if the ties then have to be replaced, there is no satisfactory way of refilling the holes in the insulation, whatever the material. The cavity insulation industry denies the existence of these problems, but in my experience they are quite common. I do not think cavity wall insulation is a good idea.

Cavity wall insulation 2

Please could you give us your views on cavity wall insulation? Our house was built in 1988 and gets very cold during winter, especially downstairs. We've had one quote so far of £260 for the downstairs part of our three-bedroomed detached house. The upstairs of our house is tiled and we have been told that we cannot have this insulated. Are there any disadvantages associated with cavity wall insulation? P.S. We live in Hampshire, although it sometimes feels like we live in northern Scotland!

If the upper storey of the house has a tile hanging then – given the year of construction – it will already be insulated, behind the timber frame that the tiles are fixed to. And since hot air rises, the heat loss through the ground-floor walls will be lower than that upstairs. In other words, the energy-saving returns on your cavity insulation will be marginal. Your house feels cold because you live in a high-exposure part of the country, with all that cold wind whipping off the English Channel in winter. This also means that when it rains, the rainwater will often be driven against the brickwork. You should be very careful about filling your cavities, because some of that water might find its way across the cavity and emerge as damp patches on the inside.

Cavity wall insulation 3

In the brochure for my bungalow it lists 'cavity wall insulation' as one of its features. I know that the cavity between the inner

and outer leaves is in fact empty. On querying this with the builder he replied that this item in the brochure was covered by the inner leaf being constructed using insulating blocks with 'Thermalite characteristics'. I have been advised by another builder that this does not meet the Building Regulations. Who is right?

It depends on the type and thickness of the blocks, and when the bungalow was built. Building Regulations change regularly. But if it was sold to you as having cavity wall insulation, and it does not have it, then you should contact your local authority trading standards officer.

Insulation inside solid walls

I have a hundred-year-old brick-built house with 9in (225mm) solid walls, and marble chippings in a cement/lime render, none of which is giving any real problems. The trouble is it's hard to keep warm, despite gas central heating supplemented by a woodburner. One of the lounge walls is north facing and I am considering putting a couple of inches of fibreglass or polystyrene inside it, in a wood frame with plasterboard skin or using the polyurethane-backed plasterboard, again about 2in (50mm), on a dot and dab fastening. I am not convinced it will not disturb what you recently referred to as the 'moisture equilibrium' even with or without a membrane. Is it a good idea or shall I just chop more logs?

Your insulation idea can be done. The problem is that by keeping the heat in the rooms it means the walls stay cold, and are therefore at extra risk of condensation. Therefore it is essential that you fit a vapour barrier on the *warm* (room) side of the new insulation, to stop warm moist air from your living areas finding its way through into the cold walls and condensing as water in the bricks. The usual scheme is to construct a frame from 50mm × 50mm sawn softwood, fit insulation into the spaces (urethane board is better than fibreglass or rockwool), staple or tack 1,000 gauge polythene sheet over and then screw plasterboard on. You can take the opportunity to add extra power points or light switches, but make sure the polythene is securely taped around all the holes. If you leave a clear 50mm gap between the new false wall and the brick wall then you will improve the sound insulation as well, but lose more internal space. Insulated plasterboard is available but it gives no provision for the vapour barrier, so is only really suitable for party walls.

Roofs

We have a problem with a very well-insulated slate roof. In the winter it keeps the house wonderfully warm but in summer it becomes unbearably hot upstairs as the hot air in the roof has nowhere to go. Even this summer it has been over 38°C. We have no vertical walls up there to put a vent and local builders have suggested air conditioning. We cannot believe this is the most efficient way of dealing with the problem. Do you have any ideas for us?

Insulation is great for keeping heat in, but it always needs to be combined with ventilation, in order to allow moisture and excess heat to escape.

I presume you mean your roof is insulated between the rafters, as opposed to insulation of the top-floor ceilings between the ceiling joists. And when you say there are no vertical walls, I guess you have a hipped roof, with four pitched sides, rather than a gable roof with two. You could either install grilles at high level and connect them to ridge vents, in place of two or three existing ridge tiles, or fit one or more small skylights which can be opened in warm weather. Avoid large roof windows, which can make the situation worse by allowing excessive solar heat gain – just like a greenhouse. A range of roof windows and ventilation accessories is available from The Loft Shop (see USEFUL CONTACTS, Loft Conversions).

Loft spaces

Can you advise me please on loft insulation. My loft has 3in × 2in (75mm × 50mm) joists with electrical cables clipped to their sides. I have roll insulation at various thicknesses between one and three inches at present but would like to increase this to 4in or 6in (100mm or 150mm) as recommended. It seems inevitable that I will cover the cables. Is this acceptable or a fire hazard? Should I run the new insulation on top of the old, trying not to cover the cables, or run the additional thickness across the joists at 90 degrees so as to cover any gaps?

Cables carrying electric current always generate heat, and burying them under insulation can allow this heat to build up. In practice, this is only a serious problem for 13A power cables, and those in your loft are likely to be only for the 5A upstairs lighting circuit. But to be on the safe side it should be a simple matter to unclip them from the joists and pass the new insulation quilt underneath. Ceiling insulation should always be draped across the joists, rather than in between them, but there should be no insulation beneath water tanks – these need warmth from the rooms below to prevent freezing, and should be securely lagged around the sides and over the top. And don't forget to lag any exposed water pipes.

Loft

You recently stated that loft insulation should always be laid across the joists. Why is this? What thickness is it sensible to lay in the loft of my huge Victorian house (no roof felt)? Finally, are any grants available?

(a) To keep the joists warm and prevent pattern staining; (b) as thick as you can afford; (c) it depends on your local authority, and grants tend to be means-tested.

You recently stressed the importance of lifting electrical cables above any insulation to avoid them becoming over-heated. Some years ago now I put down a floor in the attic with the intention of building a model railway up there when I retired. It never occurred to me at the time to lift the cables above the insulation. Is there still danger there or do you think I can relax now considering that the situation has been so for five years or more? At the same time I went all round the edges of the available space with chipboard to give a floor and covered under the rafters with insulation board to give a ceiling. I have long wondered whether I might have impeded ventilation thereby. There seems to be no harm but it is difficult to tell.

Lighting cables are usually OK. It's power cables that tend to overheat, and you have to keep an eye on the currents through them. They may need to be 'de-rated', which means you can't use them for heavy electrical loads. If in doubt, ask advice from an NICEIC electrician. The other danger is that expanded polystyrene insulation can sometimes react with the PVC sheathing of the cables and create a fire risk.

The ventilation issue will depend on whether there is a space above the insulation, and whether it is ventilated at the eaves or through gaps between the slates or tiles. If the eaves are blocked and the roof has been felted then there may be a problem of condensation on the rafters and battens.

Below-ground floor

My house has wooden floors and copious amounts of airbricks. While I am aware of the importance of the airbricks, there is a definite chill around the ankles in icy and windy weather so I wonder whether it would be practical to install baffles, around 2in (50mm) larger than the airbricks, to stop the wind blowing directly into them, but not blocking the vents. Does that sound like a good or bad idea to you?

Bad idea. Any sort of obstruction will impede the air flow below the floor and could lead to a build-up of moisture. If you are troubled by draughts into the ground-floor rooms, then draughtproof the gap between floor and skirting. But the best thing would be to insulate the ground floor by lifting the floorboards, draping an insulating membrane across the joists, and fitting insulation slabs between the joists, before re-fixing the boards. That way, you will have a warm floor, but preserve the ventilating effects of the air flow below it.

Below timber ground floor

How can I deal with cold striking up through the suspended ground floor, as the temperature at floor level can be 4°F (2°C) colder than at knee level? There is a 9in (225mm) gap between the undersides of the floor joists and the bone-dry concrete subfloor, an over-plentiful supply of airbricks which admit winds straight off the hills, and I have to look for a solution which won't cost an arm and a leg, and preferably not too much upheaval. Is there any effective alternative to taking the boards up and insulating between the joists? The area involved is approximately 30ft × 20ft (9m × 6m).

There is really no alternative to taking the boards up and insulating between the joists. It's great that you have a healthy draught underneath, as this removes moisture, methane, radon etc. There are several specialized eco-membrane products that you can drape over the joists, and which will support the insulation bats of your choice. Obviously it's an upheaval, but the benefits should be large, both in heating costs and your own comfort. A cheaper alternative would be to fix hardboard on top of the existing floor, but that would be almost as disruptive, so bite the bullet and go for the long-term solution.

Draught-proofing

I live and work in what was a derelict Georgian building now restored almost to its former glory, with original very beautiful sash windows which are a bit draughty, particularly in the bathroom! Is there a method of reducing the draught?

There are several types of draught excluder for sliding sash windows. The best ones are routed into a groove up the sides. Cheaper ones are like rows of brushes tacked to the frames.

Recycling old packaging materials

I insulated my loft some years ago. Since then I have added to the insulation using the discarded plastic foam packaging materials that come with items such as TV sets, glassware, washing machines etc. Over the years this has effectively increased the insulation and at the same time provided a handy way of disposing of packaging that would otherwise be taken to the dump. Is this something you would recommend to your readers or is it a potential hazard?

I am all for using waste packaging as insulation, and I find it very annoying that many products arrive in layers of insulated packaging which ends up as landfill. Unfortunately the UK is lagging behind other European countries, such as Germany, which require packaging to be retrieved and reused by the product suppliers. The problems that could arise are fire hazards, such as when paper-based insulation is in proximity to overheating electrical connections; or the possible reaction between expanded polystyrene insulation and the PVC sheathing of electrical cables.

(The problem when PVC-sheathed cables come into contact with expanded polystyrene is that the plasticizer leaches out of the cable, forming a sticky glue-like substance. Cable manufacturers claim that this is only a surface effect, and that it will not create an electrical hazard or fire risk, but that it should be avoided.)

Hazardous polystyrene

Our Homebuyer Survey advised we remove the potential fire hazard of polystyrene covering on one wall of the bedroom of our bungalow, which is in a very exposed rural location. Assuming the polystyrene was to reduce the cold effect of the outside wall, would it be practical to batten, plasterboard and skim this one wall to reduce its coldness?

Polystyrene ceiling tiles and wall coverings are not a 'fire hazard' as such, and there is no requirement to remove them. It's just that the fire service hates them because when there *is* a fire, the polystyrene can melt, catch fire, and drip like burning napalm. And it gives off carcinogenic fumes. So it would be just as well to get rid of it. You could easily insulate your bungalow from the inside as described, although you should incorporate a vapour barrier on the warm side of the insulation, to stop condensation occurring within the insulated wall. Better still to insulate it on the outside, using external cladding or an insulated render.

MODERN HOUSES

We are accustomed as a society to the fact that as the years go by, things get better. Health care, transport, communications – all these have improved ten-fold over the last hundred years. So it is only natural to expect that the homes built today will, similarly, be superior to those built in the Victorian and Edwardian eras. Sadly, this is not the case. The reasons for this are complex, but the underlying problem is that whilst a particular model of car, say, undergoes a constant process of year-on-year refinement, each individual car is only expected to last for five to seven years. So the manufacturer knows that if he is to achieve brand loyalty, and persuade satisfied customers to come back for more of the same, then he had better provide good after-sales care, and make sure that next year's model is better than last year's. Homes are not like that. They are expected to last for at least forty years, or a lifetime, whichever is the longer. And nobody buys a house because of the name of the builder – they buy it because of its location. So the builder knows that no matter how well he builds a property, he is never going to achieve brand loyalty or get customers coming back for another one in a few years' time. So he might as well build it as cheaply as possible and maximize his profits.

This philosophy is reinforced by the Building Regulations which govern new construction work. The Building Regulations lay down a set of minimum standards, but since modern speculative housebuilders build to the minimum anyway, they build to the requirements of the Building Regulations and not a jot more. Which is why most modern houses are flimsy, noisy and hard to heat. This often comes as a shock to people whose lifetime dream has been to buy a wonderful new house, which needs no repairs and minimal maintenance. What they often get is cracking plasterboard walls and ceilings, creaking floors and second-rate plumbing. And a builder or developer who has no interest in coming back to repair faults.

Many new homeowners are provided with a ten-year warranty from the National House-Building Council (NHBC), and are disappointed when they discover that it only covers structural defects, and not internal cracks, binding doors or constantly blocking waste pipes. The NHBC warranty is somewhat unique in that it is an insurance policy taken out by the builder, but paid for by the customer as part of the house price. If owners had to take out the policy themselves, then they might take more care to read the small print first, but then that's probably why it is done that way.

On the other hand, for those prepared to build their own homes, and who will not be trying to cut corners, modern techniques and materials mean that a very high quality product can be built for the same or lower cost than the price of an off-the-shelf house from a speculative builder. The self-build home market in Britain is growing every year, and it has never been easier for ordinary people to build a real dream home.

Dry lining

I've just read with interest your article concerning the use of plasterboard for dry lining. The walls of our (fifteen-year-old) house are finished in this way and although they are not cracking up, they are causing me a problem. I want to put bookshelves on the walls, but in such a way that I can put furniture underneath; i.e. I don't want floor-standing shelves. I would like to attach the sort of shelving system that has a vertical metal section into which shelf-support brackets are slotted. I'm sure I can fix these to the plasterboard with those special plasterboard thingies (sorry, I don't know their proper name). But, although I am fairly sure this will keep the shelves attached to the plasterboard, will the plasterboard stay attached to the wall? I'm not sure how the plasterboard is fixed to the wall (which I think is breeze block); whether it is attached directly or is on a thin wooden frame – the gap behind it is variable, sometimes negligible.

The plasterboard 'thingies' you refer to are called cavity toggles, and should only be used when there is really no alternative. You would be better off drilling right through to the blockwork and getting a good fixing in there. You can buy long screws (up to 200mm) with integral plastic plugs – 'Fischer' fixings or similar – and the builders' merchants will sell you a long masonry drill bit to suit. Use a metal detector or cable locator first to make sure you're not going to drill through a cable or pipe.

Leaky walls

I have a question on the construction of new houses and dry lining of the inner walls. My house is two years old and very well constructed to the latest standards (I assume!) except that where the dry lining is punctured, i.e. under the bath, where there are holes for the pipes to come through, there is a tremendous draught. Surely this is not correct. On the outside wall there are narrow vertical plastic vents at first-floor level; my neighbour believes these are vents into the void between the inner wall and the liner, but if that is correct then any wind will penetrate into the house via areas like the bathroom, plus the plasterboard will be at outside temperature, hence negating the wall insulation. Your advice please; should there be any circulating air in this void, or where can I go for advice?

The extent of the problem depends upon whether it is a timber-framed house, or just plasterboard stuck on to the inner block leaf of a conventional cavity wall. The vents are weep holes, situated along the top of the cavity-tray lintels. They are not there to ventilate the cavity. The draught is clearly due to some very poor construction quality, and the first thing you should do is give the builder the opportunity to rectify it. You need to engage an independent professional to make sure the work is done properly, though. You don't just want a dollop of foam gunned in to fill the gaps.

NHBC problems

I have a nine-year-old house. I have recently discovered that the connection from a washbasin has been plumbed in downstream of a WC and protrudes about 70mm into the 100mm soil pipe. This caused waste to build up and impede the free flow of waste. The builders and the National House-Building Council have declined to take any action to correct the faulty plumbing which I feel contravenes the spirit if not the letter of the Building Regulations with respect to the obstruction of soil pipes. Can you suggest any way in which I can get some action from the builders or the NHBC?

The NHBC ten-year warranty covers only structural faults.

And new houses are not even covered by the normal legal protection of the Sale of Goods Acts. If you buy a car or a stereo system then you would be protected by statutory rights, but, unbelievably, property – the biggest single investment most of us ever make – is not covered by the Act. The NHBC trumpets its warranty as being some kind of wonderful consumer protection but it is in fact a simple insurance policy, taken out by the builder but passed on to – and paid for by – the customer. And, like all insurance policies, the decision on what to pay out for in claims is determined solely by the insurer. Your problem is not untypical.

A big problem is that chartered surveyors often advise purchasers that the existence of an NHBC warranty means that a full building survey will not be needed. This is a big mistake.

Self-build

I'm considering building my own house (or more accurately contracting a builder to do it) but have no real idea where to start. Can you offer any advice?

Building your own house is a great idea. It is the norm in European countries, unlike in Britain where the market is dominated by volume speculative housebuilders. You can engage an architect to design it and run the operation for you, or, if you want to save some money and have a more hands-on experience, there are a number of good self-build books available. I recommend *The Housebuilder's Bible* by Mark Brinkley. You should also attend the National Self-Build Homes Show, held every year in London, Edinburgh, Manchester and Birmingham (contact *Build It* magazine for details) and if you want to consult an architect, call the

Architecture and Surveying Institute and ask for a list of members in your area from their practice register (see USE-FUL CONTACTS for details on all of the above).

Self build: Timber frame

I am considering buying a piece of land to build my own house on. I have been over to the States several times and am considering whether to build a timber house or stick with the traditional methods. Whilst staying with friends over in the States I have been very impressed with the houses and the level of insulation etc. A big plus is they seem to be relatively easy to erect. What are the downsides and are there any reputable UK suppliers or do I have to import direct from USA?

There are lots of 'kit' houses available from British and European suppliers for self-builders. Most of them are timber-framed, which is OK as long as they are assembled to a very high standard, but remember, a timber-framed house that performs well in Scandinavia, Germany or North America may not do as well in the damp, temperate British climate. Cold climates are dry climates; the UK climate is moderate and very wet. Other self-build systems include hay bales, rammed earth, and pouring concrete into pre-formed polystyrene formwork. There are three monthly self-build magazines – *SelfBuild*, *Build It*, and *Home Building & Renovating*, and an annual show, and a host of self-help books. First step should be buying a copy of *The House-builder's Bible* by Mark Brinkley (see USEFUL CONTACTS, Self-Build).

Timber-framed houses

I wonder if you could tell me of any of the larger builders who are currently constructing timber-framed houses in Central or

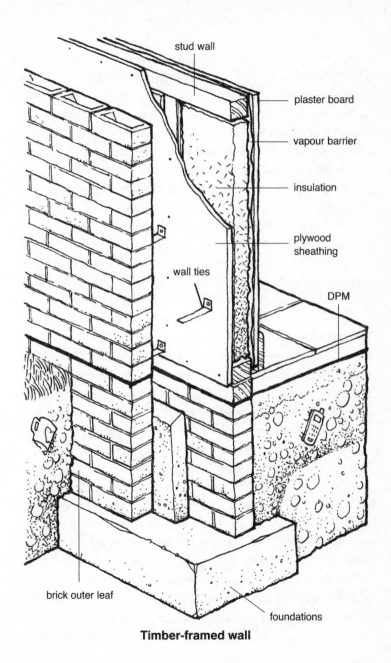

stud wall

plaster board

vapour barrier

insulation

plywood
sheathing

wall ties

DPM

brick outer leaf

foundations

Timber-framed wall

Southern England. From 1984 to 1995 I lived in a timber-framed house, built by Wimpey, in Warwickshire. I found it much warmer than a conventional brick-and-block house, and cheaper to heat. I would like to move into another timber-framed house, but am unable to find any advertised in the newspapers.

The majority of new houses being built are timber-framed, but developers do not like to advertise this fact, because of problems that have been associated with this method of construction in the past. The thermal insulation quality of timber-framed houses is not so much a product of the frame itself, as of the thickness of insulation built into it. New brick-and-block houses conform to exactly the same thermal insulation standards, and they are likely to have better structural and sound insulation qualities as well.

Timber frame

I am about to begin building a timber-frame house on the West Coast of Ireland but a relative has just given me your article on the subject. I am now very worried as I have already given the company I am dealing with a deposit. Is a timber-frame house really as bad as you say, and can you please send me some more information, or let me know where I can find out more.

The problem with timber-framed homes is that the insulation is right on the inside, next to the living space. This allows them to warm up quicker and makes them appear better insulated than masonry construction. Unfortunately, the part of the frame outside the insulation, i.e. on the *cold* side of the insulation, stays cold, and is therefore prone to condensation. It is therefore vital that there is a perfectly installed vapour barrier on the *warm* side of the insulation, to stop water vapour produced by the occupants from crossing to the cold side and condensing, where, being wood, it could cause the frame to rot. Very often the vapour barrier is inexpertly installed, or punctured by electricians and plumbers, who do not understand its importance. It is essential that the building contractor understands these principles and supervises the work accordingly, especially in a damp climate such as yours.

Timber frame – the Canadian model

Your views on frame-built houses deserve more publicity. We lived in Canada for a number of years and saw 'frame-built, brick veneer' houses being built. When we returned to the UK I queried the planning permission for this type of construction being permitted here and I was assured it was quite legal.

Good quality houses in Canada were built from solid brick, 9in (225mm) thickness of brick, I think without a cavity, and then 4 inches of studding inside this, giving 4in (100mm) of thermal insulation. Solid construction and thermally efficient.

But there was a cheaper edition than brick veneer which was 'frame built', only in rural areas where cold was cold and rain came down as snow, so less chance of rain penetration and condensation. And these are the types of houses being built in huge estates in damp, rainy Britain. More publicity condemning this dubious practice, please.

If timber-framed houses are built to a very high standard, there is no reason why they should not perform well. The problem with the current practices in the UK is, as you point out, that they are being built as cheaply as possible. The builders claim they are using the system to maximize insulation values and save the planet, but they are really just trying to maximize profits. The future for most of these houses is not promising.

Timber frame: An architect writes

How right you are, the only people likely to benefit from these
are those who will sell unnecessary damp-proofing products.
But more importantly, timber frames will lead to factory kits
and ever-increasing standardization resulting in ever-more
awful housing estates, lacking in quality, character and a sense
of locality and place. In addition I have yet to find a sealed
timber-framed building that will last for more than fifty years
in our climate. The poor souls who buy into such property are
likely to face some heavy repair bills, or the local authority, or
the Government [tax payers] will have to pick up the tab, or
there will be litigation and the only people to profit will be the
lawyers!

The most severe impact could well be the loss of traditional
building skills which ultimately will be to the detriment of the
historic building fabric.

I thought I ought to write and support your efforts to maintain good building practices rather than the 'politically correct'
legislation that seems so prevalent today.

PAINTING AND DECORATING

Most people who opt for so-called 'maintenance-free' PVC-U windows and roof-line products do so because they don't want the hassle of painting the existing woodwork. So, instead of paying someone else to do it – say £500 to £750 every five years to rub down and gloss an average terraced house – they would rather give £5,000 to some cowboy trader to rip out all the existing windows and external woodwork and replace them with plastic of no known origin or specification, and uncertain longevity. The economics just don't add up. If these people made similar decisions at work, they'd have to justify themselves with cost/benefit analyses, and they'd realize it wasn't worth it. But because it's their home, they go into a blind panic, and believe what they read in the adverts. And because almost everybody else down the street has gone for plastic windows, then they think they'd better get them as well. The replacement window and roof-line industry gets rich on this lemming-like behaviour.

The other big marketing ploys in the painting and decorating sphere are so-called 'breathable' textured external wall coatings – they aren't breathable and they cost five times the price of getting the wall painted properly – and 'one coat' paints, which a professional decorator has described as a 'pudding-like' paint which never dries (see below).

Given a modicum of care and attention, timber doors and windows will last for ever. This means a light sanding down, and touching-up or recoating on an occasional basis with proper spirit-based primer (on bare wood), undercoat and gloss. If you don't want to do it, or pay someone else to do it, then you shouldn't have bought a house in the first place. If you've never tried it then give it a go – it could change your life. Do bear in mind the toxicity of lead paint, though (see HAZARDS). This is one of the most toxic of building materials, is present in huge quantities in homes (it was used in Britain up to 1992), and is a known danger to children. The lack of public awareness, and government publicity, about this problem is very worrying.

External brickwork should not be painted – it traps the moisture. The only sympathetic coating on old houses is traditional limewash. Again, if you try it yourself you may get hooked – it's better value than watching the telly.

External walls

The external walls of my bungalow are faced with Tyrolean finish. Some of the small stones have started to drop off, particularly during heavy rain. A tradesman plasterer has advised that treating the walls with a 1:1 Feb-bond mixture may fix the backing mortar; is he correct? Although the bungalow is nearly thirty years old I am reluctant to renew the facing.

Tyrolean finish does not have stones in it. What you are describing is more usually termed 'rough-cast' (or 'harling' in Scotland). If the stones are coming off then it is a sign that the original coating was poorly applied, and there is not much you can do about it. Applying an external coat of PVA adhesive (of which Feb-bond is one trade name) would be rather like trying to stick wallpaper back on a wall by putting the paste on the outside. You may have better luck with a textured masonry paint, but it may still be a case of throwing good money after bad. If you are really worried about the appearance, then the best solution may be to have a coat of sand-and-cement render applied over the top.

I have a house built about 1900 which is rendered and painted with Snowcem or similar. It has over the years had several coats of paint but the wall facing south-south-west seems to want painting more regularly as it gets the worst of the weather. Is there a better paint or coating that is more permanent? I have even thought of cladding this wall but plastic would not look right and wood needs the same maintenance. Is there another type of cladding that would be suitable?

The problem with all external coatings is that the more hardwearing they are, the more they stop the walls from breathing. So if rainwater enters through one small crack then it will be unable to escape, and can build up to cause a serious dampness problem. Another problem can be interstitial condensation (condensation trapped in the depth of the wall material). Your cladding idea is a good one, and traditionally, exposed walls were often clad with slates or tiles hung on timber battens. This method is now known by the modern term 'rainscreen cladding', and in your case it could beneficially be used to cover a new layer of external insulation.

Conflicting opinions

We have asked for quotes from two builders to redecorate woodwork and masonry on our 1960 terraced house. The double-glazed windows are aluminium in wooden sub-frames which are horribly weathered. The walls are rendered and painted,

and badly flaking. One of the builders suggests scraping off all loose, flaking paintwork, and applying 'builder's paper' to get a smooth finish before painting with two coats of masonry paint. He also suggests replacing the wooden sub-frames and the double-glazed windows. The second builder also suggests scraping the loose paintwork and then 'stabilizing' and using two coats of masonry paint. He thinks the sub-frames can be rubbed down, repaired where necessary, and coated with two coats of timber stain preservative. We haven't the slightest idea which method is best. And what on earth is 'builder's paper'?

It sounds as though you need a professional painter and decorator, rather than a builder (see USEFUL CONTACTS, Painting and Decorating). And as for 'builder's paper' – that's the *Sun*, isn't it?

Peeling window sills

I live in a large Victorian house. Every two or three years I have to have my window ledges repainted white since the paint seems to peel off and crack. The current painter says this is normal, particularly at the back where there is more sun. However, another friend told me that if the painter strips off all the paint back to the bare stonework, the paint should last for seven to ten years. The current painter says this is not so and it's not worth the extra effort. Can you please advise?

External stone sills are subject to the extremes of the weather, but I would say that five years should be a reasonable life expectancy for a modern masonry paint. The peeling could be due to water penetration at the joint between the sill and the bottom rail of the timber window. But if it occurs over a wide area, then it is more likely due to poor surface preparation or cheap paint. It is probably not necessary to strip the paint right off, but it should certainly be sanded back hard to remove all loose or flaking areas, and then the whole surface should be given two coats of masonry stabilizing solution – this is a proprietary resin-based product, not to be confused with PVA adhesive. Then two coats of a quality smooth masonry paint, and application of an external-grade silicone sealant at the joint between sill and bottom rail.

Sealing sandy wall surfaces

We are about to re-wallpaper our interior walls but notice the plaster is very sandy and gritty. We have been advised to prime the walls with either a water-based stabilizing solution or an oil-based alkaline-resistant primer. From your experience do these actually work, or could you suggest an alternative?

Resin-based stabilizing solutions are generally only used on exterior work. For your purposes, water-based PVA should be sufficient. Make up a weak solution in water and brush it on. After twenty-four hours give it a light sanding, and if there are still any crumbly areas give them a further coating. Traditionally, decorators used rabbit-skin glue size for this purpose.

Limewash

You have described how to make traditional limewash, but you forgot to mention one vital ingredient – the 'blue'. We always had to put one of these in when we whitewashed the walls years ago, and I was told that the whitewash wouldn't work without it.

Several readers have mentioned this. It refers to a 'Reckitt's Blue' – a sachet of aquamarine pigment. This is still available in hardware stores, and is used as an artificial whitener when washing clothes. It can, indeed, be mixed into lime-wash to make the finish whiter, but it will not make any difference to the application or curing. A trick for stopping limewash flaking is to mix in casein (in the form of skimmed milk), and to waterproof it for external use, linseed oil was a common additive. For details of how to make limewash see Information Sheet 1 from SPAB (see USEFUL CONTACTS, Conservation).

Paint stripping

In my 1930s house we have panelled wooden doors which originally had a dark varnish finish. They have been overpainted several times and are in generally good condition although the paint build-up is excessive on some mouldings. We would like to strip back to the wood before redecorating and have considered sending the doors to a company that uses a caustic soda bath. They have advised us that the doors should be left for a week before repainting. How do you rate caustic soda stripping against Nitromors or a hot-air gun?

Dipping in caustic soda is quick and easy, but it is not very good for softwood doors. It can make them shrink and warp, and some carpenters say that it damages the glued joints, causing them to fall apart. Blow lamps or hot-air guns are the traditional method, but unfortunately this exposes you to lead poisoning from the paint fumes. If you use this method wear a respirator, and do not allow children or pregnant women in the house. Chemical paint strippers are the safest way of removing lead paint, although they are messy and can work out quite expensive.

Lead paint

I have read your comments on the dangers of removing leaded paint with great interest. But you did not recommend an alternative removal method.

The safest way of removing old lead paint from woodwork is to use a chemical paint stripper such as Nitromors. But the British Coatings Federation, who produce advice leaflets (see USEFUL CONTACTS, Painting and Decorating) do not generally encourage removal. They recommend that where the paint surface is in sound condition it should be sealed in by overpainting, although they stress that the householder then has a responsibility to maintain the painted surface in good order.

I feel that this is fudging the issue. If old lead paint is sealed in by overpainting, then surely labels should be posted to warn future generations that a dangerous neurotoxin lurks beneath the surface of their skirting boards. Homes in some US states already carry such legal disclosure notices.

External paint removal
Our Edwardian house has been vandalized by a previous owner. The lovely old brickwork has been painted cream. Is there a way to remove the paint and restore the bricks to their original state?

It can be done, but the method depends very much upon the type of paint and the state of the bricks. Some firms employ a basic sandblasting technique, and this is almost always disastrous, since it removes the surface 'fire skin' from clay bricks, and leaves them prone to water absorption and weathering. High-pressure steam is a gentler method, and there is also a patented water/air vortex technique for stubborn coatings. For advice call Stonehealth Ltd (see USEFUL CONTACTS, Painting and Decorating) who are specialists in cleaning historic buildings, and who operate a list of approved local contractors.

Removing paint from bricks

We are about to move into a seventeenth-century cottage. The former owners have white-gloss painted the rear back brick wall of an inglenook fireplace. The wood-burning stove has been removed!

Suggestions would be welcome on how could this paint be removed by DIY and not by a sandblasting professional. Is the latter the only choice to safeguard the lime mortar brickwork? We intend to have open fires and prefer brickwork to paint!

On a seventeenth-century cottage gloss paint is bad, but sand blasting is worse. If the bricks are hard, you may be able to remove the paint using chemical paint stripper (Nitromors or similar), but the resulting sticky goo tends to stain the brickwork. It's OK if you intend to limewash over it. Steaming off is better, and you may be able to use a DIY wallpaper steamer and scrape the paint off with a soft implement, such as a plastic or wooden kitchen spatula. Otherwise it's a professional restoration job. You could ask for advice from Stonehealth (see USEFUL CONTACTS, Painting and Decorating).

I appreciate your desire for bare brickwork, but you should understand that the original house would not have been like this. Exposed brickwork and timbers are really a twentieth-century reinvention of a past that never existed. The interior of your house would probably have been plastered throughout with lime-and-horsehair plaster, and limewashed, with earth pigments as colouring. The Society for the Protection of Ancient Buildings (SPAB) provides some good advice leaflets on this kind of stuff (see USEFUL CONTACTS, Conservation).

Pattern staining

I have night storage heaters in my maisonette. The wall above each radiator has become grey/black from the heat – carbon? If I put washable wallpaper on the walls will I be able to wash the marks off – or can you suggest anything else?

Staining on walls above heaters is usually just grime from the air. The flow of hot air creates static on the wall surface and this causes the dirt to stick. Yes, you can wash it off, and shelves fitted above the radiators will help divert the heat around the room and minimize the problem.

Bleeding knots

We have been renovating an old cottage for the past three years. A number of the doors and windows had blisters caused by oozing from knots that had not been sealed. We have stripped off the paint down to bare wood and treated the knots with proprietary knotting sealer prior to repainting. Sadly, a few months later the knots are oozing once more. I deduce that while knotting compound works well on new wood, it will not properly seal old wood that has been painted. What is the secret?

Knotting does not always work on new wood either. Some knots are very resinous, and will always bleed through. The staining is usually worse through water-based acrylic paint, but even with gloss the resin can dissolve the undercoat and form a blister. Next time try two coats of aluminium oxide primer.

Damaged ceiling

We are decorating our cottage one room at a time and last weekend started on a new project. My husband finished stripping the wallpaper and I got up the step ladder to remove the polystyrene tiles from the ceiling. However, the ceiling has been lined and the tiles stuck on to the paper. As I was getting the tiles off chunks of plaster were coming away with them. So far the other ceilings that we have stripped in the house have been fine, but this room is different.

My husband is very good at decorating and repairs but even he is not looking forward to repairing the ceiling. My question is how best to repair the ceiling. Would it be possible for a plasterer to just plaster over what is left and give us a smooth surface to emulsion? Or would the best result be achieved by dry lining with plaster board and a skim of plaster over that?

As long as a ceiling of that age is basically sound, it is usually quite acceptable to make good any holes with filler, or skim it with plaster. Remember that the original plaster will probably be lime and horsehair, and would have been designed to be covered with lining paper, rather than painted direct with emulsion.

Removing black mould

The house we're buying has been empty for twelve months, with no heating or ventilation. Consequently, the walls have black mould on large areas. Have you any suggestions for removing it? I know we need to get it heated and the windows open, but we need also to decorate. Or, do you think we should leave the decorating alone until we get the house dried out and then remove the mould? Any advice would be greatly appreciated.

Wash it off with clean water containing a splash of bleach. Much cheaper and safer than proprietary fungicide solutions.

One coat paint: A decorator complains

You should have a go at the so-called 'one coat finishes', which is the rubbish spouted by the major paint manufacturers. Joe public always seems to be looking for the quick, easy and cheap solution that just does not exist! As a decorator I often come across this pudding-like paint and its so-called amazing properties, that is its incredible ability to not flow out at all, to never ever cover in 'one coat' and if you want to overpaint, it remains in a semi-dry state permanently. It rates about as highly in my esteem as 'ready-pasted wallpaper', all thoroughly used by the 'did-it-over-the-weekend' brigade after watching the usual DIY programmes. Why they sell this rubbish is beyond me.

As you say, it is to appeal to the instincts of people who want to do things quickly, but not properly.

External wall coatings

Have you any thoughts regarding breathable external wall coatings? I was given a demonstration by a company's sales manager of the way in which the coating keeps out moisture but still permits the wall to breathe. The demo consisted of a transparent cylindrical container. Halfway down was a segment of porous building block that had been covered by the wall-coating material. I was asked to fill the top of the container with water. There was no evidence of water passing through the block – it remained dry. Then air was pumped into the bottom of the cylinder. Bubbles of air were seen to be emerging from the block of building material and coating. Pump air – bubbles. Cease pumping, no bubbles – no water passed from top to bottom. The work is also independently insured.

This is a demonstration that air under pressure passes through the coating, not that moisture vapour not under pressure would do so. So it does not mimic real conditions, and sounds like a clever sales trick. The problem with these coatings is that if you get condensation forming within the depth of the wall – i.e. the wall becomes damp from within, with liquid moisture – then it will be unable to escape. As the demonstration shows, liquid moisture will be trapped *within* the wall.

PESTS

Wherever you live, you will be competing for living space with some kind of animals or insects. Physical exclusion is always preferable to – and usually more effective than – trapping or poisoning. And people who are worried about sharing their homes with birds or bats should be aware that these creatures are responsible for keeping the insect population in check. Get rid of them and you could find your life being made intolerable by flies!

Birds

Having just acquired a bungalow with the highest roof of the adjoining properties, seagulls seem happy to sit and sun themselves (sometimes as many as fifteen). Could you please advise what can be done to deter them. We get a lot of mess from their droppings.

Birds like to sit in places where they can keep an eye out for food, and you are probably quite right that they choose your roof because it is the highest. You may therefore have problems evicting them. And note that under the Wildlife and Countryside Act (1981), you are not allowed to do anything that might injure wild birds. But there are humane physical deterrents, such as anti-perching spikes. These are rows of thin stainless steel pins sticking out from a polycarbonate backing strip. They are glued in place, and cost from around £5 per linear metre. Builders and roofers can order them from builders' merchants, or they can be bought direct from Woodland Properties (see USEFUL CONTACTS, Household Pests/Animals).

Birds in roof 1

We have an old property with a pantiled roof. We have had a problem with birds lifting the tiles and nesting in the roof space. We had the gaps filled with chicken-wire balls by a builder. However, although it deterred them temporarily, after a few months things are just as bad as before. Are the birds causing any long-term damage apart from the mess that they leave – we think they are tearing the fabric under the tiles. Can you suggest any solution?

I feel the best solution is often to 'live and let live'. When you say 'fabric under the tiles' I presume you mean sarking felt – well, a property of this type shouldn't have sarking felt anyway; it cuts down on roof space ventilation. Unless you are bothered by their noise, it is often no bad thing to have birds (and bats) nesting in a roof, as they catch lots of flies in the area around the house. If the droppings are a problem below the nest areas put some polythene or cardboard down to catch them, and, of course, make sure your water tanks all have tight-fitting lids!

Birds in roof 2

I had my wooden fascia boards replaced with PVC recently. This was partly due to the reduced maintenance aspect, but mainly to prevent birds getting in as they have been damaging the roofing felt. I was assured that the birds wouldn't get in but I now have more than ever. There are huge gaps between the straight edge of the board and my arched roof tiles. I have two questions: (a) Is there something that I can fit myself to prevent this happening? (b) Are birds in the roof a big problem?

I am personally not bothered about birds in the roof, unless their squawking youngsters wake me up early. Obviously you want to make sure your water tanks have secure lids, so they don't contaminate them or drown themselves in them. But there are a number of proprietary products which seal the spaces between fascias and pantiles, but still allow ventilation through to the roof space. They are plastic strips with flexible comb-like fingers on the top edge, which mould to the profile of the tiles. Sounds as though this is what you really wanted all along, rather than the PVC-U fascias. Try a specialist roofing supplies merchants.

Ultrasonic repellers

Do you know if ultrasonic deterrents for mice actually work? We have a pitched roof adjoining a flat roof which in turn is accessible from a bankside, and we think that the mice are using this route to get into our loft through the eaves. We wonder if an electronic device in the loft space would work.

These devices are claimed to use various combinations of electromagnetic fields and ultrasonic sound to repel rats, mice and insects and yet, curiously, to have no adverse effects on household pets. Several companies advertise these products, and claim to have independent scientific research supporting their efficacy, but when investigated by the Advertising Standards Authority, this has been found to be bogus. Some readers have claimed they are sure that the repellers have kept mice out of their homes, but there are several factors that affect the presence of mice, and it could be that installing the device has coincided with other changes affecting their behaviour. In my opinion the main effect of these devices is to remove money from gullible punters' pockets.

Masonry bees

Every summer I notice dozens of bees emerging from gaps in the brickwork of my cottage (soft red bricks, lime mortar, built 1880), and I am worried that they are burrowing into the mortar to make nests. How can I get rid of this pest?

Some homeowners get worried when they see bees emerging from holes in their brickwork, but so-called masonry bees, *Osmia rufa*, have simply adapted from their natural home in soft sandstone rocks, and it is rare for them to cause serious damage to brickwork. They do not sting, and they are solitary creatures that do not live in colonies or build nests, as such, but lay their eggs in holes and crevices that they find. If you have a lot of them, then it may be a sign that your brickwork has unfilled perpend joints (vertical joints), and it may be an idea to think about raking out and repointing with lime mortar.

Bats

My house is converted from an old timber barn, by building lightweight block walls on the inside of the timber frame. In the two summers that I have lived here, Pipistrelle bats have made my life intolerable. According to the local bat warden with English Nature, the bats are attracted to the warm south-facing wall that is in sunlight for the majority of the day. They are creating a colony within the cavity walls, their points of entry and exit being the gaps between the wooden cladding under the eaves. I know that the bats are a protected species and I have no desire to harm them. However the noise they create within the cavities, particularly in the small hours, is

sufficient to ruin a good night's sleep – night after night, all summer long.

English Nature's suggestion was to create non-return doors: due to their small size – these bats use gaps as small as three-quarters of an inch – its proposal is entirely impractical. I have attempted to seal off the gaps by means of expanding foam, but other openings, as yet unseen and unknown to me, are still being used.

I resent being forced out of my bedroom by these 'flying mice' to get a good night's sleep, or being required to adopt a siege-like attitude and create a fortress of my own home to relieve myself of this nuisance.

Bats, which are suffering a dramatic decline in numbers, are voracious insectivores, and perform a valuable service in keeping insect numbers down. They are being deprived of roosting sites in houses by the ubiquitous plastic ventilation grilles, and by the current trend for filling cavity walls with insulation. The spraying of timber treatment chemicals in loft spaces has also taken its toll on the bat population, although the Wildlife and Countryside Act (1981) achieved a notable success in clamping down on this practice. British bats are completely harmless; they do not use nesting materials and, unlike mice, they never nibble cables or wires. There is no known health risk associated with British bats or their droppings.

Most bats roost in roofs between April and June. *Pipistrellus* like to nest in cavity walls, and can be noisy for a few weeks during the breeding season. You may be able to lessen the noise nuisance by building an insulated sound-proofing stud wall on the inside. But if you are determined to evict them then English Nature should put you in touch with the local bat worker. Further information from The Bat

Conservation Trust (see USEFUL CONTACTS, Household Pests/Animals).

Cluster flies

Over the past five or six years we have restored an old stone farmhouse in France. The inside has been replastered and the outside has been repointed. But we have a big problem with flies which seem to be laying eggs in the wall and hatching out indoors. Most of the flies seem to emerge from around the window frames and door frames, but there are big wooden beams in the wall, too. We have someone locally who could introduce a course of spraying, if that seems the best idea, but what should we use? (My French isn't so good that I could buy something over there.) Or is there something we could paint on to the woodwork, which is treated with wood preservative but not gloss painted?

The insects in question are probably cluster flies, *Pollenia rudis*, *Dasyphora cyanella* and *Musca autumnalis*. These are parasitic on earthworms, and so are commonly found in rural locations, especially properties surrounded by grassland. They actually hatch outdoors, and then find their way into houses, often through gaps round window frames, but also through gaps between roof tiles. They seem to prefer some houses to others, but the best answer to keeping them out of living rooms does seem likely to be sealing gaps around window and door frames. The best way to do this is to seal the joints externally, filling large gaps by pointing and finishing off with a properly applied mastic joint.

Be warned, though, that people whose homes are invaded by cluster flies often have great difficulty keeping them out. Merlin Pest Control Services (see USEFUL CONTACTS, Household Pests/Animals) supply a factsheet on cluster flies.

PLASTERING

The term plastering refers to spreading any wet material on to a wall. 'Plaster' can be lime, clay, cement, gypsum or chalk, mixed with each other and/or with sand, earth, straw or lightweight aggregates. It has been ever thus. Unfortunately, mention plaster to any modern builder in Britain and he will know only one type – pink gypsum, or calcium sulphate. This is a wonderful material which sets hard in ninety minutes and gives a smooth trowelled finish on plasterboard or dry internal cement-rendered brickwork. But expose it to any degree of long-term moisture and it starts to dissolve. Many of the so-called 'rising damp' problems in ground-floor flats in old Victorian properties are actually gypsum plaster efflorescence due to the combined influence of internal condensation, raised external ground levels and leaking window sills. The original lime-and-sand plaster coped with all this without complaining, but the gypsum can't hack it.

To be fair to the gypsum plaster industry, they make a large variety of products for use in different circumstances. British Gypsum, for example, make and market thirteen types of plaster for the British building trade, including special formulations for application to plasterboard, brickwork and lightweight blockwork. But the average builders' merchants only stocks two – bonding backing coat and multi-finish skim coat – so these are the materials that jobbing builders use, to the exclusion of the more specialized products. British Gypsum have an excellent technical advice department and can arrange next-day deliveries to most parts of the UK, but most builders carry on regardless.

It is also a shame that British builders are afraid of using lime plaster. It is easy to use, and hydrated lime is available in bags at most builders' merchants. Mix it one–to–four with washed sharp sand, cover it with polythene sheeting and leave it to 'sweat' overnight, and it will match the lime plaster used on most Victorian houses. Animal hair reinforcement is also easily available from specialist suppliers. Builders have been persuaded that lime plaster 'won't work', probably by the propaganda of the cement industry. But its cause is not helped either by the 'lime loonies' – a group of mostly middle-class conservation enthusiasts who have discovered the joys of working with lime, but who insist that the only way to do it is to use traditional lime putty, preferably slaked in oak vats from quicklime fired in medieval kilns. This dotty purist approach makes real working builders very suspicious, and hardens their belief that the hydrated lime in bags from the builders' merchants is a 'different material', which will only work if mixed with cement. But hydrated lime works fine. I plastered my house with it.

Stained plasterboard ceilings

The recent storms have caused rainwater to come through the plasterboard ceiling of my daughter's ten-year-old house. A builder has said that this will cause the plaster to crumble and the ceiling will have to be replaced. Is there a less expensive way of dealing with this, as the ceiling appears to be intact?

The recent storms have been so extraordinary that they have caused many roof leaks, even in homes that have never leaked before, although they are quite likely to be a 'once in fifty years' event. Modern plasterboard with a gypsum plaster skim finish is not the best at coping with a soaking, but as long as the ceiling is still intact, and shows no signs of sagging, then it should dry out, and not need replacing. Even when there is serious water damage, it is usually possible to cut out and replace small damaged areas, and it is rarely necessary to replace a whole ceiling.

Skimming plasterboard ceilings

Is there anything that can be done to improve ceilings that appear to be just plasterboard whitened with emulsion paint, but where you can see the joins etc?

Many recently built homes are not plastered internally, and the plasterboard walls and ceilings are finished simply by painting or wallpapering directly on to the plasterboard. There are no advantages to this, apart from cutting the developer's costs. The disadvantages are unsightly cracks and poor sound insulation. This practice is especially widespread with new timber-framed housing developments. You could employ a plasterer to skim the ceilings with Thistle Board Finish plaster. He should first scratch through the emulsion paint to provide a good key, and prime the surface with a solution of PVA adhesive in water. Joints between the boards should be taped with hessian scrim.

Restoring an old croft

I am contemplating bringing a derelict croft house back into use. Any internal cladding of the stone walls has fallen off and only traces of laths remain. My options seem to be rendering in concrete, rendering in plaster or lining with heavy plasterboard on a wooden framework! Are there other options and have you an opinion on the best way forward?

All these three suggestions would seem to me to be most unwise. Applying modern materials to old buildings usually ends in tears. You need to find out what type of internal plastering system was used originally, and try to replicate it as closely as possible. I suggest you contact the Society for the Protection of Ancient Buildings (SPAB) for advice (see USEFUL CONTACTS, Conservation).

Lime render

We are renovating part of an old house which has walls of thick slate and lime mortar. If we were to render the inner walls should we use a lime render and would this allow a plaster finish?

Lime render, lime plaster. The only difference is the grade of sand. If you mean can you use gypsum plaster then the answer is no.

PLUMBING, HEATING AND DRAINAGE

In a temperate climate like Britain's, homes need heating for three-quarters of the year. And since over 70 per cent of us own our homes, or are responsible for the heating in the homes we rent, it is no wonder that when the heating goes wrong, we are prone to being held to ransom by the trade. The fact that almost every house or flat has its own central heating system – with boiler, radiators and controls – is one reason why Britain is so inefficient in its use of energy. Other European countries make much better use of energy, with blocks of flats and even whole streets sharing heating systems.

The majority of us use natural gas as a fuel, which heats water in a boiler, to be pumped round a wet radiator circuit. Oil, solid fuel, and LPG (liquified petroleum gas, or propane) are also used to fuel the same type of heating system. The principles are very simple, but the equipment gets more complicated by the year. It's very similar to cars. The first few cars I owned were noisy, dirty and not particularly efficient. But when they went wrong – which was often – I could usually open the bonnet, spot the problem, and fix it with a screwdriver and a pair of pliers. My current car is quiet, clean and hardly ever goes wrong. But when it does, I open the bonnet and I haven't a clue how to fix it. It has to be towed into a garage where they plug it into a computer

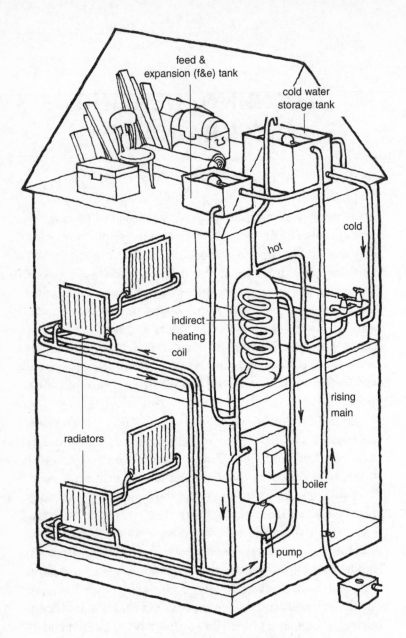

Traditional central heating circuit

which diagnoses the fault, and the remedy is often the whole-sale replacement of a huge chunk of electronics, costing hundreds of pounds.

Where old central heating boilers differ from old cars, though, is in the fact that they don't wear out as quickly. A boiler consists of a cast-iron vessel with a burner underneath it. The water is circulated through it and around the radiator system by a separate electric-powered pump. So there are no moving parts, and nothing much to go wrong. The old pilot lights were pretty infallible and cost maybe £25 per year to run, but this was deemed to be wasteful, so electronic ignition systems were introduced. When these go wrong the parts have to be replaced, at a cost of maybe £150, or six years' worth of pilot light fuel.

Nevertheless, the industry is geared up to 'upgrading' the nation's boilers, which means selling new, complicated boilers with lots more electronic circuitry, rather than keeping the old ones going. At the forefront of this sales push are British Gas Services, formerly known as the Gas Board, but now owned by the Centrica Corporation. British Gas Services operate the Three Star Service contracts, whereby customers pay an annual fee as a kind of insurance against breakdowns. Except that many readers report that when they call the engineers in, they are told either that their problem is not covered by the terms of the Three Star Service contract, or that the boiler is beyond repair because parts are no longer available. An increasing number of readers report being told this in the course of their annual Three Star boiler safety check.

This idea that boilers can become 'obsolete', or that 'parts are no longer available', is disputed by some independent gas engineers, who point out that just because a particular manufacturer no longer supplies original catalogue-numbered parts, this does not mean that equally effective replacement spares are not available from other sources. Pressure switches, pumps, fans and timers, for example, are all pretty much standard components which will fit a variety of appliances. Potterton may no longer supply a cut-to-length section of asbestos rope for the door seal of a 1969 floor-standing boiler, but the equivalent modern material is available by the reel from plumbers' merchants.

Going back to the car analogy, it's like saying that a 1975 Ford Escort is beyond repair because Ford no longer manufacture replacement gear sticks. There are always replacement parts that will fit the bill – witness the huge number of Ford Escorts still being driven around.

But the main reason to be careful about British Gas Services engineers' advice to buy a new boiler is that the engineers are paid commission to sell them. British Gas Services have denied this, but the engineers themselves confirm that they receive what are known as 'team rewards' for selling equipment and services to Three Star customers. The prices that British Gas Services quote for supplying and fitting a new boiler are also consistently high – in the region of £2,500 to £3,000 for a boiler whose trade price is nearer £500.

So if you have trouble with your boiler, or are thinking of upgrading, then it is always best to get two or three estimates from independent CORGI-registered gas engineers before coming to a decision.

Apart from central heating problems, most readers' queries concern poor water pressure, noisy plumbing systems, toilets that won't flush, and leaking shower enclosures. These are all things that should be within the remit of any

half-decent plumber, but unfortunately there are lots of guys
calling themselves plumbers who don't seem to have a clue.

Heating – electric

Is there such a thing as electric-fired central heating? Not
Economy 7 or storage heaters but something that does exactly
the same as a gas-fired system?

Electric flow boilers do exactly the same job as gas or oil-
fired boilers, heating primary water which is pumped round
a conventional wet radiator circuit. It is claimed that this is
more efficient, and more controllable, than other forms of
electric heating, and allows conventional central heating to
be easily installed in homes with no access to mains gas.
One supplier is Electroheat, whose boiler prices start at
around £500 (see USEFUL CONTACTS, Plumbing and
Heating).

Relative costs of fuels 1

We heat our house by a modern conventional oil-fired boiler
and, up to now, our domestic hot water too. However, the price
of oil has increased from 10.5p per litre in April 1999 to 22.7p
per litre now. Standard rate electricity has remained constant at
6.4p per unit. Would we be better off heating our water by
electric immersion heater or is it still better to use oil, given
that the boiler is already working to heat the house?

Relative costs of fuels 2

I was interested to learn that it is possible to have an electric
boiler doing the same job as gas- or oil-fired boilers. We currently have an electric panel heater system operating from a
time clock. Could you tell me how the running costs of an
electric boiler compare with gas or oil, please?

Relative costs of heating by different fuels are difficult to work out, as the suppliers' invoices record their calorific values in different ways. Prices also vary in different parts of the country, and between different suppliers. The standard 'unit' of electric power is the kilowatt-hour (kWh), which will heat a one-bar radiant electric fire for one hour, and costs around 6p. Off-peak electricity (e.g. 'Economy 7') costs between 3 and 4p per kWh, but usually with a higher standing charge, and is used with 'night storage heaters', which many people find inconvenient. Natural gas piped into the house ('town gas') costs around 1.3p per kWh, but gas boilers may be only 65 to 75 per cent efficient, giving a truer cost of nearer 2p. Heating oil and LPG (propane), which are delivered by tanker and stored in special tanks outside the house, provide roughly 10 kWh per litre, so at current prices this is around 2.3p per kWh – say 3p allowing for boiler efficiency – still slightly cheaper than off-peak electricity and half the price of standard rate electricity. (All 2001 prices.)

Anyone thinking of switching from one fuel to another, or considering upgrading to a new boiler, needs to calculate the pay-back period for the costs of the new installation. In most cases installation will cost thousands of pounds, and this will take many years, or even decades, to show a profit. So it is usually better to stick with the system you've got, unless you have a very large house and/or very high heating bills, and can accurately calculate that a new instal-lation will start saving you money within five years.

Combi boilers

After twenty trouble-free years with a 'bog standard' indirect gas-fired central heating system we are about to have a change, in order to recapture the efficiency of our system when it was

younger. All we hear is combi – combi – combi, extolling the
virtues as being 'you only pay for the gas you use, the radiators
heat up quicker, and no need for a hot water tank'! But we
cannot get any real advice regarding the advantages of the
traditional indirect system, apart from the fact that you can use
a power shower off an indirect system but not a combi system.
What are the pros and cons of the indirect and combi systems?
Combination, or 'combi' boilers are only really suitable for
one-bedroom flats, as they allow hot water to be drawn
from only one outlet at a time. So if you are taking a shower
and someone else turns on the kitchen tap, then you are in
trouble. Also, in winter, when the incoming mains water is
colder, you will get less of a flow of hot water, and it can
take ages to run a bath. There should be no difference in the
speed with which the two different types of boiler heat up
the radiators. Some heating engineers try to sell combis
because they are easy for them to install, but in your case
you already have a cold water storage tank and hot water
cylinder, so I can see no advantages of a combi boiler at all.
And before you rush out to buy a new boiler, it may be
worth asking a CORGI-registered gas installer for an opinion on the existing one.

Combi boiler – slow bath filling
I have recently had a new central heating system installed,
using a combination boiler instead of the ordinary type used
previously. I have now found that the water pressure is extremely low (it takes ages to fill a bath). The plumber says this is
because a combination boiler takes its water directly from the
mains and the mains pressure is low (although, apparently,
within the guidelines). Is there anything that can be done to
increase the pressure?

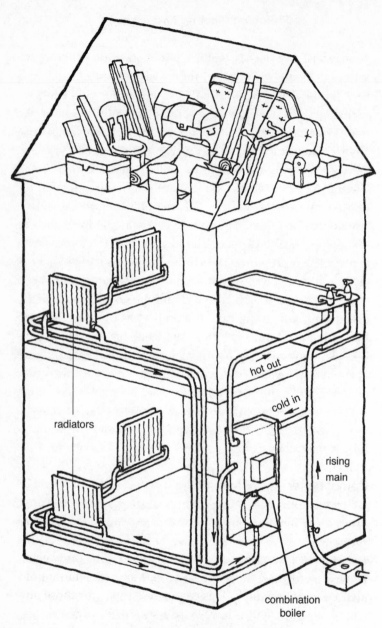

radiators

hot out

cold in

rising main

combination boiler

Combi central heating circuit

Combination (or combi) boilers depend entirely on mains pressure, so there is no header tank in the loft as a back-up supply or from which to provide a boosted pressure. Check that your plumber has used 22mm pipe for both inlet and outlet for the new boiler, rather than 15mm. But apart from that, there's nothing you can do. The water flow has to be limited by the thermal capacity of the boiler. To be able to heat up water at the rate it would normally flow out of the tap in a conventional system, the boiler would need to have an enormous rating. This would be very expensive, and greatly over-sized for domestic heating purposes. Hence the compromise of a smaller unit and a low hot water flow. Combi boilers do not provide a good flow of hot water, and they are only really suitable for small flats with showers, not bigger properties with baths.

Combi boilers – waste of energy
We live in a flat-roofed 60s terraced house without a water tank, and have a combi boiler (Worcester Hi-flow). Jeff, it is *so wasteful* of energy you wouldn't believe it. Well, I suppose *you* would! We can dry two washing machine loads in a day in the airing cupboard it's in. It's about ten years old so I imagine it'll give up the ghost soon. But what do we replace it with? This week, being energy week, I heard a 'condensing' boiler being mentioned. What is it? Is it expensive? Is it suitable for our house; and if not, what is? Where do we go for independent information?

Readers have also pointed out that combi boilers can waste water, since up to 8 litres has to be run through before hot water arrives at the taps. This can increase bills for those on metered supplies, and is a waste of a scarce resource.

I am not keen on condensing boilers. I recommend a

conventional boiler (around £500) feeding a hot water cylinder. If you have no room for a water tank in the loft you can get a combined tank and cylinder, but pressure will be poor. Contact two or three CORGI-registered gas installers for prices (see CORGI block advert in Yellow Pages under 'Gas Installers').

Combi boiler won't fire

The central heating radiators in my one-bed basement flat were hot at the bottom but cold at the top. Following a friend's advice I bought a 'bleeding key' from a plumbers' merchants and bled the air out of them. They are now completely cold and the boiler refuses to fire up under any circumstances. What on earth have I done wrong?

I guess your flat has a combination gas boiler. These are not fed by water from a header tank but rely on mains water pressure. What has probably happened is that there is a slight leak in one of the radiator valves which has allowed air to be drawn into the system. This is not unusual, and is not a disaster. You have done the right thing in bleeding the air out of the radiators. Now all you have to do is recharge the boiler up to working pressure. There should be a flexible metal hose somewhere around the pipework feeding the boiler, and opening up the valves at either end of this will allow mains water to flow into the system. Make sure you locate the water pressure gauge before you start and turn the valves off when you reach one atmosphere pressure.

Putting additives in combi systems

I understand that in central heating systems where steel radiators are connected by copper pipes it is advisable to add inhibitors to the water to slow down corrosion. How is the inhibitor fluid added to the combi boiler system?

The corrosion you mention is a result of electro-chemical reaction between the two different metals. This corrosion is also responsible for the formation of sludge in the system, which can block radiators and clog circulating pumps. In a conventional wet central heating circuit, inhibitor is poured into the feed-and-expansion tank ('header' tank) in the loft. A combination boiler operates on a sealed system with no header tank. The easiest way to introduce an inhibitor – or any other additive – into a combi system, is to inject a concentrate into one of the radiator vents. These are available from plumbers' suppliers, or for further information call Fernox (see USEFUL CONTACTS, Plumbing and Heating).

Noisy boiler

My new Baxi back-boiler was installed when I moved into this semi-bungalow eighteen months ago. It has always made a loud clattering noise when it first switches on. The installer said it was an airlock and put a full bottle of Fairy Liquid into the header tank and for a while that seemed to rectify the problem. It is now as bad as ever. Do I give it another bottle of Fairy Liquid? What else can I do? It's driving me mad!

Washing-up detergent is no solution for any plumbing problem. It is bulked-out with salt and so will cause corrosion within the system. I suggest you ask the manufacturers for their comments, and contact your local authority trading standards officer with the installer's details.

Condensing boilers

I am considering buying a condensing oil boiler for our house, which we are in the process of renovating. All the current plumbing is being replaced. I would be interested to hear your comments on condensing versus conventional boilers.

Condensing boilers – both gas-fired and oil-fired – are promoted as being hugely efficient converters of fuel into heat. Efficiency gains of 15 per cent are commonly claimed by manufacturers and retailers, but this is actually a myth. They would only achieve this sort of advantage if they were constantly running in fully condensing mode, which would mean an operating temperature of 56°C (as opposed to the usual 82°C for a conventional boiler). In practice, in a domestic central heating system, a condensing boiler will be firing-up from cold, running for two or three minutes, and then turning itself off again, just like a conventional boiler. It will thus only be running in condensing mode for a few seconds in each on/off cycle, and this is the period when a plume of steam can be seen shooting out of the flue (a phenomenon known as 'pluming'), which some owners and neighbours find alarming. Energy efficiency savings will be slight, and the industry has yet to produce any reliable independent figures to support its claims.

In return for this theoretical efficiency, condensing boilers are more complicated, need more regular servicing, and have many more parts to go wrong and be replaced. St Albans City Council, for example, have found that condensing boilers installed in their council homes are less reliable than traditional ones, and are costing around £1 million per year in repairs and maintenance (*St Albans Observer* – 5 October 2000).

So condensing boilers are really only worth installing if you have a very big house, or hotel, and very high fuel bills. And it is worth noting that if the boiler does actually run in fully condensing mode (56°C), then that is as hot as the water flowing from it will ever get, which means radiators will be cooler, and may need to be replaced with larger-sized models in order to emit the same amount of heat to the rooms. The domestic hot water supply will also only reach 56°C, which is, incidentally, below the British Standard recommended minimum of 60°C.

Condensing boilers

All the hype I read about condensing boilers led me to believe that I should tear out my twenty-year-old conventional boiler and install one of these gismos. Being a sceptic, I asked if there was any downside. After some waffling, I was told that my system would need to be chemically cleaned every three or so years at a cost of up to £200 a time. Apparently, if this work isn't done, it can foul up the boiler and cause the system to be permanently on! Surely this will eliminate most of my savings. Maintenance and servicing on condensing boilers is certainly more extensive, and expensive. Neither the manufacturers nor the Government's energy-saving promotional literature make this clear. If your conventional boiler is giving no trouble after twenty years, then it is highly unlikely that replacing it would save you any money, or save the planet any energy.

Kettling noise in boiler

My five-year-old boiler is making increasingly loud 'kettling' noises, and I have been told that this is due to limescale, and that the whole system needs to be cleaned out with a 'Power-flush', at a cost of £550. My local plumbers' merchants tells me that for £500 I could buy a new boiler. Is it worth paying so much to descale the present one, especially since the problem will presumably recur?

'Kettling' may well be caused by limescale on the heat exchanger. This traps steam bubbles which expand and explode, causing the noise. Powerflushing will only clear out the limescale if descaling chemicals are introduced into the system first, and if the scale is removed by chemicals then it may be possible to drain the system down manually without the expense of the Powerflush. 'Sentinel' descaler costs around £20 from Plumb Centers and can be added to the system and left to act slowly. I would give that a try before embarking on the expense of either a Powerflush or a new boiler.

Noisy pipes

We recently moved to a refurbished 1930s house. The master bedroom has polished floorboards. When the heating is on, we hear a high-pitched ringing noise, presumably from the pipes. Can we remedy this by carpeting the room?

Central heating systems make noises for a lot of reasons, but bare floorboards should not be one of them, and whilst carpeting the room may muffle the sound, it would be better to fix the problem at source. Noise can be caused by thermostatic radiator valves, or may be due to the circulating pump being on too high a setting. The high-pitched ringing noise may also be caused by a small blob of loose solder running up and down inside the pipes when the pump is circulating the heating water.

Pipes can also be noisy if they are not clipped securely enough to the joists, or if they are clipped too securely. (Pipes need to be supported but also allowed to expand and contract.) A common problem occurs where pipes have been run across shallow notches in floor joists, and the floorboards have been screwed down tightly on to them. So it would pay to do a bit of underfloor investigation before you pay for that new carpet.

TRVs

I find myself wondering why you described thermostatic radiator valves as 'an infernal nuisance' (see CONDENSATION). We've had them for about eight years and so far they've worked as expected. But I know from your columns that you always have sound reasons for your views, so what is behind your comment?

TRVs are often set too low, so that while part of the house is getting warm, the rooms with the TRVs stay cold. This means that moist air from the warm (and often wet) rooms – e.g. bathroom and kitchen – finds its way into the colder parts of the house and condenses on or within the cold walls. The most obvious symptom of this is black mould growth, usually low down on the walls and in stagnant corners. TRVs are also sometimes mistakenly used instead of fitting a room thermostat, and sometimes they can all shut down at the same time, but leave the boiler firing up and pumping hot water around itself, which is a waste of fuel. In my experience, TRVs are often used simply because their large size means they are easy to turn on and off, whereas many people find conventional radiator valves difficult to turn. But this is not a good reason for fitting TRVs – it would be better to fit new radiator valves with larger knobs. In my opinion TRVs are only useful in rooms with other heat sources, such as kitchens – especially if the central heating boiler is also in the kitchen – and living rooms with open fires or stoves – then they can save fuel by shutting down the radiator when the room is warm.

Heating controls

My central heating radiators all have thermostatic valves, apart from the one in the bathroom, which is supposed to provide a safety outlet in case the boiler overheats. The thermostatic valves have a 'frost' setting, which I intended to use when away from home in the winter, but as the bathroom radiator is uncontrolled, it stays hot all the time, even if I turn the temperature control on the boiler to its lowest setting. The bathroom is too hot, and I am wasting gas. What can I do?

Your central heating system is missing one vital component – a room thermostat to turn the boiler off when the house has reached the desired temperature. Thermostatic radiator valves in themselves do not affect the boiler; they simply shut down the radiators, but the boiler will continue to pump hot water around the rest of the system. When you are away from home you should leave the thermostatic valves on full, the boiler heat setting turned right down, and the room thermostat on the frost setting. Contact a CORGI-registered gas installer to have a look at your system.

Central heating: controls

What would you advise for a central heating system that blows either hot or cold, but nothing in between? The wall thermostat has to be turned to 24°C to turn it off. Any setting between these two levels has no effect. Two 'heating engineers' have so far failed to rectify the problem, and three different thermostats all produce the same result. The hot water, incidentally, remains exceedingly hot on the minimum boiler setting.

At the time you wrote your email (26 September), it was actually quite warm in Britain, so I would say that the 24°C reading indoors would not have been far wrong. And a four degree differential (or 'hysteresis') is about what you'd expect on a normal cheap room thermostat wired as an on/ off to the boiler. However, you may find that the thermostat can be persuaded to perform better by changing the wiring so that the small 'accelerator heater' in it is brought into the circuit. Plumbers often use only three-core cable ('twin and earth') to wire up room stats, whereas they really need four-core ('triple and earth'), with the live and switched-live conductors routed through the thermostat, and a spare neutral connected to the accelerator heater. The current through this, when the thermostat is 'on', keeps the thermo-stat closer to room temperature, and can reduce the hyster-esis to plus-or-minus 1°C. If re-wiring presents a problem, and if your room thermostat has no exposed metal parts (and the air grilles are proof against small fingers), then you may be able to sacrifice the earth wire and use it as the neutral connection to the accelerator heater. This is probably not a DIY job. For totally accurate control you will need a more expensive digital thermostat, such as the Honeywell CM67. Hot water temperature is controlled separately, by a thermostat on the side of the hot water cylinder. Turn this down to 60°C for hot but not scalding water.

Underfloor heating

What are the advantages of 'underfloor heating' as against 'rads' (radiators). If you had to choose from either one (to go with a condensing boiler) to go into a new bungalow which we hope to get built within the next few months – what would you choose, and why?

I have never lived with underfloor heating, but people who have it seem to be very evangelical about it. The advantages are that you don't have radiators taking up wall space and getting in the way of furniture placement, the floor is nice

and warm to walk on, and the heat is spread evenly throughout the room.

Disadvantages are that underfloor heating works best on
solid floors – concrete, brick or tiled finish – which have
their own disadvantages. It also needs fitting in conjunction
with underfloor insulation, and so means a lot of excavation
and building work. Of course, if you are building from
scratch then this is not a problem. UFH *can* be used under
timber floors, and there are various systems involving metal
plates to spread the heat around. But obviously you would
have to make sure that the floorboards were totally dry
before fixing, to stop shrinkage gaps opening up. And then,
if the heating was left off for any great time, the boards
could absorb moisture and swell and buckle.

Because the floor itself becomes the emitter, rather than
radiators, then it may take some time for the house to warm
up and cool down – i.e. response times are slow. Obviously
the underfloor piping has to be installed to a very high
standard, as it would be very disruptive to take up the floor
to repair leaks. But the biggest difference between UFH and
radiators is that the water temperature from the boiler has
to be lowered, otherwise the floor would be too hot to walk
on. The water temperature is adjusted by using valves to
mix cooler water from the return pipes with hot water in
the flow pipes – another complication. Many installations
have UFH below a solid ground floor, and radiators
upstairs.

Flushing radiator system
There are four radiators in my one-bedroom flat. The two
situated closest to the boiler are working but the two at either
end of the flat are not. It is not an airlock problem. I think the

system needs flushing through. Is there any way I can do this myself?

First try turning the two hot radiators down or off and see if that forces some hot water through to the others. You may need to turn the pump up a notch. If that does the trick, then it's just a case of balancing the radiators. If not, then the next step is to try draining the system down to see if that removes the blockage. If that fails, then use Fernox or Sentinel Central Heating Restorer to clean the system out before draining down and refilling. If you have a conventional gravity-fed system then this can be added to the feed and expansion tank, or 'header' tank, in the loft. If your radiators are on a closed pressurized system with a combi boiler then it can be injected into one of the radiator bleed valves.

British Gas Services and the 'Powerflush'

Some of my central heating radiators get very hot, whilst others are barely warm, even after bleeding. I have heard that the radiator system should be balanced, but the British Gas Three Star Service engineer does not seem keen on this, and recommends that the system is 'Powerflushed' instead, at a cost of over £600. Can you tell me how to try balancing the system myself, before I incur unnecessary expense?

Powerflushing is rarely needed, and you should be aware that British Gas Services engineers get paid commission for selling this service. Balancing the system is easier, and will often direct more heat to sluggish radiators, but it is a time-consuming process, and engineers and plumbers often cannot be bothered to do it. But it is a relatively simple DIY operation. At its most basic, balancing involves restricting the flow through the radiators nearest to the boiler, so that more heat reaches those further away. Each radiator has two valves – the on/off valve (usually, but not always, on the right-hand side), and the balancing or 'lockshield' valve at the other end. The balancing valve is shielded by a loose cap which can be removed by undoing a screw, and the valve can then be adjusted using a small adjustable spanner.

Open all the on/off radiator valves fully and then, starting with the radiator nearest the boiler, turn the balancing valve right off and then open it one-quarter turn. Do the same with the next radiator, opening it three-eighths of a turn, and so on down the line, until the last radiator has the balancing valve fully open. Further 'fine tuning' may be needed to ensure that the heat is evenly distributed around the whole system.

A more sophisticated approach is to use a pair of clip-on thermometers on the flow and return ('in' and 'out') pipes either side of the radiator (e.g. Brannan pipe thermometers from B&Q – about £12 per pair). Again, starting nearest the boiler, adjust the balancing valve until you get a temperature drop of 11°C across the radiator, and then move on.

Balancing radiators
Our local B&Q say they have never heard of Brannan pipe thermometers, and neither have our local builders' merchants or heating suppliers. As I would very much like to balance our system (it was drained down to fit two new radiators) and the price you quoted for these thermometers seems very reasonable, I wonder if you could suggest another source or the address of the manufacturer so that we could order them from our nearest stockist.

Several readers have reported this problem, but Brannan insist that their pipe thermometers should be available through B&Q. The B&Q product number is 212 098 33 and the B&Q barcode number is 501 140 533 4053.

Balancing radiators: A professional view

I think your advice on balancing radiators missed the mark somewhat and I would recommend the following method of working: Open up the lockshield valves on the larger radiators to three-quarters full and turn down the smaller ones, regardless of where they are in the system, to half a turn. Switch on and check all radiators to ensure that they get fully hot at the same rate. Those getting hot too quickly should have the lockshields turned down, whilst those not getting hot quickly enough should be opened up slowly and progressively. This operation should be repeated over, say, half a dozen cycles, until all radiators heat up at the same rate, which is more to do with their thermal load than their position in the system. This is a time-consuming and in some cases costly exercise, which, coupled with the customer's reluctance to pay for additional time and extras such as inhibitor, accounts for most inefficient systems and the early demise of pumps and combi boilers.

OK, that is certainly a version of radiator balancing. But most manufacturers recommend that the return pipe to the boiler should be 11°C cooler than the flow pipe, in order to make most efficient use of the fuel, and the way to achieve this is to adjust the radiator valves as I have described. In a correctly designed central heating system, the radiator sizes will all be matched to the heat losses of the rooms they are in, and the pipe diameters will vary so as to distribute the hot water most efficiently to where it is needed. Badly designed systems will need more adjustment.

Boiler spares

Our Vulcan Boiler has given stout service over the past thirty years, but now we are told the parts to keep it functioning are no longer available. If we have to have a new boiler could you advise on a suitable system?

Before you decide to scrap the old boiler, I think you should get a second opinion. When heating engineers say that parts for old boilers are no longer available, what they often really mean is that catalogue-numbered parts from the original manufacturer are no longer available. That does not mean that standard replacement parts from other sources could not be used to keep the boiler going. You need to find an engineer who is prepared to make an effort to keep your boiler running, rather than one who is after the commission from selling you a new system (see USEFUL CONTACTS, Gas, CORGI).

Low-level radiators

I have replaced a window with patio doors on to a roof terrace, and in so doing, I have removed the central heating radiator from below the window. I would like to replace it with a slim low-level radiator on the skirting below the doors, thus using the original pipework, but none of my local plumbers' merchants can supply such a radiator, or suggest where I might get one. Can you help?

It is not a bad idea to fit a radiator below patio doors, to stop condensation on the glass. But you should make sure that it will not be stepped on, by means of a projecting sill or similar. Skirting level radiators are often used in commercial premises, below plate-glass windows, for example, but they are not much used in houses, which is why your plumbers' merchants will not stock them. Try Hudevad (see USEFUL CONTACTS, Plumbing and Heating).

Leaking flue

About two years ago we had our gas central heating boiler replaced. It was situated in the same position as the old boiler. The new flue cowl and new boiler were replaced by the same person, a friend of the family. Since it was installed we have had a problem that when the rain is driven into the side wall where the flue cowl is situated it leaks through into the boiler and into the kitchen. Is there a type of cover that will prevent the rain leaking through the flue?

It depends on the type of boiler. You should start by asking the manufacturers for their opinion. But also check that it was installed properly – it should be at a slight downward angle to prevent this happening.

Problems with flue discharge

My gas central heating boiler flue is set well above head height but only 2ft below the eaves soffit. The cage over the outlet has a solid metal panel on to which the gases discharge and then vent through the mesh sides and top. This has resulted in the wooden soffit board above rotting in only six years. Having replaced this I wonder if I should drill a series of holes in the solid plate to allow the gases to escape more directly. Would you recommend this?

The type of outlet you describe is typical of a balanced flue. The air feeding the boiler enters around the outside of the flue pipe, and the exhaust gases exit through the middle. The central covering plate is there to stop local wind conditions from interfering with either inlet or outlet, and

drilling holes in it could upset the equilibrium. In the worst
case, this could result in a build-up of deadly carbon monoxide within the house. You should contact the boiler manufacturer and ask if they can supply an alternative flue
outlet which will direct exhaust gases away from the eaves.
Or you may consider fitting an alloy guard plate above the
flue and below the soffit board, to intercept condensation
from the exhaust gases.

Air in radiators
I have a conventional central heating system with boiler, pump
etc., and thirteen radiators. Of these, two have to be bled
regularly to release air and no matter how often I bleed them,
within a week or two they need bleeding again. There is no sign
of any water leak. How can the air be getting into the system?
The two problem radiators are probably on the return, or
suction, side of the pumped circuit, and it is quite likely that
there is a leak in one of the radiator valve joints. On the flow
side of the pump, a leak would result in water dripping out,
but on the return side it can draw air in, with no sign of water
leakage. The only cure is to remake the joints in turn, making
sure they are thoroughly sealed with jointing compound.
Start with the first joint on the flow side, i.e. 'upstream' of the
two problem radiators. Then it's a trial-and-error process of
elimination until you find the guilty joint.

Air in radiators
Eighteen months ago British Gas Services fitted a new boiler to
supply heat to my water and central heating system. Ever since
then the heated towel rail in the upstairs bathroom goes cold
at the top. Consequently I have to bleed it. This occurs every
two to three weeks. All other radiators function satisfactorily.

What is causing this and how can I cure the problem permanently?

Sounds like a design fault in the system. Air should be automatically vented through the expansion pipe, but for some reason it is finding its way into the towel rail instead. But why did this not happen with the old boiler? Maybe British Gas Services changed the speed setting on the circulating pump. You could try turning it down and see if this makes a difference. Otherwise, you can fit an automatic bleed valve on the end of a length of vertical pipe, on the 'feed' side of the towel rail, but if I were you I'd try to get British Gas Services to come back and sort it out free of charge first.

Air in system

We have a conventional central heating system approximately eight years old. Every twenty-four or forty-eight hours the central heating pump will make horrible noises and the radiators will not heat up. The only way to rectify the problem is to access the pump in the loft and release what appears to be a small pocket of air through a release valve attached to a 'T' connector close to the pump. There is never any air in the radiators as they have already been bled. Twelve months ago a family friend moved a first-floor radiator a few feet for convenience and the above problem is usually accompanied in the first instance by loud knocking in the radiator around the vicinity of the control valve and can only be stopped by slightly moving the valve. This has been going on for months and I am at a loss as to the build-up of air.

Try turning down the pump speed, if possible. But if that doesn't work then you'll probably have to move the pump to a lower position in the system.

Gas in radiators – hydrogen?

I have had a new boiler fitted. When it was fired up and set to heat the domestic hot water it heated the radiators. A non-return valve was fitted and this solved the problem. Unfortunately I had to bleed the bathroom radiator every day, until eventually the engineer said there must be a leak in the system. This is unlikely as the pipe work is all visible and there is no sign of a leak. Thinking that air may be drawn in via the expansion overflow pipe, he sealed this off, all to no avail. The bathroom radiator has been replaced, and Fernox Inhibitor added, but now the bedroom radiator (the one farthest from the boiler) has to be bled every day. Any suggestions?

Leaks on the return side could allow air to be drawn in without necessarily letting water out. But another possibility is hydrogen or hydrogen sulphide gas being generated by metal corrosion. The fact that replacing the bathroom radiator stopped it having to be bled supports this as a possibility. If the bled gas smells like rotten eggs, then this is a sure sign of hydrogen sulphide. It may also burn with a yellow flame, although this is not a recommended way of testing.

You could try giving the system a thorough clean out using Fernox Restorer, before draining down and refilling, using Fernox Protector (see USEFUL CONTACTS, Plumbing and Heating).

Oil-fired boilers

I am considering converting a solid-fuel central heating system to an oil-fired one, which I hope will be more efficient and less hard work, and certainly cleaner. I have been told that the boiler can be situated outside the house, thus eliminating noise. What is your opinion?

Modern oil-fired boilers are much smaller and cleaner than

in the past, and many models are designed to be fitted within kitchen units. The differences between oil and gas boilers are the possible smell of the fuel oil if there are any leaks, and the minor extra noise of the fuel pump. It is a neat idea to mount the boiler outside on the wall, which eliminates the possibility of smell and noise, and makes servicing easier. One such model is made by Thermecon (see USEFUL CONTACTS, Plumbing and Heating).

Gas fire in bathroom

Please would you tell me if it is allowable (i.e. Building Regulations, CORGI recommendations) to fit a coal-effect gas fire in a bathroom. We are remodelling – to use an American term – a 1901 five-bedroom house to suit two fifty-something marrieds for the rest of their foreseeable futures. The room we are turning into a large bathroom was formerly a bedroom, hence the fireplace and flue. The plumber is digging his heels in and hence our question. The bathroom is centrally heated, so the fire will be for effect only. We do not have any children. I can't see why not, as long as the flue and the ventilation conform to the relevant standards. There may be a problem if you have a mechanical extractor fan in the bathroom, which may try to draw air down the flue, hence drawing in carbon monoxide when the fire is burning. You may therefore need a separate air inlet from the outside to a floor vent adjacent to the fire to prevent this happening. The only other problem might be possible corrosion of any electronic ignition parts etc. due to high humidity in the bathroom – this is a reason why heating engineers are not keen on boilers in bathrooms. Why not call the manufacturer and ask their opinion? And check that your plumber is a CORGI-registered gas fitter.

Poor water pressure

We have very poor mains water pressure, which means that only one cold water tap can be used at a time. In addition, since we live in a bungalow, the pressure from the storage tank in the loft is minimal. It takes twenty-five minutes plus to fill a bath, and showering is interfered with if someone turns on a kitchen tap. Plumbers have suggested raising the storage tank in the loft, and/or a complicated system involving a series of electric pumps and thermostatic shower controls. Is there nothing more straightforward that could improve the water pressure?

Poor mains water pressure results in a limited flow, which means that only one tap can be used at a time. This situation can be improved by using a water-pressurized storage system. Combined with an unvented direct hot water cylinder, this can improve the flow to both cold and hot taps without the need for raised header tanks or electric booster pumps. For further information contact Dualstream (see USEFUL CONTACTS, Plumbing and Heating).

Low water pressure

If a system suffers from low mains water pressure, a water-pressurized system would suffer the same fate, wouldn't it? Or am I missing something? In the same vein, four years ago I bought a house which had very low mains water pressure and flow (1 bar and 4 litres per minute). After pressurizing (sorry!) Yorkshire Water they eventually discovered a mains leak and about a year later got around to fixing it. There was no surface evidence of the leak but you could hear water flowing using a long stick with one end in your ear, the other on a hard piece of ground. The repair improved the figures to 3 bar and 15 litres per minute.

A water-pressurized storage system doesn't increase the

pressure, it improves the flow, so that the same pressure can be delivered from two or more outlets simultaneously. Obviously it is always worth checking first that incoming mains pipes are of sufficient size, and not furred up. But some properties are in areas with low water pressure, and the Dualstream system is a good way of improving flow, and avoids the use of electric booster pumps.

Poor water flow

I have had the water board and plumbers out to try and find out why the flow of water from cold taps reduces when more than one tap or appliance is being used, e.g. the electric shower and the washing machine. It has been confirmed that the standing pressure from the mains supply is at 11 bar and we believe we have a direct supply. It has been suggested that the fact that we are supplied from the mains by a half inch copper pipe is contributing to the lack of flow and local plumbers have tested and found no blockages or inoperative stop valves. Before I instruct a replacement of our 50m supply pipe I would value any comments on why we have low level of flow inside the house. Is the supply pipe too small?

It certainly sounds as if the bore of the pipe is too narrow. Whilst this will not affect the standing pressure reading, it means that there is simply not enough room inside the pipes for the water to get through quickly enough to feed more than one outlet at a time. The service pipe connecting the house to the mains would normally be in at least 22mm pipe. 11 bar is a comparatively high pressure for a mains supply, so it is not a pressure problem, but very likely a flow problem. 50m is also a long length for a supply pipe, so if you get it replaced, then it may be worth having an even larger bore pipe put in – maybe 32mm.

Low flow from new taps

I recently changed the kitchen taps in my bungalow from the conventional 15mm pipe single hot and cold to a mixer tap with smaller bore supply pipes, and the hot water pressure is now much lower. Cold water supply is from the mains, and the hot water is from a header tank in the loft. The hot water pressure has remained good to the bathroom basin tap which has a 15mm supply pipe. I do not understand why having a different size pipe should lower the pressure. Is there any way of overcoming this problem?

Many kitchen mixer taps are of Italian or French origin and have 10mm or even 8mm feeds, soldered on to 15mm tails for the British market. Reducing the pipe diameter does not lower the pressure, but it does lessen the flow, which is especially noticeable with the small vertical head of pressure that you will have from a roof tank in a bungalow. There is no solution, short of an electric booster pump.

Noisy tanks

I live in the top flat of a three-storey 1970s purpose-built block. Recently the cold water tank in the loft, which feeds all three flats, has started making a dreadful noise when refilling. I have called in a local plumber but he has been unable to find a solution. Can you suggest any remedy?

There are several 'silent fill' ball-float valves available for this kind of problem, such as the Torbeck and the Fluidmaster. I am surprised your 'plumber' isn't aware of them. Your local plumbers' merchants should be able to advise you of a suitable model for your situation.

Noisy system

Our problem is plumbing noise. We have a new central heating and water system, with the boiler in the utility room and the tank in the loft, and the noise of the system can be heard in the bedrooms and lounge. Our plumber doesn't seem to have any idea what is wrong. The cold water flow, alone, is noisier than the radiators. We have done all the obvious things but must we now resign ourselves to a noisy life?

When you say 'the obvious things', presumably you have tried adjusting the mains water flow and central heating pump speed, and made sure that there is no air trapped anywhere in the pipes. Ball valves in cisterns can be replaced with 'low noise' valves such as the Torbeck, to stop water hammer. You should also ensure that all pipes are clipped at regular intervals and you could also try lagging them with thick foam sleeving to stop vibration and resonance.

Showers

I was about to arrange for a shower cubicle to be installed (professionally) in a corner of my bathroom, the internal walls of which are constructed of plasterboard on timber studding. Thus, two of the cubicle sides would be of plasterboard (suitably tiled) and two of glass (side and door). But from your comments it seems this is not a good idea, so could you please let me know why plasterboard is unsuitable and suggest how this problem might be overcome?

Ordinary plasterboard consists of a slab of plaster-of-Paris sandwiched between two sheets of paper. Both of these materials absorb water readily and so are unsuitable for shower cubicles. The water will always be absorbed through the grouting between the tiles and will wet and soften the plasterboard underneath. After a couple of years the tiles will fall off, exposing spectacular outbreaks of mould growth. Shower cubicles are better lined with marine-quality ply-wood (marine ply) or one of the proprietary brands of lining boards (Knauf Aquapanel or similar). The only plasterboard suitable is British Gypsum's moisture-resistant (MR) board.

Showers – plasterboard cubicle

You have said that constructing a shower cubicle with plaster-board walls is a mistake. This concerns me as I am converting my garage and have lined the walls with plasterboard and built internal studwork and plasterboard walls which will form the sides of the shower cubicle. The local building inspector has inspected the work and did not comment on this practice as incorrect. Surely if the walls are properly skimmed with plaster and then fully tiled this will be OK? Am I correct in thinking that your article referred to shower cubicles being built that were then not plastered or tiled? I would appreciate your com-ments as the work is not yet completed and if you think I need to change the design then it would need to be done now.

This kind of thing would not be the concern of the building control officer. You should use marine ply, or one of the proprietary lining boards, or at the very least a waterproof plasterboard which the manufacturers confirm as suitable. The tiles should go straight on to the boards, with no plaster.

Noisy shower pump

Some time ago we had our bathroom modernized and, because of poor water pressure, had a power shower installed. We now seem to be getting continual noise from the shower pump; there is a whirring and knocking noise as though it is trying to function although not in use. The refurbishment is now out of guarantee and the company that did it do not want to look into the problem. Can you offer any solution?

Shower booster pumps are activated by flow switches which detect water running through the pipes and complete an electrical circuit to start the pump. It sounds very much as though one or both of these switches may be causing the problem, and they are not difficult to replace. I suggest you contact the manufacturer for their advice.

One-piece shower enclosure

We stayed in a mobile home in France this summer. It had a shower with a one-piece plastic interior lining – wall, floor, ceiling. It didn't look at all bad, and the long-term advantages of cleaning and maintenance must be tremendous when compared with tiles, grouting and caulking. Is this kind of product available for domestic use here?

Leaking showers are a perennial problem. The typical British version has a shower tray set into a corner, with two sides enclosed by a glass or plastic door system and the other two sides tiled and grouted. The weakest point is always the joint between the tiles and the shower tray, and the usual thin smear of silicone mastic is unable to cope with the movement when an adult stands in the shower.

One-piece shower enclosures are available in the UK – enquire at any plumbers' merchants – but they are expensive, starting from around £700. Self-assembly shower cubicles with three walls and a door are also a good design for avoiding leaks, and cut out the need to tile the walls. I have never seen them on sale in the UK, although a US model can allegedly be ordered from B&Q warehouses, again for around £700. They can also be bought in European DIY stores for around £300, including tray, enclosure and shower taps. You can easily bring one back on a roof rack.

Showers – silicone seal

You have said that the weakest point in a shower is always the joint between the tiles and the shower tray, and that the usual thin smear of silicone mastic is unable to cope. Is there nothing that one can use that will do the job satisfactorily or is there a particular mastic or method of applying it that would give optimum results?

Silicone mastics will absorb around 20 per cent movement, and the weight of an adult on a plastic shower tray, or a resin shower tray on a timber floor, may move it by 3 to 4mm, so the mastic joint has to be at least 20mm deep. The mastic joint should be as thick as it is deep, so you need a 20mm square bead of mastic all round. The joint should be clean and dry before application and, if necessary, treated with the manufacturer's recommended primer. Shower trays and enclosures should be thoroughly cleaned with methylated spirits before application. Very few builders follow these basic principles.

Staining tiles

We have recently had installed at great expense a completely new tailor-made shower enclosure, completely tiled in white. The terracotta from the back of the tiles is now apparently leaking through the grout (in spite of re-grouting), giving a red/brown stain between the pristine white tiles. Can you suggest a make/type of grout, or grouting procedure which eliminates this problem? Or is there a product for applying to the grout to cover the staining?

Sounds like the tiles might not be suitable for use in showers. What did it say on the box?

Re-enamelling baths

I have almost finished renovating the house I moved into eighteen months ago. I have reached the bathroom, which contains a large cast-iron bath. I was intending to replace this, but have recently had the suggestion put to me of having it re-enamelled. Do you have any advice as to whether this is a viable option? Does it work, what would be a reasonable cost, and what should I ask potential re-enamellers?

Enamelling is a factory process which involves heating the metal to a very high temperature and melting a new vitreous surface on to it. This cannot be carried out in situ, although some firms claim to be able to use a heat process to re-enamel small areas, to repair chips and cracks. What is usually advertised as 're-enamelling' is the application of a two-part epoxy resin coating over the whole bath. It will never be as good as the real thing, but if you like your existing cast-iron bath and would like to keep it in place, then it may be worth considering. Prices are from around £150. Try Renubath (see USEFUL CONTACTS, Plumbing and Heating).

Drilling tiles

I have recently tiled a bathroom with standard white wall tiles and now I need to refit the shower-head rail to the wall. The only reference I have found suggests that I screw the fixings between the tiles into the grout. I would rather drill through a tile but apart from the fact that I should use a masonry bit I am unsure as to how. I presume a slow speed rotation is preferable to a higher drill setting and that I should place 'sticky-backed plastic' over the area to be drilled. Another complication is that the wall is plasterboard without easy access to the non-tiled side.

You can drill through a tile with a sharp (i.e. new) masonry bit. Use a bit of masking tape to stop it slipping around. If you get into the hollow between the timber studs then you'll have to use a cavity toggle, which means a much bigger hole. Best to locate a stud first (using a metal detector or cable locator to find the plasterboard screws) and fix into that.

Incidentally, plasterboard is not a good material to use for shower enclosures, unless it is moisture resistant (e.g. British Gypsum's MR board).

Mould removal

Firstly, I have resealed round my shower tray and bath with a silicone sealant which incorporates a fungicide. Nevertheless black mould has reappeared. The tray and bath are both made from plastic (perspex, polycarbonate?). Is there any proprietary treatment, safe to use on plastic, which will remove it and prevent further invasion? Secondly, I have regrouted the tiles in the same area and patches of orange coloured substance (or growth) have appeared. What is this and is there an appropriate treatment for it?

Both are fungal growths, and bleach will remove them. Once silicone has been stained, though, it is very difficult to clean up.

Toilets

A builder has told me that you are allowed to install a macerator toilet only if you have another, conventional toilet in the house as well. Is this strictly true? I would like to do away with the huge bathroom/WC in the downstairs room of my (Victorian conversion) flat, in order to use the space. I would instead create a smaller shower/WC in a corner upstairs. But the distance from the drains is apparently too far to have a normal WC. Is there any way round this?

Building control officers do not like macerator WCs because they are unreliable, and they are right to insist that you have a proper toilet as well. Macerator WCs use an electric-powered mincer to chop up the contents of the bowl and pump it through a 40mm waste pipe. They were originally marketed for basement conversions below the level of the main drain – in which case they represent the only possibility for installing a bathroom. But they are notorious for breaking down, particularly as the macerator teeth are easily snagged by cotton fibres – plumbers say that women should not be allowed near them!

But there are very few situations where a normal 100mm WC waste pipe cannot be installed in an older house. The pipe needs a fall of 1 in 40, which can usually be achieved within the ceiling space of a Victorian house. And if not, then the pipe can usually be raised at the bathroom end or lowered at the outlet end to achieve the required fall. Ask an experienced architect or surveyor to design your new bathroom for you (see USEFUL CONTACTS, Architects and Surveyors).

Macerator toilet

Do you ever come across vibration problems caused by the above in bathrooms where the unit is disposing of waste from the bath, shower, toilet and washbasin? My neighbours have one mounted on the wooden floorboards and its use wakes me at all hours of the night when they use the bathroom. The repetitive low frequency cycle drives me mad.

Yes, I know. This is another disadvantage of the stupid things. All I can suggest is that you tell the neighbours what the problem is, and if they don't act, then go to the local Environmental Health Department. Noise pollution is an increasing problem, and they should investigate.

Unsightly pipe runs

My daughter recently bought a very nice house (built late sixties), but the bathroom is dreadful, with exposed pipework running across the wall at various levels. Boxing-in would not be easy and usually looks just what it is. Have you any suggestions please?

From the sketch you sent me I can see that the plumber has run all the water and waste pipes from the bath, basin and WC horizontally across the wall into a service duct in the corner. This is careless work, but not untypical in situations where tradesmen are working to a fixed price and supervision is poor. There is no satisfactory way of covering up the exposed pipework, and the only option is to employ a conscientious plumber to re-route the pipes at floor or skirting level. Either that or paint them in bright colours in the style of post-modern architecture!

Quarter-turn taps

As our kitchen mixer tap is showing its age and O-rings are no longer available for the spout seal, its replacement has become necessary. We are attracted to the ceramic disc, quarter-turn type but have heard varying reports as to their suitability in hard water areas and the cost of replacing disc assemblies should this become necessary. Your advice on the relative merits of ceramic discs and the more traditional washer-type of tap would be appreciated.

If you think it is difficult to find O-rings to fit the swivel arm of your old tap, then wait until you try to fix a leak in a ceramic disc tap – some of them need three different-sized O-rings, and plumbers' merchants never seem to stock them. And if you give up, and decide to buy a whole replacement disc assembly, you will find that every manufacturer makes a slightly different model, and yours is either obsolete, unavailable, or will take three months to order from Italy or Germany.

However, you may be able to find O-rings (including one to fit your old tap) from various other sources, such as hydraulic suppliers, bearing factors and agricultural engineers. Or you can buy a pack of about 1000 assorted sizes, for around £16 from RS Components (see USEFUL CONTACTS, Plumbing and Heating).

Intermittent hot water

Can you please suggest a remedy for a bathroom that only enjoys intermittent hot water? We have a second bathroom where the hot supply is fed from the main cylinder through approx. 40ft (12m) of attic space, via a plastic pipe, which regularly loses its supply (apparently) due to a build-up of air in the pipe. I have been told that this is because the level of the building is higher in the bathroom than at the lowest point (i.e. the beginning) of the pipe and that it is one of the pitfalls of a house that is over 300 years old. We have had a 'non-return' valve fitted in the pipe and this does seem to have helped; however, we do keep losing supply and are only able to recover it following a complicated process of forcing cold water back through the hot tap using a hose whilst someone reconnects the hot from the cylinder to the valve in the attic. As I am sure you can imagine, this is all rather unsatisfactory, but as yet no one has been able to offer a solution (NB I have been told a pump is not practicable). Please help.

This problem sounds like it has nothing to do with the age of the house, and everything to do with the incompetence of the 'plumbers' you are employing. It sounds as though your system has been installed without any logical design. You need advice from someone who knows what they are talking about – look for The Institute of Plumbing registration.

Multipoint boiler

The fifteen-year-old boiler in my flat has broken down again, and it is time for a replacement. I don't need central heating – my oil-filled radiators suffice – but I do need enough hot water for one bath every day. To save money, I am considering getting an immersion heater or a gas-heated water cylinder, rather than another boiler, but I am being quoted between £1,000 and 1,700 for this, which seems excessive.

You could fit a 'multi-point' gas boiler to the existing pipework. These cost from around £350, and are the modern equivalent of the old 'geyser'-type water heater. They cannot be used for central heating, but will provide limitless 'instant' hot water. They have balanced flues, and so need to be sited against an outside wall.

Plumbing: Trace heating

Many years ago I came across an electrical wiring system known as 'trace heating', which was used to ensure that water supplies on farm land and within exposed farm buildings did not freeze in cold weather. I believe the system involved an electrical heating cable being secured to the length of the supply pipe. Do such systems exist for domestic use? Where would I get one, and is it a DIY project?

Trace heating is a useful way of ensuring that long runs of water pipe do not freeze. It is used widely in commercial and industrial buildings, but is also available for small-scale domestic use. Short runs use low voltages and currents and could be a DIY job; larger installations require more power and should be installed by a qualified electrician. Your local electrical trade suppliers should be able to give you more information.

Water softeners – electrical

Could you give me your opinion on the magnetic and electric 'limescale removers' that wrap some cable round the rising main. I had one of these systems installed eighteen months ago. The only way I can monitor it is observing the bath water! I still get hazy water in spite of foam lotion and when the water is let out I still get an invisible but tactile scum adhering to the sides of the bath so I am a bit sceptical about the result.

I'm a chartered electrical engineer so I feel I ought to know the answer to this – but I don't. We see these adverts for electrical gadgets that cost only a few pounds per year to run and connect to wires wrapped round the incoming water pipe. There is a photo of a cut-open hot-water cylinder and various testimonials assert that the system prevents new hard water effects, and even removes existing problems, in 98 per cent of cases. I find it hard to believe. Have you any first-hand knowledge to share with us?

Instead of installing a proper ion-exchange water softener, which requires plumbing-in and the monthly application of a dose of salt, manufacturers of these devices advocate cutting into the mains pipe and inserting a chrome tube containing a magnet. There are also electrical versions which involve wrapping coils of cable around the pipe.

The companies who market this equipment produce lots of glossy brochures with artists' impressions of pipes, water, wires, and coloured blue and red arrows showing how their patented electro-magnetic waves will save your immersion heater. They are not so keen on producing independent research supporting their inventions, though, because there isn't any. Well, perhaps – in anticipation of the abusive letters that the manufacturers of these devices will be writing to me – I had better qualify that.

Work at Cranfield University has shown that, under certain conditions, some magnetic water conditioners do reduce limescale formation. The bad news is that nobody knows exactly what these conditions are, or why the devices work when they do work. There are theories, but none of them tells the whole story, and no experiments have stood up to the test of scientific repeatability.

What is known is that the devices can be made to work in closed industrial processes – i.e. where the same water is recirculated at a known flow rate and constantly remagnetized. These conditions do not exist in the average home's plumbing system, where the device is fitted to the incoming pipe, and the water passes through it once only, and at a varying rate of flow.

The manufacturers' literature does not make this clear. And it often makes selective use of the research by reproducing data from the experiments which worked, but omitting the data from those which did not. On the other hand, those who market the devices claim that British Water, the trade association, is dominated by companies which sell ion-exchange water softeners, and there are even dark mutterings that favourable research is being deliberately suppressed by the salt manufacturers. Skulduggery indeed in the murky world of water treatment.

Many readers ask whether these magnetic or electrical water conditioners actually work, and the answer has to be ... maybe. But since they cost between £50 and £150, and since proper ion-exchange softeners now cost as little as £180, it would seem sensible to pay the extra and buy something that is proven to work.

Water softeners – blue staining

Since installing an Ecowater Sensatronic 518 water softener in 1995 any water marks left in baths and sinks have been tinged with blue, which we understand is due to copper sulphate being leached from the pipes. Even though we have slightly reduced the hardness setting on the computer from the correct figure, this has not solved the problem.

Is there a solution to this problem apart from bleeding untreated water into the system (as recommended by the manufacturer), which rather defeats the object one would have thought? More importantly, do we run the risk of pipe failure in the long term?

Soft water dissolves salts – which is why rainwater (soft) extracts calcium and magnesium salts from the ground it passes through to become hard. So if you have corrosion within your pipe system – possibly due to reaction between mixed metals (copper and steel, or copper and zinc), then the softened water will be washing it out and depositing it on the bath and basin. It sounds as though your water may be *too* soft, and the manufacturer's suggestion is the correct one – to increase the hardness by mixing a proportion of unsoftened water into the supply. This does not defeat the object, but adjusts the hardness/softness to a suitable level, where you get the advantages of softened water, but not the blue staining problem. It is simple to bleed unsoftened water into the supply, by opening the bypass valve a little. You should aim for around 50mg/l hardness, and the manufacturer should advise you on how to test for this.

Trade association British Water publish ten free fact sheets on all aspects of domestic water treatment (see USEFUL CONTACTS, Plumbing and Heating).

Drainage – soakaways

I understand that there is the possibility of a rebate from my water company for homes with soakaways. Is there any easy way to tell if surface water runs off to a soakaway, without digging big holes in the garden?

Find the inspection chamber where your waste water joins the main drain. This may be either outside the kitchen door, or sometimes in the front garden. Lift the lid and check that you have the right inspection chamber by getting an accomplice to flush the toilet or run the kitchen tap. Then get the accomplice to pour a bucket of water down a yard gulley. If the water ends up in the inspection chamber then you are connected to the main drain; if not, then it may be going to a soakaway.

Soakaways: Claiming rebates 1

Regarding soakaways and the reduction in the sewerage rate of a house that uses them, I wrote to my local water supplier, Anglian Water plc, on the subject, but all I got back was a meter installation form. Could you please clarify whether I am eligible for a reduction in my water rates, as I do have a soakaway for all the roof water from my three-bedroom house.

As I have lived in this house for thirty years, who knows, I might even get it backdated!

I have contacted Anglian Water and they apologize for the mix-up. You should, by now, have received an application form for a surface water drainage rebate. This rebate results from a change in the charging scheme for water services introduced by Ofwat, the water regulator, in April 2000, and applies to any property where surface water or roof water does not drain into the sewer. All the water companies should have introduced the rebate by April 2001, and you may be able to get it backdated for a year, but not, unfortunately, any further.

(Rebates vary between different water companies, roughly between £15 and £35 p.a. This rebate is available to consumers who pay a fixed annual charge for water and drainage – those who pay by water meter will have their bills reduced by a percentage figure. In order to qualify for a rebate in any particular year, the application must be made before 31 March.)

Soakaways: Claiming rebates 2

After writing to Severn Trent Water about this, I received a form asking for information and a freehand sketch of my property. This duly completed and returned, I was visited a week later by a water inspector who told me that although 92 per cent of my plot complied, the first 3yds (3m) of my driveway sloped towards the road and because of this 8 per cent length of driveway they were entitled to charge me 100 per cent for surface water removal. I was also told there was no percentage reduction for soakaway maintenance. Another no-win situation.

It sounds as though it would be worth digging a trench

across the drive to divert the surface water into the surrounding ground. Even if you had to pay someone to do it,
the cost would probably be repaid by the first couple of
years' rebates. Some of these privatized water companies
will do anything to avoid paying this rebate.

Drainage – septic tanks

We have recently moved into a house in Suffolk, dating from
the late eighteenth century. The property is not connected to
mains drainage (there isn't any in the village). All sewage from
the house, and some rainwater drainage, run into a set of
underground brick containers, with concrete tops and two
inspection/access covers. These are about 50yds (50m) from the
house, and 8 to 10ft (2400 to 3000mm) from a drainage ditch
that runs along the boundary of our property but isn't ours. I
noticed that there was a lot of black slime in the ditch downstream from our cesspit, and that there were signs of a steady
outflow – though very slight – from the bank on our side. After
heavy rain (and we've had plenty of experience of that lately)
there is a quite a strong sulphurous/sewage-works smell. Concerned that the system wasn't working properly, I sought
advice. A charming and knowledgeable young man in a Land
Rover explained that the levels and quality of final effluent
could not be improved with the existing system, and that the
only solution would be a 'packaged sewage treatment system',
which could be installed for £7,863 plus VAT. He said that the
original system was well constructed, but that it was no longer
appropriate. Might he be correct in his verdict? Or am I being
sold something that I don't really need? As a regular cyclist, I
have noticed 'the smell' quite often in the surrounding lanes of
Suffolk, so it would seem to be something that people learn to
live with. The problem here is that we are going to be offering

bed and breakfast, and guests may not wish to be either reminded of Spanish holidays or acclimatized to the smell.

A considerably cheaper option for your problem would be to install a pumped aeration device in the last chamber downstream. There is at least one of these on the market, which is configured to fit an existing bulb-shaped septic tank. I wouldn't have thought it beyond the wit of man to adapt one to fit your system. The parts probably cost around £50. It will qualify you for the necessary 'permission to discharge' certificate from the Environment Agency, but, be warned, all these systems pong a bit when the wind is in the wrong direction. The trick is to get them emptied before the guests arrive. It would also be an idea to redirect the rainwater straight into the ditch, so that it doesn't flush the septic tank through unnecessarily.

If you do decide to go for a new system, then it is still quite permissible to install a plain septic tank, costing around £500, and have the run-off filtered through the ground using 'Y'-shaped rubble-filled drainage channels. Reed beds are also quite the rage, being environmentally friendly and all that. See Building Research Establishment Good Building Guide 42, 'Reed beds' (see USEFUL CONTACTS, Construction Literature.

Rainwater collection

Following your recent comments on surface-water drainage, I have tried to obtain details from local builders' merchants of tanks suitable for installing underground for collecting rainwater. At present the roof water and surface water run to a rubble soakaway. The only suggestion so far has been for a GRP (glass-reinforced plastic) septic tank. I have also contacted the manufacturers of plastic oil tanks, but they inform me that they are only suitable for installation above ground. Can you recommend any suppliers?

A new GRP septic tank, which would cost upwards of £500, would contain unwanted baffles and chambers, and would be an unnecessary expense. Most people who install DIY rainwater collection systems use recycled orange juice tanks. These hold 1,500 litres, and can be purchased from Tank Exchange (see USEFUL CONTACTS, Rainwater Collection/Recycling). Two or more can be linked together to provide extra storage.

Recycling rainwater does not just save on water company drainage charges, but if you pay for your water via a meter, then by using rainwater or filtered 'grey' water (bath and shower waste) for garden irrigation, flushing WCs etc, you can save even more. Advice on partial or complete systems can be obtained from Aquarius Water Engineering (see USEFUL CONTACTS, Rainwater Collection/Recycling).

Drain smells in conservatory

I have had a conservatory built at the back of my terraced house, and find that at times it is unusable because of the drain smells emerging from the vicinity of the manhole cover. Does this mean there is something wrong with the drains, and is there any solution short of relocating the manhole?

Even the best-constructed and ventilated sewer will be smelly on occasions. It sounds as though your conservatory has been built over an existing manhole with a loose-fitting cover. Now that the manhole is inside, it needs to be fitted with a special double-sealed cover, which is screwed down on to a rubber gasket. These are also available with tray-type lids which can be tiled to match the surrounding floor finish.

Unblocking drains

Having previously paid £80 call-out fee to a plumber to unblock a drain (when it turned out to be caused by food in the sink outlet) I feel I should learn how to do this myself. But I really haven't a clue what to do, and I am afraid of flooding the floor, which is the ceiling of the flat downstairs. Any tips for a complete idiot?

Clearing blocked kitchen waste pipes is easy. There is a U-bend below the sink where the offending detritus collects. This is known as a trap. Not because it traps solids, but because it forms a water-seal to stop foul air from the sewer rising up into the house. To clear a blockage, you put a bucket or bowl underneath, unscrew the two plastic collars holding the 'U' to the inlet and outlet pipes, and wriggle it free. It will be full of grease, hair, rice and unidentifiable black sludge, which you scrub off into the bucket and flush down the toilet.

This is not a pleasant job, but it's better than paying a small fortune to someone else to do it for you. If, instead of a U-bend, you encounter a bulbous plastic object, this will be a bottle trap, which you remove by unscrewing the whole thing. In both cases, once you have scrubbed everything clean, reassemble in reverse order and run some clean water through while you check for leaks.

Very old U-bend traps were made from lead pipe. These often incorporate a small screwed-in plug to facilitate cleaning, but which will probably not have been opened for fifty years. If you use too much force on this plug you could damage the whole pipe, so it is best to first try the traditional remedy of the rubber plunger. But note that plungers will not always work on sinks or baths with integral overflows – these are connected to the waste pipe below the outlet but above the level of water in the trap, so the plunger simply pushes air through the overflow and does not disturb the blockage. Try blocking the overflow with a wet flannel.

It may also be worth trying soda crystals poured into the outlet and left overnight. These dissolve grease, and are sometimes effective on kitchen sinks, although less so on baths, where hair is the culprit.

Blocked waste

In your comments about unblocking drains you mentioned that because 'hair is the culprit' in bath outlets, soda crystals will only have a minor/moderate effect in unblocking them. Therefore, my question is, what will be effective in unblocking bath outlets which are blocked by hair?

You just have to remove it by physical methods. I always find that a kebab skewer with a forked end is a useful tool for digging out hair from waste traps. Poke it down, rotate it, and pull it out. If this doesn't work then the really drastic solution is one of the acid-based drain cleaners, but obviously these are highly corrosive, and not good to have stored around the house.

PVC-U

All materials are subject to decay, but this is not something that is much discussed by salesmen, who prefer the idea that their products will last for ever. Adverts for PVC-U replacement windows and cladding, for example, often give the impression that the material is 'maintenance free', and, for the scientifically uneducated, this must sound like a wonderful thing. Unfortunately, it is simply not true.

A recent reader's letter describes a typical scenario. The reader lives in a fairly modern purpose-built block of flats, and someone on the residents' committee has decided that, in order to 'reduce maintenance costs', all the windows, fascias and soffit boards should be replaced with PVC-U, at an estimated cost of over £100,000. The current annual amount they are spending on exterior maintenance is, of course, zero, because the windows, fascias and soffits have not actually been painted since 1976.

Imagine if we adopted the same approach to our clothes. Or teeth. Don't bother to clean them or look after them. Just let them rot away and then buy some plastic ones. Society would judge anyone who behaved like this as foolish, or deranged, or both. They would be sent for psychiatric counselling and their children would be taken away from them. But when it comes to the buildings that we live in, it seems to have become socially acceptable to allow them to rot.

The PVC-U salesmen exploit this inertia by reassuring us that it really is all right to neglect our homes. It is not our fault that the windows have rotted, they say; it is because they were made from that pesky old-fashioned stuff called wood. Time to get modern and use space-age materials that will last for ever.

Only they won't. PVC-U inevitably becomes discoloured, and brittle, and, because of its high thermal expansion coefficient, it can even crack. This last problem is especially common in PVC-U replacement fascias and soffit boards, which need very careful fixing and – dare I say it – mainten-ance? – if they are to remain intact for more than a few years.

I have been very interested in your comments on PVC not being 'maintenance free', as I live in a block of flats in which some windows are PVC and some are not. Would it be desir-able for the PVC windows to be repainted when the other windows and the rest of the woodwork are redecorated every few years? If so, is paint suitable for woodwork to be used or is a special paint preferable? At present the management com-pany does not have the PVC windows done.

The biggest maintenance requirement for uPVC or PVC-U (the 'U' stands for 'unplasticized') products is to keep them clean. The plastic surfaces seem to attract dust and pollut-ants – possibly by electrostatic attraction – and white PVC-U can quickly become dirty. And since dark surfaces absorb more ultraviolet light than white surfaces, this exposes PVC-U to extra ultraviolet light, which causes embrittlement, and shortens its life. So all PVC-U windows and roof line products should be washed with detergent at least once a year – more frequently in towns or areas close to the sea. ICI/Dulux make Weathershield PVC-U paint – for use on weathered PVC-U windows – which will need rubbing down and re-coating every few years, like all paint-work. Since ICI used to provide the raw ingredients used to manufacture most PVC-U windows, it would seem likely that they developed this paint for good reason, and this must raise the question of whether PVC-U has any real long-term maintenance advantages over timber.

I live on an estate of houses with much white boarding – soffits, fascias etc. Firms come around offering maintenance-free white PVC. Some firms cover the surfaces of the existing wood soffits with thin plastic boards; others insist it is better to remove the original wood and replace entirely with PVC. Few of us still have the original woodwork which, of course, has the disadvantage of needing repainting at intervals. Grateful for your views on which is the best option.

'Maintenance-free' PVC-U is something of a myth. It won't last for ever. It becomes brittle through exposure to sunlight, and permanently discoloured by airborne pollutants. PVC-U must also be fixed using slotted holes to allow for thermal movement. If this is not done then the boards can buckle and split. Fastening PVC-U boards over existing timber is a real bodge job, as it will trap moisture underneath, and the timber will rot. Why do you think there are so many of these firms around touting for work? It's because they are making a fortune for doing not very much. For the money they charge you could pay to have the woodwork main-tained and painted for fifty years.

Fascias and soffits

Please explain to a bemused pensioner the merits or otherwise of an offer by an established cladding company to PVC-clad a bungalow's fascias, soffits etc. and in so doing to cut off the soil pipe at soffit level and re-tile the resulting hole in the roof. When I asked whether or not this meant venting any pong into the roof space I was told, 'Oh no, sir – we fit a non-return valve'! (a) Is this legal? and (b) What is the point?

This is, indeed, a very strange offer, and whilst not being strictly 'illegal', it is contrary to the recommendations of the Building Regulations. Presumably by 'non-return valve' they meant 'air-admittance valve' – these are usually only permitted in addition to an existing vented soil stack, not as an alternative. I would have nothing to do with this company, and your local authority trading standards officer might be interested to know why they are specifying this unnecessary work.

We live in a semi-detached bungalow. We have the rainwater downpipe for the front of the two properties discharging at the front corner of our bungalow, and our neighbour has the corresponding pipe for the rear. He is going to have his original wood fascias, guttering etc. replaced with PVC, and wants us to do the same. Ours is quite sound, and we do not care to replace with PVC in any case. What do we need to be aware of with regard to jointing etc.? How can we be sure it has been done correctly, and what redress would we have if there were problems in the future?

The main thing to be aware of is that most of this kind of replacement PVC-U work is carried out by unskilled, unqualified cowboy companies, who are unlikely to still be trading in twelve months' time, when the gutters start leaking. You should make it clear to your neighbour in writing that you will hold him responsible for any problems caused to your property as a result of his actions. You should also commission a condition survey from an independent surveyor, which should include a photographic record of the guttering as it is now (see USEFUL CONTACTS, Architects and Surveyors).

Roof-line products

The wooden flashing around the roof of my house will soon need replacing. Although it has been regularly painted (every three years or so) parts of it are now so rotten that it should be replaced. Some of my neighbours have had PVC (or something like it) flashing fitted, complete with new guttering. One paid £6,000 and the other £1,100. The low cost seems to have come from a number of factors: the two guys involved had just set up in business, they gave no guarantee and they did not remove the old wooden flashing but put the plastic over the top. My neighbour says they did an excellent job as far as he could see but they were probably also on some VAT fiddle as well. My question is: should I replace wood with wood or would PVC do? And, if PVC is preferred, should the old wooden one be removed first?

By flashing you mean fascia boards, barge boards and soffit boards. Personally I wouldn't touch PVC-U with a barge pole, and especially not the version which just covers up the rotten timber – all it can do is continue to rot out of sight. Replacement timber, if thoroughly primed and undercoated on ALL surfaces before installation (most was not), should be good for many years, and unlike PVC-U it won't end up poisoning us all in the long term!

ROOFS

The roof is the first line of defence against the rain, and leaks can seem very dramatic – although the total amount of moisture entering the house may be insignificant compared with a leaking gutter dripping against an outside wall, or the condensation introduced into the house by daily showers. It's that drip, drip into the saucepan that makes it seem like a desperate situation.

The roofing trade is notorious for providing a refuge for cowboys, which is a shame for the many skilled, conscientious roofers who get tarred with the same brush. So, although I am always loathe to recommend trade associations, I do suggest that readers with roofing problems should always use members of the National Federation of Roofing Contractors or the Flat Roofing Alliance (see USEFUL CONTACTS, Roofers). Membership of these bodies does not mean that a roofing company is 100 per cent wonderful, but it does mean that if something goes wrong, then you will at least have a point of reference to start chasing them. The main things to beware of are:

- Victorian houses where original slate roof coverings have been replaced with interlocking concrete tiles. These are heavier than the original slate and the extra weight can cause deflection of the rafters.

- Cement fillets around the edges of upstands instead of proper lead flashing.

- Anything sprayed or painted on top of a roof (usually black bituminous stuff, but sometimes red paint).

- Anything sprayed underneath a roof – i.e. insulating foam.

Spray-on foam treatment

We live in a 1920s three-bedroom semi in a small village. We are on the side of a river valley and get a lot of wind here. Every year gusts of wind dislodge one or two slates. Some just move a little, others slide right off the roof. I keep replacing the slates that have moved, but obviously a solution is needed. The roof is in its original 1920s condition with no underfelt.

There are adverts in the papers for a 'foam spray solution' for old roofs. These are guaranteed for twenty or so years. Is this the easiest way forward, or should we look to get the whole roof redone? I have heard conflicting reports about the foam-type repair, varying from 'fantastic' to 'waste of money'. As the damage is only slight each year could we just keep on repairing the occasional damage instead?

The fact that slates are slipping every year probably indicates that the nails which hold them to the timber battens are rusted through. Roofers refer to this as nail fatigue or nail sickness, and it is definitely time to have the roof stripped off and re-covered. Having foam sprayed on to the undersides of the slates may sound like a wonderful high-tech solution but it is actually a bad idea. It is at odds with the recommendations of the Building Regulations, which require a clear 50mm ventilated gap between insulation and roof covering. The foam sets hard and removes the two vital attributes that allow a traditional roof to last and perform so well for so long – the ability to breathe and the

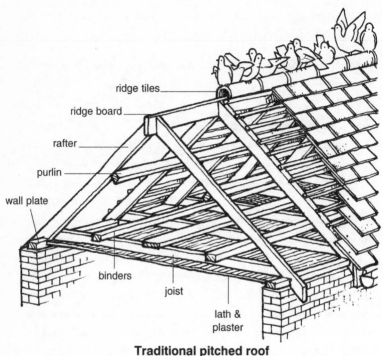

ridge tiles

ridge board

rafter

purlin

wall plate

binders

joist

lath & plaster

Traditional pitched roof

ability to move. The foam completely encloses the timber battens and the top surfaces of the rafters, which almost guarantees that they will rot. The foam also sticks tight to the slates and makes it almost impossible for them to ever be re-used. You will also probably find that the cost of the spray-on foam solution will be three or four times that of having the roof re-covered in the traditional way. Try to find a roofer who will remove the existing slates carefully, and re-use as many as possible. Also make sure that the roofer uses a breathable sarking felt, and allows it to sag between the rafters. The ridge tiles and any hip tiles should be rebedded using lime-and-sand mortar to match

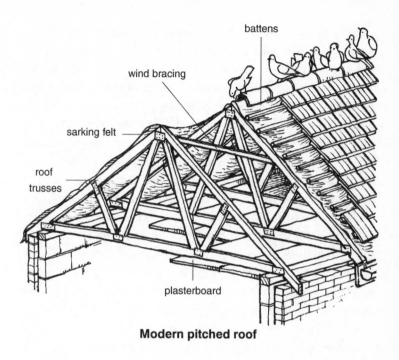

Modern pitched roof

the original; do not allow the roofer to use sand-and-cement.

Foam roof undercoating

My son and his partner live in a 1930s ex-council property. It has a tiled roof and although it appears to be perfectly weatherproof, he is anticipating that he will have to do some maintenance. He wonders about getting it 'Renothermed'. This appears to involve having the interior of the roof sprayed with a white substance, which they say overcomes almost all roofing problems (slipping tiles or slates, lack of underfelt, leaks and condensation, freezing pipes and tanks, nail fatigue). They have BBA [see over] approval, are members of the British

Urethane Foam Contractors Association and are BSI registered. Your advice as to whether this treatment would be worthwhile would be very much appreciated.

See answer to previous question. In addition, note that the firm does not 'have British Board of Agrément approval' – BBA testing is paid for by the company, and only tests what they ask to be tested. In Renotherm's case, the test confirms that the foam sticks to tiles and slates. It does not mean that this is a good thing to do to a roof, and does not test for possible condensation and rot problems in the enclosed timbers. The British Urethane Foam Contractors Association is a trade association, and again, membership of this does not prove that it is a good thing to spray foam on roofs. Neither is the company 'BSI registered', although their paperwork may have conformed to BS5750 – which became obsolete in 1996, and was replaced by ISO 9001. Renotherm used to claim in their advertising that this made them 'government approved', which was not true, and was stopped following a ruling by the Advertising Standards Authority.

The National Federation of Roofing Contractors (another trade association, but one whose members repair roofs using traditional methods – see USEFUL CONTACTS, Roofers) publish a technical bulletin on spray-on coatings of this nature, and a spokesman told me that they would only recommend it as a stop-gap measure to extend the life of an old building – a farmer's barn, for example – for another few years. They do not recommend it for use in houses.

Flat roof coverings

The flat roof of my rear extension is leaking (it has the normal bituminous roofing felt covered with stone chippings), and a number of firms are offering apparently foolproof solutions, such as fibreglass, rubber membranes, and jointless glassfibre-reinforced plastic coverings. These systems are all promoted with a variety of impressive-looking glossy brochures and promises of 25-year guarantees. What is your opinion?

Flat roofs in Britain are notorious for leaking, and the problem does not usually lie with the roof covering material, but with poor workmanship. 'Flat' roofs actually need a fall of at least four degrees, a requirement which is often neglected. And if the timber roof joists are not thick enough, they can sag in the middle, allowing water to pond, and find its way through any minor defect.

The problem with most of the 'instant fix' flat roof repairs on the market is that they simply cover the existing leaking flat roof with a new waterproof coating, and will not remedy the underlying causes of the leak. This is throwing good money after bad. For example, covering a leaky flat roof with a rubber membrane can trap moisture underneath, which results in blistering and further damage later on.

The GRP (glassfibre-reinforced polyester) and glassfibre flat roofing systems are often advertised as having 'no joints', as if this was an advantage, but in fact a large flat roof area exposed to sunlight should always have movement joints to cope with thermal expansion. If there are no joints then there will almost certainly be expansion damage later on. And the 25-year 'guarantees' are usually meaningless. Also, the prices charged by these companies are often greater than the cost of getting the roof re-covered properly using tried and tested traditional methods. Modern high-tensile roofing felts should last for fifty years if they are installed properly (see USEFUL CONTACTS, Roofers).

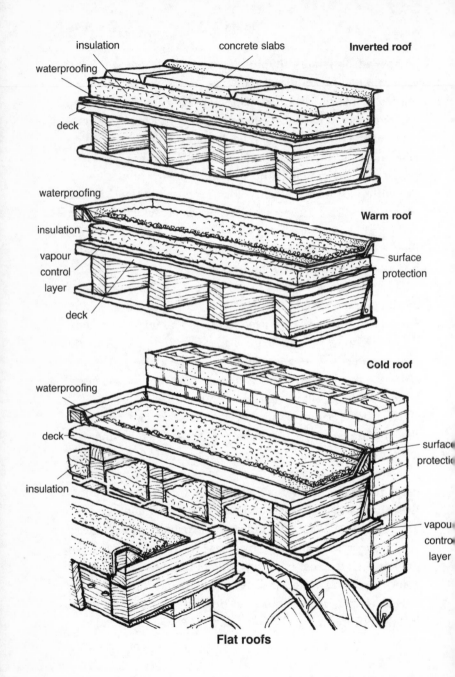

Inverted roof

insulation
concrete slabs
waterproofing
deck

Warm roof

waterproofing
insulation
vapour control layer
deck
surface protection

Cold roof

waterproofing
deck
insulation
surface protection
vapour control layer

Flat roofs

Flat roof repairs

Where can I obtain information on DIY flat roof repairs? I am an accomplished DIY enthusiast and am confident that I can carry out the necessary work properly but would like some tips on the correct method to adopt.

Try the Flat Roofing Alliance which publishes a free booklet, 'The Householder's Guide to Flat Roofing', and a more detailed handbook for £17.50 (see USEFUL CONTACTS, Roofers).

Flat roof problems

We expect to have to repair or renew the flat roof above our kitchen fairly soon as it has begun to bubble. Would you recommend replacing with glassfibre or is something else preferable for a flat roof?

The first thing to do is find out why the roof is bubbling. It may not be the surface that is at fault, but something more basic to do with the structure, insulation etc. Trade association, the Flat Roof Alliance, recommend that repairs on flat roofs should be carried out using products that are compatible with the original surface. If the existing roof is built-up bituminous felt, as most domestic flat roofs are, then bituminous-based repair systems will give a better result. Repairs to the membrane, however, are usually dealing with the effect and not the cause of the failure. The real cause could be many things such as structural movement, condensation, damage to the surface, excessive foot traffic, inadequate solar protection etc. For a satisfactory long-term solution the cause should be identified and dealt with, not just the effect.

Replacing old slates

A question about my son's house (typical solid, generously proportioned south London terrace): The roof needs attention because of slipping/cracked slates (the nails have given up the ghost). Builders have said that, although it would be possible to reuse a lot of the slates and buy in replacements for the damaged ones, it would be very expensive. They have suggested using concrete 'slates', but I seem to remember you warning about the increased weight and consequent stress on the supporting timbers. Is there a product that he could afford and that would not be too heavy? He is a hard-up young musician, so every penny counts, but I don't want him to do anything that could lead to expensive problems in the future.

Artificial *slates* are OK. Concrete *tiles* may not be. (The former are thin rectangular black things the same size as the old Welsh slates. The latter are big thick heavy red or black concrete things with knobs at the ends.)

Internal lining

Our house, built 1936, has no felt between the rafters and battens. The slates have been back-pointed years ago but much of the mortar has dropped out over time. Consequently the attic is draughty and dusty and when I drop the trapdoor and the loft-ladder there is always a shower of dust and small debris into the room below. I have considered stapling clear plastic sheeting to the underside of the rafters. This would stop the bits dropping and enable me to see through the plastic to check for any deterioration etc. Is this a good idea or is there a better one?

Your polythene sheet idea wouldn't do any harm, but it would probably be quite noisy when the wind blows and would be prone to tearing. Heavy-gauge bubble wrap may be better, and there is even one with a silver face which adds to the insulation value. But why don't you consider insulating between the rafters and boarding over them, or alternatively fixing insulation-backed boards direct to the undersides of the rafters. You are supposed to fit a vapour barrier on the 'warm' side of the insulation, and make sure there's a ventilated gap above the insulation.

Lining the rafters

I have a Cotswold stone tiled roof with traditional lime-mortar torching under the tiles. It has been suggested that I could insulate the loft space and cut down dust, by fixing aluminium-faced polystyrene block insulation under these tiles between the rafters. Do you recommend this? Should a ventilation gap be left under the tiles?

Polyurethane has a better insulation value than polystyrene (Kingspan or Cellotex or similar). You should try to leave a clear 50mm air gap between the insulation and the tiles, so if you have 100mm-deep rafters you can fit 50mm insulation board. Alternatively, you could screw whole sheets of insulation board to the underside of the rafters, rather than cutting pieces to fit in between the rafters. This is probably a better method, although it will cut down headroom if you are hoping to use the loft space for anything. Whichever method you choose, for a really professional job fix a vapour barrier (1000-gauge polyethylene) on the inside of the insulation and finish off with OSB board (oriented strand board, or 'sterling board').

Sarking felt 1

I would be grateful if you would kindly advise me how to repair small tears to internal roofing felt. The outside tiles appear to be sound and are not leaking.

If the roof is not leaking then there is no need to repair the felt. Sarking felt is a fairly recent product, whose main purpose is to make life easier for roofers. Once the roof tiles or slates are on, it serves no further purpose and can actually cause problems by cutting down ventilation.

Sarking felt 2

My valuation survey report says that the roof of my 1930s semi has no underfelt, and that it will have to be brought up to modern standards by stripping off the tiles and battens and re-roofing, including felt. The roof seems to be in good condition, both internally and externally, and there are no signs of any leaks, past or present. Is re-roofing really necessary?

Since the 1960s it has been common building practice in Britain for roofers to drape 'sarking' felt across the rafters before battening and tiling. The term 'sarking' comes from a bygone age and referred to close timber boarding laid across the rafters to prevent wind-driven rain and snow penetrating through the gaps around tiles and slates. Sarking is a good second line of defence in areas of high exposure, and the original boarding is still used in exposed areas in Scotland. In fact, the Scottish version of the Building Regulations specifies close-boarded sarking for certain areas.

But for less exposed parts of the UK sarking felt is less of a necessity, and has generally been adopted simply to make life easier for roofers. When re-tiling an old roof, roofers used to have to work in sections, stripping and re-covering an area in a day, so as to leave the roof weathertight. With sarking felt they can strip the whole roof covering off in the first day and felt it, and then take their time with the replacement tiling or slating. Sarking felt has two disadvantages:

- The idea that it is a failsafe second line of defence encourages roofers to take less care with the final tiling or slating. This is especially notable with regard to calculating and laying the correct headlap (vertical overlap) to cope with prevailing weather conditions. Tile manufacturers (and the Building Regulations) specify a minimum lap, to prevent wind-driven rain and snow being blown up under the lap and into the roof space. This may be as much as 60mm or 75mm, and if this measurement is adhered to, then no roof should leak. But by shrinking the headlap to 25mm, roofers can save one or two complete courses of tiles or slates (thus saving themselves £30 in materials), and if the water gets in then the sarking felt will catch it – as long as it stays intact – for maybe fifteen or twenty years. After that, the roof will start to leak in severe weather conditions, and there will be no alternative to complete re-roofing.

- Sarking felt cuts down on the natural ventilation in the roof space; especially if it is stretched too tight (it is supposed to sag loosely between the rafters) or if it is one of the new impermeable plastic varieties. With the current high standards of ceiling insulation, roof spaces are very cold in winter, so the water vapour, which finds its way up from the bedrooms, is trapped in the loft by the sarking felt; it condenses against the cold surface of the felt, and can drip down and stain the plaster on the ceilings. Some readers have reported a steady dripping of condensation from the felt, and have even thought that the roof is leaking. It is notable that other European countries, including those with cold northern climates such as Germany and Denmark, do not use sarking felt, but prefer to keep the natural ventilation that comes from air passing through the gaps between the tiles or slates.

If a roof really needs re-covering, due to a large number of rusty nails and/or a large number of slipped slates or tiles, then it is probably worth letting your roofer use sarking felt as part of the new installation – as long as it is installed properly according to Buildings Research Establishment standards, and adequate ventilation is provided in the form of special vents at eaves and ridge. But if an old roof is in sound condition and not leaking then there is no need to strip it off simply to install a layer of felt. This recommendation indicates a misunderstanding by the valuation surveyor.

Leaky tiles

Our rear addition roof was lost in the 1987 hurricane and replaced with artificial slate. It leaked in several places and as we are lucky enough to have a long-standing friend who is a roofer, we asked him to strip the 'slates' piecemeal and re-lay/replace as required. It was a horror story, as many roofs are, considering the number of 'roofers' who came out of the woodwork in 1987.

When he finished everything seemed fine. That is until we had heavy rain with a strong westerly wind. The roof is in two parts, the front and what I believe is known as the rear addition. The valley between faces west. No matter what he has done since, including leading, tar paint etc., it still leaks and it is driving me witless. The leak appears low on one side of a beam over the loo ceiling but there is no hole so the water must get in high up and drip off at the lowest point. I have been told this is a notoriously difficult area to seal once it springs a leak. Have you got a solution? We just cannot afford to strip off the roof and start again.

It sounds as though there isn't sufficient vertical lap between the slates, and between slates and valley gutter lining, to cope with the wind-driven rain. The minimum figure depends upon the pitch of the roof and the exposure conditions, and is given in Building Research Establishment documents (or ask your local authority Building Control department). If your roofer has failed to comply with the required lap then you should get him to do it again properly. There is no alternative.

Leaks between tiles

In 1985 we built a new kitchen on our 1957 semi. The roof has been leaking since about 1990. The flashing and tiles have been checked on numerous occasions, all to no avail. Last year we bit the bullet, and had the roof completely redone (it turns out the original builder had not used big-enough joists for the size of the roof). And guess what? It is leaking again!

The roof is a very shallow pitch, Redland concrete tiles. The leak comes through the ceiling towards the edge of the pitch, about 3ft (900mm) in and towards the outside wall. This only happens when it rains heavily, so we have ruled out a leaking pipe. Any ideas? We are getting desperate as we are trying to sell the house!

I suggest you call Redland and ask them the minimum headlap they recommend for that particular tile for the given pitch. My guess is that there isn't sufficient lap, and the rain is either getting blown in, or tracking back under the edges by surface tension.

Loft conversions 1

I would like to make a storage area in my loft. The ceiling joists are 3in × 2in (75mm × 50mm). Would I need to strengthen them or not?

Many older houses were built with 75mm × 50mm ceiling joists over the upper rooms, and whilst these are capable of supporting the weight of the ceiling, and a few suitcases and boxes of Christmas decorations, they should not be loaded with too much else. (Having said that, many homes have 250-litre water storage tanks resting across two 75mm × 50mm ceiling joists!) The current Building Regulations require much more substantial timbers. 75mm × 50mm ceiling joists would only be allowed to span 1.4m, and if you wanted to use the loft as a habitable room then you would need to add at least 150mm × 50mm joists, which would allow you to span 3.5m. So the short answer is, it depends how much weight you want to store up there. The Loft Shop (see USEFUL CONTACTS, Loft Conversions) produce a free guide to the Building Regulations and Loft Conversions.

Loft conversions 2

We are planning on converting our loft in our late Victorian house and have had several companies round to quote. All but one have said that they will have to insert steel beams (joists?) to support the floor of the conversion. However, one company has said that we don't need steel beams as the internal wall below is loadbearing and they can span from the outside wall to this wall using wooden joists (beams? – you can see I am not too hot on terminology!). To complicate matters, this wall has been knocked through on the ground floor as well! They say that this is OK as the load is spread out to the side walls by the ground floor – arch principle. They seem a reputable company and have come recommended by a friend who used them, and their quote is cheaper by a couple of thousand than the others, so I'd like to use them too. I know that the building regulations inspector will have to inspect their work – I'm worried that he'll insist on there being a steel beam put in instead, causing huge disruption and extra cost. Hope you can advise me on this.

Can't possibly say without seeing the house. But since the final word will rest with the building control officer, why not contact him directly and ask what he thinks? Also, you would be better getting the whole scheme properly designed by an architect or engineer in the first place, and then getting builders to tender for it, rather than letting the builders do the design.

Loft ladders

I have heard a couple of horrific stories from friends regarding accidents putting Christmas decorations down/up or out of/into lofts when balancing on chairs/inadequate ladders etc. We went to buy a loft ladder this year but houses like ours (1960s-style, speculative jerry-built, I'm sure you know the type) have such a mass of trusses and what-have-you one would need something very neat that folded away probably on to the hatch itself. Any suggestions?

You are right to be concerned. Most serious accidents are caused by falls, and it is a good idea to install a proper retractable ladder for loft access. The Loft Shop (see

USEFUL CONTACTS, Loft Conversions) do a range of folding loft ladders that are mounted on the door of the hatch. The narrowest is about 540mm, which will often fit into an existing hatch width. But if your roof trusses are at 400mm or 450mm spacing, then it is still relatively easy to enlarge the opening by cutting through one ceiling joist and supporting the cut ends on trimmers to the adjacent joists. With care, this can be done without even damaging the surrounding plasterboard ceiling.

Thatched cottage

Please could you advise on the implications of buying a semi-detached thatched cottage, some parts of which are believed to date back to the seventeenth century. It has been restored, has exposed ceiling and wall beams, four stone fireplaces, high-vaulted ceiling to the kitchen, fairly recently installed central heating by gas-fired Aga. We have always lived in up-dated houses built c.1930 so have no experience of life in such a property. Would welcome any advice you could offer.

Thatch is an attractive traditional roofing material and very good for insulation – both thermal and sound. People who live in thatched houses have nothing but praise for the material. Its insulation properties are second to none, keeping a home warm in the winter and cool in the summer. And estimates of longevity are actually greater than you might think. Norfolk reed thatched roofs (the best quality material) have been known to last for over a century, with sixty years being a reasonable minimum, and even a straw roof can last a good forty years. All thatch needs re-ridging every fifteen to twenty years, and localized damage needs prompt repair, on the 'stitch in time' principle.

The other perceived problem with thatch, that of fire risk,

is also the subject of much heated (sorry) debate. The idea that sparks flying out of the chimney and landing on the thatch will set the roof alight is pretty far-fetched, as anybody who has ever tried to light a bonfire will know. But there are various kinds of spark arresters on the market, usually consisting of fine wire-mesh cowls sitting on the chimney pot. Insurance can be higher than for other houses. Certain insurance societies are offering reduced premiums to householders who have their thatch treated with fire retardants, even though the chemicals in question do not appear to have received any kind of official approval. The waters are further muddied by the fact that the manufacturers of the fire retardants are actually *owned* by a leading agricultural insurance society. The efficacy of the fire retardants is also questionable; when I asked a thatcher who had used it how he disposed of the chemically-treated waste straw he replied, 'Oh, I just burned it.'

For details of qualified thatchers contact your local authority building conservation officer, or call the National Council of Master Thatchers Associations (see USEFUL CONTACTS, Roofers).

Which guttering?

Regarding metal gutters, which would you recommend, aluminium or cast iron? I have found that aluminium tends to oxidize under the paint leaving a white powder. Is there a cure for it?

Cast-iron guttering is best, but expensive. Zinc alloy is a good one – available from builders' merchants in France! I painted mine with Hammerite alloy primer and plain black Hammerite finish, and have had no problems.

Repairing cast-iron gutters

What is the best way of repairing a leak in a cast-iron gutter? The painter has put a blob of silicone sealant in, but the leak has come through again. The rest of the gutter is in good condition.

If the leak is at a joint, then the two sections should be separated (undo or cut off the nut and bolt holding them together). Then clean off and paint the exposed metal and reassemble using traditional linseed oil putty as the sealant. If you are going to the trouble of refurbishing one joint then you might as well do the whole lot, and it will last you considerably longer than modern plastic guttering. Cracks can be repaired by conventional electric arc welding, using cast-iron welding rods.

Moss growth

The moss on my roof is getting more abundant and I am concerned that it may cause damage to the tiles. I have been advised of various remedies including a chemical solution, although warned that it may cause blotchiness to the tiles. One other interesting suggestion is to affix copper wire at various points of the roof. Can you advise?

Lichen and moss growth on roofs is a totally natural occurrence. Some people find it unsightly; others welcome it as a sign of natural weathering and ageing of a house. The only serious damage is likely to occur on soft old red clay tiles, where the roots of button-type mosses can eat through and eventually create a leak. Even this can take a century to happen. Lichen and moss growth occurs more in country locations than in cities, where air pollution prevents it. The problem with chemical treatment is not just staining, but the fact that it has to be repeated regularly. The idea of copper wire laid along the ridge is that the copper oxide is washed off by the rain and flows down the surface. Again, this can lead to staining, and water running off copper on to other metals can cause severe corrosion – aluminium gutters and window frames are especially at risk. Personally, I'd learn to love the moss, or else pay a roofer to scrape it off every few years.

Moss growth – copper wire on roof

I have read in a couple of places that stretching copper wire along the ridge of a roof will prevent the build-up of moss. However there has not been any detail as to what type of wire is suitable – single or multi-strand; its gauge, where to get it and how to fix it. We live in a large bungalow with two sections of roofing of a fairly shallow pitch, each having a central ridge, and clad with concrete tiles which accrete moss quite quickly.

I don't think the size of the copper wire matters – it is just a convenient way of allowing a trickle of copper oxide to flow down the roof.

SOUNDPROOFING

According to a report from the World Health Organization, noise is the most widespread pollutant on the planet, presenting a significant threat to health, well-being and quality of life. And figures from the UK's Chartered Institute of Environmental Health show a consistent year-on-year rise in noise complaints to local authorities.

With noisy neighbours, the Institute recommends communicating with them as the most effective way of dealing with the problem. This is often easier said than done. As I write this I am trying to ignore my neighbour's dog which barks from eight in the morning till ten at night. When I first politely drew this to the neighbour's attention she told me that it was natural for dogs to bark. On the second occasion she accused me of harassment and said she would call the police if I complained again. The local Environmental Health Department say that barking dogs do not constitute a 'statutory nuisance' under the Environmental Protection Act (1990), and that they are unable to take action.

So, since we now live with so much noise – traffic, dogs, television, amplified music – and since the legislation is so useless, it may be easier to soundproof our homes than to deal with the noise at source.

Noise from outside, such as traffic and barking dogs, should first be approached by draughtproofing around doors and windows and fitting secondary glazing. Secondary glazing is not to be confused with double glazing, which

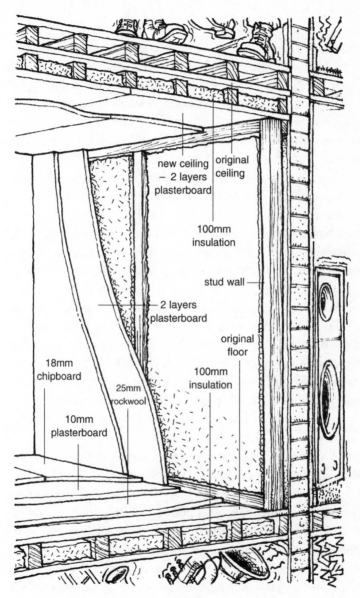

Soundproofing

has a small sealed gap – around 15mm – between the two sheets of glass, and is good for thermal insulation. Secondary glazing creates a bigger air gap between itself and existing windows – 100 to 200mm – and this is better for reducing noise. Fitting secondary glazing is cheaper than complete replacement double glazing, and offers the advantage of retaining the original fenestration pattern in older houses.

Noise from immediate neighbours – whether through walls or floors – enters in two ways: impact sound and airborne sound. Impact sound is most likely to be the footsteps of the people in the flat above, and becomes worse when they follow the latest trend for taking up the carpets and having bare wooden floors. The solution involves physically separating the floor and ceiling, so breaking the path of the vibrations. The best way to do this is to construct a new floor above, with joists between, but not touching, the original ceiling joists below. This will raise the floor level slightly, and doors will have to be trimmed to fit. Alternative, but less effective, solutions are to re-lay the existing floor so that it 'floats' on acoustic rubber strips, or to construct an insulated false ceiling in the downstairs flat.

Older houses converted into flats during the last ten years should have a fair measure of soundproofing, supervised by the local authority Building Control Officer, but earlier conversions may have escaped their attentions, as might buildings where planning relaxations were granted – to preserve ornate Victorian ceilings, for example.

Airborne sound, if loud enough, can make the walls and windows vibrate as well, but its usual entry route is via gaps. If you can smell your neighbours' cooking or cigarette smoke, then you will probably also be able to hear their noises, travelling along the same paths. In terraced houses, a common route is through the cracks which open up between front walls and party walls; locating these gaps, and sealing them with a flexible filler, can sometimes achieve good results. Chimney breasts in party walls are also a route for sounds and smells, when the internal brick lining of the flues may have broken down.

More serious soundproofing of a party wall involves constructing a new timber stud wall close to, but not touching, the original brickwork, filling the space with sound insulation quilt, and finishing with high-density plasterboard or plaster on metal lathing. Proprietary plasterboard sheets with soundproofing quilt already attached, such as Gyproc's Triline system, can be fixed straight on to the existing wall with dabs of adhesive (see USEFUL CONTACTS, Plastering, British Gypsum).

Readers can obtain a free leaflet, 'Improving sound insulation in homes', from the Building Research Establishment website, www.bre.co.uk/acoustics/soundsin_homes.pdf

Noise through plasterboard walls

You recently discussed the advantages of old building methods over modern ones and referred to modern plasterboard partitions acting like a drum skin in transmitting sounds. My own house is built to 'modern standards', and the walls of the bedrooms surrounding the bathroom transmit all sounds with embarrassing clarity. I am in the process of erecting fitted wardrobes down the bedroom walls and I wondered if there is a soundproofing sheet which I could fit to reduce noise transmission?

You can fit a special plasterboard sheet with soundproofing

quilt attached, such as Gyproc's Triline system (see USE-
FUL CONTACTS, Plastering, British Gypsum). Better still
construct a separate stud wall with 50mm × 50mm timber,
with a 50mm gap between this and the original wall. Fill
between the studs with 100mm soundproofing quilt and
finish with two layers of 12.5mm plasterboard with stag-
gered joints.

Noise through floors 1

You wrote recently about how to soundproof houses against
noise from neighbours, but didn't cover my particular situation.
My problem is with airborne sound – television, music, loud
conversation (occasional bedroom noise!) – from the flat below.
While not deafening, it is irritating. I live in a top-floor conversion flat of a large Edwardian terrace (conversion pre-building
regulations of the early nineties). Some of the floorboards have
'dished' and there are gaps between the boards. All are covered
with underlay and carpet but I suspect there is only airspace
between the boards and the lath and plaster ceilings below. An
architect friend has suggested laying a product called Fermacell
(a sandwich of dense fibreboard and insulation material) on
the floorboards. This, however, will raise the floor level 30mm
and will involve lifting skirting boards and, possibly, the
fireplace. It is also expensive – £1,500 for just one room – plus
costs of redecorating and relaying carpets. As my problem is
not severe, merely irritating, can you suggest cheaper solutions?
Airborne sound travels through gaps, so you could try
sealing the gaps between your floorboards by lining the
floor with hardboard, which would be a lot cheaper than
the Fermacell and is only 3mm thick. Before you fix the
hardboard – with serrated 20mm hardboard nails every
150mm – you might as well lift a few floorboards and put

some glassfibre or mineral wool quilt between the joists. Be careful not to bury any power cables under the quilt, but let them sit on top of it, otherwise they may overheat. After the hardboard is fitted (rough side up), seal the junction between the floor and skirting board with decorator's flexible filler applied with a mastic gun.

But before you do anything, why not see if you can get your neighbours to contribute to any proposed works. After all, I'm sure they can hear you too, and it is in both your interests to upgrade the soundproofing of your properties.

Noise through floors 2

I have recently bought a rather nice flat, rebuilt from a burnt-out hotel *c*.1947. Lovely high ceilings, 2.8m, elegantly decorated, so that for once in my life I don't want to alter anything. The problem is that I can hear my neighbours above change their minds. Nice young couple only there at weekends and holidays, but they usually have guests so that's four minds I can hear changing – and a lot more besides. They are aware of the problem (noise goes both ways) and have had two layers of rock wool 800mm put between the joists underneath their floorboards and above our main bedroom ceiling. Made a big difference and now all we can hear is their boards creaking (a bit) and their loo flushing.

Now we would like to do our bit. What can we do to insulate our ceilings without spoiling the decor? Don't mind losing a bit of height (say 200mm) and re-coving. If we are shown to be doing our bit then I think we could persuade them to do the rock wool treatment over our sitting and dining rooms.

Another potential problem is that they are talking grandly of 'putting down a hardwood strip floor' (money no object I gather). That would seem to nullify all the insulation efforts. Will have to try and persuade them otherwise. Local builders don't seem to have much of a clue.

If your upstairs neighbours are going to spend money on a new floor then this would seem like an ideal opportunity to effect a complete acoustic break, so that they put in new floor joists between your ceiling joists. You could offer to contribute to the cost, and keep your existing ceiling intact. Alternatively, they could lift their existing floorboards and lay the new ones on acoustic rubber damping strips on top of the existing joists – not as effective, though. Details in the BRE leaflet (see USEFUL CONTACTS, Soundproofing).

Polished floorboards

I have just bought a two-bed top-floor flat in a Victorian conversion, which is a bit grotty, and want to do three things, apart from painting etc. The main one was to strip the floors, polish them and put rugs down. However the lease states 'to cover and keep covered with carpet and underlay all floors except kitchens and bathrooms'.

Has anyone come up with a system of insulation that has an effect equal to carpet and underlay, i.e. lift the floorboards, add loft insulation between the joists and run a 5mm thick rubber strip along each joist before putting the floorboards down again? As this is apparently a standard clause, do people either ignore the clause completely and just strip the floors or respect it totally and stick to carpet? The sanding hire people say most people ignore it but I do not want to upset the people downstairs.

You are right to consider the result of your actions on your downstairs neighbours, as stripped wooden floors are a major source of irritation, and can lead to serious disputes. In your case, your lease clearly states that the floor must be carpeted, and this provision may have been imposed by the local authority when they gave planning consent and Building Regulations approval for the conversion of the property into separate flats. If you ignore this then you could find yourself on the wrong end of legal action from the neighbours and the freeholder.

There *are* various ways of installing soundproofing divisions between flats, but they are a lot more complicated than the scheme you describe, and are not guaranteed to be 100 per cent effective. The effect of heels on a polished timber floor can be like drumsticks on a drum, and it might be heard not just downstairs, but next door too. My advice is to accept that your flat is not suitable for bare floors, and to stick with the carpet. Console yourself with the thought that polished wood floors are a fad, and they will not always be as fashionable as they are now.

Noise from bare floors

We bought and remodelled an older home. My husband tore out layers of carpet and padding. We got the floor back to the original hardwood floor, but now you can hear everything that goes on in the house from outside. Is there a product or something that can go under the house to solve the problem? We have a crawl space basement. Also is there anything else that can solve this problem without destroying what we have already finished?

Maybe you have discovered just why the previous occupants had all that carpet! I don't see why you couldn't fix glassfibre insulation between the floor joists, and finish off with moisture-resistant chipboard screwed to the undersides of the joists. Ideally you should have a layer of polyethylene sheet on top of the insulation (i.e. on the warm side) as a vapour barrier, to stop warm moist air from the living rooms causing condensation in the basement.

False ceiling

My builder just attempted to improve soundproofing in my bedroom from the flat above. He was going to rip down the ceiling and start again with fibreglass insulation followed by a double thickness of plasterboard hung from metal strips which apparently (somehow) don't touch the old ceiling. However, when he started to pull off the old ceiling he found, to his surprise, that it was already stuffed with fibreglass insulation. So he left the ceiling as it was and simply hung more plaster-board from metal strips then plastered over to finish. It hasn't made that much difference.

The trouble with suspended ceilings is that they are hanging from the joists above, and so can act as a sounding board for transmitted sound. They only really work with new joists spanning the whole room. And whilst false ceilings can help in stopping airborne sound from the bottom flat going upwards, they are less useful the other way round. There is a lot of ignorance in the building trade about this. Extra insulation on top of the new plasterboard may have helped, but it sounds as if it's too late now.

Brick wall

I have a neighbour who proposes to have built, a 6ft (1800mm) high brick wall to replace a 4ft (1200mm) high fence, to cut down the traffic noise. Her house is only some 20ft (6m) from her boundary with a pavement and busy road. I am not sure the wall will give her the relief she expects from such a large outlay but have no experience in this matter. She would ideally like to sit in her garden in the lee of the wall in some peace. Also, would she need permission for the wall?

Boundary walls under 2m high (1m if within 1m of highway) do not need planning consent unless you are in a conservation area. Solid brickwork is a good direct sound blocker, although there will still be airborne sound refracted around the sides and over the top. But in general, if the wall blocks the view of the traffic then it will also block its noise. It may be possible to construct a quiet corner by returning the wall down one or both sides of the garden, as well as just along the front. Brickwork is expensive, but if built to a high standard, with an attractive facing brick, then a garden wall of this nature will also add to the value of the property.

STRUCTURES AND MATERIALS

Most readers' queries about structural matters concern the removal of internal walls, and the difference between a load-bearing wall and a non-loadbearing wall. There is no mystery to this; if an internal wall has something resting on top of it – floor joists, ceiling joists or another wall – then it is loadbearing, and it would be unwise to remove it or cut holes in it. However, the vogue for open-plan living means that some people will always be determined to buy old houses and rip the guts out of them. Many thousands of Victorian terraced houses have had the central spine wall knocked through at ground-floor level, and this used to be done by leaving two nibs or piers of brickwork at the sides and sliding in an RSJ (Rolled Steel Joist) to pick up the floor joists above. Rather belatedly it became clear that by concentrating the load on the two nibs, there was a chance of settlement, causing cracking damage right up the house, and possibly to neighbouring properties as well. So the preferred method is now to insert a rigid steel frame, which spreads the load right across the original span. There are plenty of cowboy builders around who still prefer the old RSJ trick, though.

Neither should it be assumed that because a wall is non-loadbearing, then it is a good idea to knock it out. Internal partition walls provide soundproofing, thermal insulation, can prevent fire from spreading and in older houses they may also have a bracing or stabilizing effect on the side walls (see also CHIMNEYS, chimney-breast removal).

Also remember that if you turn two rooms into one, then you lose the wall space for bookshelves and furniture. And, because of the strange way in which British estate agents value property, a house with fewer rooms may be worth less.

Loadbearing walls 1

My flat is the top two floors of a Victorian terrace house, and I would like to knock out the separating wall between two lower rooms to form a through lounge/diner. The partition wall is only timber and plaster, but my builder says it is a loadbearing wall. Can this be true?

Yes, the wall between the front and back rooms in these types of houses is called the 'spine wall', and, although it is of timber construction, it supports the weight of the floors and the roof above, and contains internal diagonal bracing which strengthens the whole building. If the bracing is cut through or removed then there could be serious structural movement. This type of wall should only be removed or altered under supervision from a qualified structural engineer.

Loadbearing walls 2

Can you tell me a simple way of identifying a loadbearing wall? I'm a bit stuck because I can't find clear information anywhere! I want to remove part of the internal wall between my kitchen and dining room. There is no wall directly above and the joists run parallel to the one I want to remove which is made of concrete aggregate blocks. Two builders have told me it isn't loadbearing but I just want to make sure. We contacted a structural engineer but he just said that if two builders have said it isn't loadbearing then it should be OK – didn't seem to want the business!

I can't really add to what you've already been told. If you're confident that there is no load on it, then, by definition, it isn't loadbearing. However, depending on the age of the house, there is a possibility that this wall may be providing a bracing or tying effect on the outside walls, so you really should seek professional confirmation before undertaking any work. Also, this wall will be performing other functions, such as fire-stopping, soundproofing and thermal insulation. You may wish to consider what effect these changes might have on the rest of the house before you knock through.

Lintel above window opening

We want a window put in an internal wall. The house was built in 1966 and the wall is 10ft (3m) wide and constructed with breeze blocks. The aperture is to be 4ft wide × 3ft high (1200mm × 900mm). Does this require a lintel above? Our first quote stated one was to be provided. My husband queries the necessity.

Almost certainly. But when you say 'internal wall', do you mean an internal partition wall? If it is really non-loadbearing, and you only have to support the weight of one course of blocks, then it may be possible to support them on a hefty timber window frame. But who is designing this installation? If a builder, then does he have qualifications in structural engineering? If he makes a mistake, then you could end up with expensive repairs for cracking damage.

Loads on floors

We have a large collection of books spread through most rooms of our house, and anyone who has tried to lift a pile of books will know how heavy they are. In addition, our grandchildren, staying overnight, have recently found that jumping off their beds makes the floor bounce most satisfactorily! What are the normal weight limits for bedroom floors? Our house was built in 1973 with brick-and-block walls.

Your 1973 house will have been built to the current Building Regulations, and the floors should be able to support at least 150kg per square metre. So a 4m × 5m room will be able to carry a load of 3000kg, or 3 tonnes. If the books are spread across the floor, though, they may cause bending of the joists, and cracking of the plaster ceiling below. It would be preferable to concentrate the load near the ends of the joists; i.e. bookcases against the front and back walls. The same principle applies to the grandchildren.

Changing room layouts

1930 semi-detached houses such as ours have kitchens too small for all mod cons and no room under the stairs for a toilet. The house itself is big enough for our needs and we do not want to build an extension. Is it possible to alter the layout of the ground floor/staircase to provide the areas we need? Can you suggest anything – or refer me to any other source?

It is always possible to change rooms around, but you need to take care. Non-loadbearing partitions are easy to remove; loadbearing walls are much more difficult – and expensive. Moving a staircase is also usually a fairly complicated procedure, and I would have thought that there is an easier way to install a downstairs WC than moving the staircase. A good architect – preferably one with engineering skills – will be able to advise you on what is possible (see USEFUL CONTACTS, Architects and Surveyors).

High alumina cement

My daughter has recently made an offer on a flat in a three-storey block of around thirty flats which was built about 1973. Her solicitor has advised that high alumina cement may have been used in its construction. The block is brick faced and has a tiled roof but she was told that the floors are of concrete. Can you tell us the implications if this material has in fact been used in the construction.

High alumina cement (HAC) sets and hardens quicker than ordinary Portland cement (OPC), and so it has been used extensively to make structural concrete. But it has gradually become apparent that in hot or damp conditions concrete made from HAC can undergo a molecular process known as 'conversion', which makes it unstable and crumbly, and some buildings have actually collapsed. It has not been used for structural purposes in Britain since 1985 (1943 in France, 1962 in Germany!). The first thing is to find out what basis the solicitor has for suspecting that it may be HAC, and then to get it tested to confirm. If it is HAC then I would have thought your daughter would have great difficulty getting a mortgage.

Sagging concrete beams

I live in a small block of twelve flats built in 1976/77 with integral garages in the basements. The ceiling of each garage contains concrete beams 40cms wide. Recently, whilst installing a shelf in my garage with the up and over door closed due to inclement weather, I noticed that some of the beams (normally covered by the door when it is open) showed signs of a distinct sag. On some of the beams the sag was spread along a major part of the length; on others it was concentrated in an 18in (450mm) (approximately) length in the centre. The amount of sag varies between 20 and 30mm. I duly reported my findings to the flats' management committee, comprised of six elderly residents, who do not feel that my query is worth following up. I would appreciate your views as to whether such a sag on concrete beams is normal – is it possibly due to settlement – or could it be something more serious? I would just add that many of the beams shows signs of a white fur and pieces of concrete, some as large as 2in × 3in (50mm × 75mm), have come off the beams over the years.

Concrete beams do suffer from 'creep', which may cause them to sag over time, but the kind of movement that you describe, over such a span, does seem to be excessive. Also, any evidence of efflorescence or spalling of structural concrete beams of that age would appear to be worthy of urgent investigation and perhaps a call to your insurance company. If your insurers, or their loss adjuster, decide that the damage is due to poor construction, then you may have a case against the developer and/or contractor – if you can track them down.

SURVEYORS

If you have bought a home that is older than you are, then your mortgage valuation survey may well have recommended further investigation by 'specialists' for timber and dampness defects, drains, cracks, heating system and electrics. Even if you thought to avoid these nasty-sounding problems by buying a recently built property, there may still have been some bad news in the surveyor's report, such as a recommendation for further investigation of the state of your cavity wall ties.

For many people, especially first-time buyers, this turn of events can be confusing, because, having commissioned a survey and report from a chartered surveyor, they thought they had already paid for an authoritative investigation. The last thing they expected was a list of other people they should consult because the chartered surveyor did not wish to express an opinion.

For, sadly, when you engage a chartered surveyor, you are not necessarily employing an experienced construction professional. More often than not you are getting someone who got an A level in Geography, spent three years in the classroom at a 'new university', and then got a job in a surveying practice. There, they will have been taken under the wing of a slightly older surveyor, who probably advised them to 'forget everything you learned at college' (no big problem), and took them out to do a couple of mortgage valuation surveys. These entail filling in the blank spaces on a printed form, such as, 'State whether main water, drainage, electricity and gas are connected', an acceptable reply to which will be, 'All mains services appear to be connected but have not been tested.' You could do better yourself.

A clue to the limited nature of surveyors' investigations can be had from the clothes they wear to work. Most surveyors turn up in their best suits, hardly well equipped for climbing up into the loft or having a poke round in the gutters. They won't even want to get down on one knee for fear of dirtying their trousers, which rules out looking at the drains or even lifting the edge of a carpet. In fact, the standard Homebuyer Valuation includes the stock phrase, 'Furniture, wall hangings, floor coverings, insulation material and stored goods have not been moved.' So if you are selling a house and you don't want the buyer's surveyor to notice some particularly dodgy detail, just hide it with a few tea chests or a bit of carpet. I once looked at a place where a huge crack between the main house and the kitchen addition was covered with a calender of pastoral scenes. The surveyor had missed it completely.

Even when they do try to 'investigate' a bit deeper, most surveyors manage to give the impression of being totally ignorant. In one study, 93 per cent of surveyors questioned did not know how to use an electrical moisture meter correctly to diagnose dampness problems in walls. The result is that, rather than risk making mistakes and laying themselves open to future compensation claims for negligence, surveyors always recommend 'further investigation' by others of tricky subjects like dampness. So their reports give carte blanche to cowboys to come in with estimates for thousands of pounds worth of unnecessary work, all sanctioned by the surveyors and, therefore, by the mortgage lenders.

But why get a survey done at all if it is likely to be so inadequate? The answer lies in the Building Societies Act (1986), which requires a written valuation report to be obtained on the occasion of each advance. Since demutualization, most of the building societies are now actually banks, and are not governed by this rule. But old habits die hard. As Adam Smith pointed out, all professions are a conspiracy against the public.

Types of surveys

We are always told that we should not rely on the mortgage valuation, but should pay extra for a more detailed survey. But having done just this during the recent purchase of my terraced house, I feel that it didn't tell me any more than I could see for myself. Should I have paid even more for a full survey? What exactly are the advantages and disadvantages of the different types of survey?

Good question. The basic valuation (£150 to £250) is carried out on behalf of the mortgage lender, for them to judge whether the property has sufficient collateral for them to lend money against it. Even though the buyer pays for the valuation, in law the documentation belongs to the lender. So if the surveyor fails to spot a costly defect, then you would not be able to sue them afterwards.

With the Homebuyer Survey and Valuation (£300 to £350) you are engaging the surveyor to work for you directly, so if he fails to spot a defect then you may be able to sue him. But obviously surveyors are aware of this, which is why they hedge the wording of their reports so carefully. Hence the prevalence of phrases such as, '. . . xyz *appears* to be in good order', and, '. . . floor coverings and furniture have not been moved', because surveyors know that in order to be found guilty of negligence in court, it is not enough to prove that they have missed something – it must be shown that the defect was clearly *visible* or that they should have been able to infer its presence from *symptoms visible* to them at the time of the inspection. This accounts for surveyors' use of electrical moisture meters on walls, even though they know that the readings are meaningless. Because a judge in a famous court case ruled that a surveyor would have been able to spot some hidden dry rot if he had used a moisture meter on the wall nearby, since that case surveyors have always recommended that clients should have further investigation by damp-proofing and timber treatment companies.

The wording on the Homebuyer Survey and Valuation report form is set by the Royal Institution of Chartered Surveyors (RICS), although some firms of surveyors amend the wording in their own versions of the form. Also, the quality of the survey varies according to the type of surveyor. Most Homebuyer Surveys are carried out by General Practice (or GP) members of the RICS, who are often little more than estate agents or valuers. A more specialized surveyor will belong to the Building Surveying division of the RICS, and may also have engineering experience or qualifications, in which case he may be more knowledgeable about building construction, and more confident about making judgements about the state of a house.

The more expensive Building Survey (£450 to £800) should be a much more thorough investigation, carried out by a Building Surveying RICS member, or a structural engineer. You would expect anyone undertaking a Building Survey to wear overalls, and to bring a set of ladders so that they can access the roof space (although they are still unlikely to go up on to the roof, and will state in their report that they have not done so). They should lift manhole covers to inspect the drains, and may use tools to lift carpets and floorboards (although this may not be done if the sellers are still in occupation, and do not give their permission).

Types of surveyor

When we moved house four years ago I was very disappointed by the performance of the surveyor, who I felt did very little for his fee, landed us with a huge bill for damp-proofing (which turned out to be unnecessary) and failed to point out the things that we really should have spent our money on, like the leaking roof. We are planning to move again in the next couple of years, and would like a better service. Can we get a survey from a different kind of professional (an engineer, perhaps) and would this be acceptable to the building society?

The RICS has a near monopoly on simple mortgage valuations, because of the 'panel' system operated by the major chains of estate agents. But Homebuyer Surveys and Building Surveys (which can include valuations) are carried out by professionals who belong to other organizations as well, including the Architecture and Surveying Institute (ASI), the Association of Building Engineers (ABE) and the Institution of Civil Engineers (ICE). Finding someone who is going to provide you with the quality of survey that you expect is a matter of contacting members of these bodies, finding out if they do domestic survey work, and quizzing them with regard to their experience and attitude. Valuations from members of these professional bodies should all be acceptable to mortgage lenders.

Homebuyer surveys

I am hoping to move house but the survey has concerned me. I have had the 'expert' builders' quotations – on the advice of the surveyor – and the roof is apparently 'shot to pieces'. I also need a damp course to the ground floor etc., etc., etc. I really don't know whether to go ahead with the purchase now or not. One quote yesterday came to £14,000! Apparently I need a whole new set of UPVC windows, as well as fascias, soffits etc, which are rotten. I made the mistake of asking the various builders to quote for points marked in the survey and they really have gone to town. Where can I obtain honest advice? My mortgage company (on the basis of the survey) is withholding money until the damp(ness)/timber treatment is carried out to the surveyor's satisfaction – so I need to make up the shortfall AND pay for the work.

Please advise – I don't really trust any of the opinions given. The surveyors are so careful about protecting themselves that apparently nearly everything 'probably' needs replacing.

In general I advise against damp-proofing, timber treatment, PVC-U windows and PVC-U fascias, as these items are usually (a) unnecessary; (b) damaging to the house and (c) damaging to the environment. The roof may or may not need repairing, depending upon age, type etc. 'Shot to pieces' seems to imply some kind of war damage which, as far as I am aware, is uncommon in present-day mainland Britain. It sounds to me as though you need independent advice, rather than asking contractors to quote for specific items. When builders are called in to quote for work on newly purchased homes they tend to smell mortgage money and worried new owners, and react accordingly.

Party wall problems

We have recently had plans drawn up to add a single-storey extension across the whole of the back of the house, and these have been passed by the council. I have read in a book that cognizance has to be taken of the Party Wall Act (1966). The architect is very sanguine and says just go and chat to the neighbours, but my understanding is that we need written permission from the neighbours on both sides. Both are elderly and I cannot find a specimen consent letter not written in intimidatory legalese. Do I really need written consent?

You should seek expert advice from a surveyor experienced in party wall legislation. You will have to pay a professional fee for this, but it could save you a lot of trouble in the future. Call the Architecture and Surveying Institute (see USEFUL CONTACTS, Architects and Surveyors) and ask for suitably experienced local practitioners from their practice register.

Dodgy surveyor

I bought an Edwardian ground-floor flat a year ago and was ordered by the surveyor to have a new damp-proof course in place wherever there was an external wall. I got this done and thought that damp would never be a problem. Then I read your article stating that 'rising damp' is a myth and also found that in two rooms that were treated there is a serious damp problem caused by condensation I imagine. I've paid £300 plus VAT for completely pointless work. Do I have any comeback?

It depends what you mean by 'ordered by the surveyor', and the wording of his report. You could try suing for negligence and damages, but your costs may come to more than the £352.50. The Royal Institution of Chartered Surveyors (RICS) have an arbitration system for disputes with their members, and this may be the best first step. In any event, you should contact the surveyor in writing and make your feelings known, and see what the response is.

Surveyors: What are they for?

Why do I have to pay for a survey before I can buy a house? The things that the surveyor comes up with are laughable. What I want to know are the things I can't see for myself, i.e. structural deficiencies etc., but I have to seek further professional advice on such matters because 'fixed floor coverings have not been lifted' etc. However, it is very helpful to be told that 'the interior decoration requires some attention' and 'the kitchen units would benefit from some updating'. Having average eyesight I can spot that myself.

It's all to do with the Building Societies Acts (1986). Building societies – unlike banks – were bound by these acts to commission independent valuation surveys before lending money against a property. Now that most building societies have been demutualized – i.e. they are effectively the same as banks – then there is no legal reason why this charade should continue. But the whole property industry is hamstrung by inertia and complacency, and it is difficult to see the surveying profession changing practices that it has been doing for years. It's a bit like the First World War soldiers' lament – 'We're here because we're here, because we're here because we're here . . .'

House log book

In an article several months ago in one of the financial sections mention was made of a 'house log book'. I have made enquiries in various bookshops but to no avail. I am wondering if you can give me any guidance as to how I might obtain such a book in which to record bills, location of taps and other useful information for a prospective purchaser.

I think the house log was just somebody's bright idea, and doesn't exist in the real world. In my view it would be totally impractical, and lead to disinformation and fraud, much like the Government's proposed sellers' packs.

TREES AND PLANTS

Buildings and trees have an interesting relationship. On the one hand, most people like seeing mature trees, as they have a softening impact on the urban landscape, and are homes for insect and bird life. On the other, trees have recently become demonized by insurance societies following a series of expensive subsidence claims. As a result, surveyors are now very quick to recommend 'further investigation' of trees near houses, and some arboriculturists (tree surgeons) are quick to recommend felling. The surveyors' and insurers' main fear is that as a tree grows, its roots will extract increasing quantities of water from the soil, causing drying shrinkage (especially in clay subsoils) and subsidence. In reality, subsidence and cracking that can be directly attributed to the presence of a tree is extremely rare. There is always seasonal drying and shrinkage in soils, anyway, but trees seem to get the blame for this whether they are guilty or not. And there are many cases where trees have stood for a century or more within touching distance of a house without causing any damage at all

Decisions on whether mature trees should be removed or left standing should be taken only after joint consultation between an arboricultural consultant and a structural engineer – the one to access the condition of the tree and its roots, and the other to look at how these factors are likely to affect the building. If a mature tree has historic or landscape value, then there are simple steps that can be taken to prevent its roots from damaging a building, and keeping the tree may actually add more to the value of the property than removing it.

For further advice call Michael Brightman of The Tree Care Company (see USEFUL CONTACTS, Trees).

Surveyor says cut it down

The surveyor's report on my London house drew attention to a sycamore tree in the garden, and recommended that it should be felled. But there are no signs of cracking in the property and I am reluctant to cut down a beautiful mature tree, which also shades the garden from the southern sun. Is there any evidence that trees actually damage buildings?

The idea that trees and buildings don't go together is largely myth, but surveyors are paranoid about being sued for negligence, so they prefer to recommend their removal. The fear comes from the idea that tree roots extract water from the subsoil, and where this is shrinkable clay – i.e. in London and most of southern England – then it can result in shrinkage, foundation movement, and subsidence. In reality, more subsidence is caused by leaking drains making the subsoil wet and plastic, but since this is happening out of sight below ground it generally gets overlooked. Trees are a more obvious target. The Building Research Station published some research in 1949 suggesting that in certain circumstances fast-growing trees such as poplar, elm and willow close to houses might cause problems, and this has been misinterpreted and thought to apply to all trees and all houses. Local authorities often prune or pollard trees because of their supposed threat to buildings, but some experts say that this is pointless, and just makes the tree extract more water in order to recover.

Ironically, cutting down a mature tree on a shrinkable clay subsoil can sometimes cause cracking where none existed before. This is because the tree, the soil and the house are existing in equilibrium, but when the tree is removed, the excess water causes the subsoil to expand, pushing the foundations upwards.

Should I prune my willow?

Is it too late, now that my willow is in bud, to have it lopped in order to safeguard my house?

You can prune your tree at any time, but whether it would stop it causing damage depends upon a number of factors, such as height of tree, distance from the house, depth of foundations, soil type, height of water table etc. Or when you say 'lopped', do you mean 'felled' – i.e. cut down completely? Again, it depends upon the circumstances; old houses often live in happy equilibrium with trees, and removing them can lead to surplus water and soil swelling. It all depends on the individual circumstances.

Damage from roots

I have a problem in that surface roots from a neighbour's tree are damaging the surface of the drive and terrace. Is the neighbour liable for this damage? Would I need their permission to root prune?

You are free to prune whatever grows on your side of the fence – as is the case with overhanging foliage – as long as the tree is not protected by a tree preservation order. But it would be a shame if your pruning damaged the tree or made it fall over. Younger trees have more chance of recovery following root pruning than mature ones. If the roots are really causing damage to a particular structure, then the best bet would be to dig a narrow trench next to the building, cutting through the roots, as deep as you can manage, and drop a sheet of thick polythene down it. Tree roots grow towards moisture, so they'll turn back when they hit an impermeable barrier.

Virginia creeper
Our house, built in 1958, has a large Virginia creeper covering the front and side walls up to roof level. I am concerned that this plant may cause damage to the mortar between the bricks, although I have seen no evidence of this so far. In general, is it a good idea to have such a plant attaching itself to the walls or would I be better advised to remove it?

I believe the term Virginia creeper can apply to more than one species. But in general this type of plant does not damage masonry, unlike ivy, which roots in the mortar joints.

New trees and new house
I have recently purchased a house on a newly built development that has a small paved and planted front garden containing three trees *Prunus avium plena* (wild cherry) each about 3 to 4m tall some 1.5 to 3m from the house front wall. As the trees develop will they pose a threat to the house foundations?

The possibility of foundation damage due to tree growth is much exaggerated. It is usually only fast-growing species such as willow and poplar which can upset the moisture balance, and then they only cause a problem on highly shrinkable clay soils. Modern houses are built with deep concrete foundations, which are often supported by piles, and are most unlikely to be affected by trees. Count yourself lucky to have a new home with established trees already in place.

WINDOWS

Most people who have double-glazed replacement windows fitted to their homes do so under the impression that they will last till the end of their days. Unfortunately this is often not the case. Sealed double-glazed units have a limited life-span, and the seal will eventually fail, resulting in misting-up between the two panes of glass. In the highest-quality installations this may not happen for thirty years. Some experts say twenty years is a reasonable life expectancy. But poorly installed windows can fail much sooner – sometimes within a year – which can come as quite a shock to people who swallowed the sales pitch that their new windows would be maintenance-free for ever.

The sales techniques used to flog double glazing are much the same as those for any other building gimmick, except that double glazing is now apparently approved by the world's leaders. The Kyoto Accord on reducing carbon emissions committed nations to cutting down fuel consumption, and the British government is amongst those concentrating on reducing home heating energy in order to reach their Kyoto targets.

The only problem is, double glazing requires energy to manufacture and install, and the pay-back period, in terms of both energy and money, is very long. Taking the average British home, and replacing its existing windows with new double-glazed units, it would probably take around a hundred years of reduced heating bills to cover the cost of the installation. So the salesman who recently persuaded a 95-year-old man that new windows would save him money in the long run surely deserves some kind of award.

In any case, there is no way that new, sealed double-glazed units are going to last a hundred years. They are doomed to eventually fail because of the way they are made. The two panes of glass are joined at the edge with a polymer compound, which by its very nature is slightly vapour-permeable – i.e. it will always allow a small amount of water vapour to enter from outside. So to keep the glass from misting up, each double-glazed unit also incorporates a desiccant – a drying agent – housed within a perforated alloy strip running around the edge. This desiccant absorbs the invading moisture and prevents misting. But eventually there will come a day when it can absorb no more. It will be saturated, and then there will be free water between the panes, which will form as mist on the glass. How long this takes depends upon the quality of the materials and work-manship.

In ideal circumstances the sealed glass unit will be mounted in drained and ventilated recesses in the window frames, positioned on special setting blocks, and with spacers at intervals around the edges to support it when the window is opened or subjected to wind loads. When this is not done – which is very often – the resulting stresses on the glass can break the seal. Units fitted into timber windows using ordinary putty or oily mastics can also fail quickly, as these dry out the sealant and cause it to crack.

When the seal is broken, any water collecting at the bottom edge of the glass will find its way through and saturate the desiccant. And once these double-glazed units mist up inside there is nothing – but nothing – that can be done to remedy it. Thousands of windows in hundreds of homes already have this problem, and the numbers are set to grow.

Do the boffins at the Department of Trade and Industry know about this – the ones who are madly promoting the use of replacement double glazing in existing buildings? I very much doubt it. (See USEFUL CONTACTS, Windows and Glazing, for independent advice on new glazing.)

Repairing damaged frames

Can you offer advice regarding dry rot in the bottom transom of window frames? I am thinking in particular of the use of fillers or even splices as a repair.

Windows are unlikely to suffer from dry rot, as this requires high humidity and so only occurs within enclosed spaces. Your windows are more likely to have been damaged by wet rot, caused by water running down the glass and getting in behind poorly maintained paint and putty. Once the transoms, bottom rails or sills have started to rot, there is really little point in trying to patch them up with filler, especially if the joints have been weakened, and it is better to engage a skilled carpenter to cut out and replace the damaged sections. Surface damage on otherwise sound sections of timber is best filled with a two-part epoxy filler such as Nickerson Chemical's Timbabuild, a specially formulated repair paste. Nickerson can put you in touch with people who do the repair work (see USEFUL CONTACTS, Timber Repairs).

New timber windows, or new sections, should be given two good coats of primer before glazing, and the paintwork should be inspected annually and, if necessary, touched up to cover any damaged areas. The life of timber windows can be greatly extended by opening them at regular intervals to release water trapped between the sashes and the frames.

Sliding sash problem

I have recently bought a flat in a Victorian house with sliding sash windows. These all work well, apart from one in the kitchen, which will not stay open. The cords on both sides are in good condition, but the window falls shut unless it is propped open with something. How can there be a fault with this one window?

The most likely cause is that the sliding sash in question has had a glass breakage, and been re-glazed with 4mm glass in place of the original 3mm. On a large pane, this can represent a significant weight difference. On a top sash, it will result in the window refusing to stay shut, and on a bottom sash, in its refusal to stay open. You should be able to spot a new pane of glass by looking at the putty and paintwork. Your options are to have the offending pane re-glazed, or to add extra weights to the sash weight hanging inside the box frame. Both are almost equally troublesome.

Secondary glazing – for sound reduction

My brother-in-law and I are seeking to fit secondary glazing to our houses for different reasons. My requirement is to bolster the soundproofing effect of my existing double-glazed units because of road noise. He wishes to improve the heat insulation of single-glazed windows on a north-east-facing wall. What are your views regarding secondary glazing for these purposes? Do you have recommendations regarding glass thickness or aluminium versus PVC?

Secondary glazing is best for noise reduction, double glazing for heat insulation. But secondary glazing will also help to keep the heat in, by cutting out draughts, and your brother-in-law may achieve good results by using a single pane of 'low-E' glass from Pilkingtons. In both cases get the thickest glass you can – 6mm if possible. Alloy frames are better than PVC as they are less obtrusive and longer lasting.

Secondary glazing – how to clean

I have bought a house with secondary glazing already fitted. We are on a busy main road, and it does seem to cut the noise down very well. The problem is cleaning it from the inside. The original outer windows and the secondary glazing are vertical sliding sashes, but whereas the original timber sashes slide past each other so that you can reach both top and bottom of each sash, the secondary glazing gets stuck in the middle. I have tried every possible combination of up and down, but just cannot reach the bottom half of the top pane.

This is a drawback that the manufacturers fail to mention when they sell secondary glazing. The only way to clean the outsides of most inner sashes is from the outside.

Windows

I have an old house (1730) which was a laundry building to a manor house. It was extensively refurbished in the 1920s and the front of the building fitted with metal windows which I think were called Crittall. These do look 'part of the house', and I have resisted the temptation to replace them. I am now about to build an extension and I would like to fit similar windows to match. Can you advise if these can be found anywhere? I realize this is a strange request, but I think the house with extension will look better with the same style of windows.

Crittall steel windows are still available from the original suppliers. Steel windows are also supplied by other members of the Steel Windows Association (see USEFUL CONTACTS, Windows and Glazing).

Double glazing – leaking vents 1

Have you encountered this before? We have moved into a lovely house in Aberdeenshire with A/S Spilka Industri (Norway) wooden-framed windows, with Jon Hole Vaksdal sealed double-glazed units in them. Recent high winds and driving rain made me realize that water can get in through the draught strips, even when they are shut. I'd like to make new curtains, but not if they are going to have to be waterproofed! Can you offer any advice?

Double glazing – leaking vents 2

I read with interest your recent reply to a letter concerning double glazing, noting that replacement double-glazed windows should always have permanent ventilation slots at the top. We had windows replaced two years ago and unfortunately when it is very windy, the wind howling through the closed vents produces a noise like elephants trumpeting! At times the noise drowns out the TV. Is there something wrong with our windows' vent system or is this inevitable with window vents? Other readers have complained of wind noise, and also of rain being blown in through window vents, even when they are shut. The idea of these 'trickle vents', as they are known, is to provide a gentle flow of ventilation, to make up for the fact that the replacement windows have probably sealed off all the natural ventilation that was occurring before. But trickle vents should always be designed to cope with the prevailing weather conditions, and if they are noisy, or leaky, then this is because they are simply poor quality and not fit for their designed purpose. Your installers have an obligation to rectify this. A soundproof trickle vent is available from Renson, and Glazpart claim to supply a weatherproof vent (see USEFUL CONTACTS, Windows and Glazing). Both can be fitted to existing windows, although this may be more than a DIY job.

Double glazing – misting up

Several years ago I had my windows replaced with double glazing. After a few years, the south-facing ones became subject to occasional, unsightly internal misting. As there was a ten-year guarantee I claimed for renewal of the windows. The insurance company claimed that the condensation was normal and therefore refused the claim. What is your opinion?

One of the great unspoken truths of sealed double-glazed units (SGUs) is that eventually they will all mist up. This is because the sealant that joins the two sheets of glass together has to be flexible, otherwise the panes would crack at the edges as the enclosed internal air space expands and contracts. But flexible sealants, by their nature, are also vapour permeable, so moist air is constantly finding its way from the outside into the air space. SGUs cope with this by incorporating a desiccant material, contained within a perforated alloy strip around the edges. Eventually this will become saturated, and then the SGUs will mist up inside. Timescale should be twenty-ish years in a perfectly made and installed window. But in poorly made ones it can be a lot less. Five months has been reported.

So, in a way, the condensation *is* 'normal', in that it will happen eventually in all windows. But I would have thought you could expect that a ten-year guarantee would reasonably cover you against misting within that time. Depends on the small print, I suppose.

Misting up

Remisting between panes. I have twice had this problem on
large windows, and have cured it by drilling a small hole
through the glass at the top and bottom of the outside pane.
This allows a bleed of comparatively cold dry air to pass
through the cavity, absorbing moisture as it does so. This cure
has so far lasted for several years without further problems.

This may prevent misting up, but the convection current
will also carry warmth away from the inner pane, thus
lowering the thermal insulation value of the SGU. In the
long term, the insulation effect will be little better than for
single glazing, but at a considerably higher cost.

Misted up

My house was extended about ten years ago, before I bought it,
with new UPVC double glazing. Several of the windows on the
south side now have condensation between the panes, which I
assume means that the airtight seal is no longer effective. Can
they be repaired? I cannot trace the builder, and the double
glazing has no manufacturer's markings.

No, it cannot be repaired. It is an inevitable consequence of
fitting sealed double-glazed units. The salesmen never mention it, though.

Replacing failed SGUs

You have warned against double glazing; but I have it – some
of it large 8ft × 6ft (2400mm × 1800mm) sheets. It seems to
last about five years and costs the earth to replace. My glaziers
say they cannot replace it with single (thermal, toughened)
glass because this cannot be fitted in the plastic frames (which
are excellent). Is there no way of doing this?

Yes, it can be done, but you need glaziers who know their

trade better than the ones you have. But then again, if your glaziers knew what they were doing, then your sealed glazed units would not be failing after five years.

Georgian look?

I'm forever replacing putty and re-painting our mock-Georgian window frames. Not only is it a constant battle against leaks, but single-glazing means pools of condensation throughout the winter. You've described the pitfalls of UPVC (both in commercial and practical terms) but my wife is adamant that she wants to enjoy the comfort of double glazing and I don't want to continue with high maintenance. Can I satisfy both of us and still maintain a 'Georgian' look?

Yes. Modern high-performance sealed glazed units can be as thin as 14mm, so this makes it possible to double-glaze your existing timber windows, or new timber replacements. It is claimed that timber windows can achieve minimal maintenance if they are painted with high-build microporous paint, which needs a rub down with steel wool and a single re-coat every seven to ten years. And this gives you the warmth of timber, which is superior to PVC-U reinforced with aluminium. You need a vented and drained dry glazing system (no putty or mastic bedding) to keep the SGUs from misting up prematurely.

Leaking leaded lights

I have a house built in the 1930s with small leaded windows. When it rains heavily, some of the windows leak badly and pools of water form on the casements or window sills causing the paintwork and the wallpaper to deteriorate. I have tried putting putty or wood filler on the horizontal sections but it is a very protracted job and I have had little or no success. Is

there a product on the market to insert between the lead and
the glass or is the answer to have new sections made?

The material to use is made to a traditional formula and is
called leadlight cement. Unfortunately it needs to be applied
while the windows are lying flat, so it will be necessary to
remove them from their frames. You should scrape out all
areas of loose old cement, and make sure that none of the
soldered joints have corroded, as these can also be points of
leakage. The new cement is then brushed into the joints, and
the excess cleaned off with whiting (chalk). For professional
restoration look under 'stained glass suppliers' or 'leaded
lights and windows' in Yellow Pages. These firms should
also supply leadlight cement; or call James Hetley, who also
supply books on leaded light work (see USEFUL CON-
TACTS, Windows and Glazing).

Patio door won't open

We have recently had new double-glazed UPVC windows and
doors installed, and quickly found that on days that are dry
and sunny the key will not move smoothly, or at all, through
the locking mechanism on the sliding patio door. On Sunday,
we experienced our first difficulty unlocking and locking the
door. It was a sunny day. On Monday it could be used, as it
was a cooler day. On Tuesday morning (overcast) the door
could be used, in the afternoon (sunny) it could not.

The company says that it will only look at the door, which
they say we may be using improperly (it's only a door, not a
space rocket!), provided we settle our balance. The work would
then be done under the warranty.

It is clearly a problem with thermal expansion. They have
not left sufficient clearance to allow for this. There should
be a minimum of 5 to 6mm all round if the door is white, 7

to 8mm if it is brown (dark colours absorb more heat from
the sun and so expand more). You should not pay the
company any more money until they have fixed the problem, and make it clear, in writing, that you will pay them
the outstanding money not later than one calendar month
after the work has been completed satisfactorily. This is the
normal legal position under the Sale and Supply of Goods
Act (1994) – it includes installed goods – which states that
you are entitled that products be 'satisfactory' (to British
Standards, not yours), and free from 'major and minor'
defects. You are under no obligation to accept less.

Warranties are usually worthless, and are honoured as
and when the company feels like it or if enough fuss is
kicked up.

Chances are that your problem is multiple, i.e. the lock
clearances are insufficient for the plastic's expansion. So it
binds. It's a simple adjustment but needs someone who
knows the mechanisms to do it and who will adjust while
leaving the door secure. In addition, the rollers can be
adjusted up and down which can compensate for any lack
of adjustment in the lock.

Under recent case law since the Construction Act (1996)
and the new Civil Procedure Rules became effective, you
have to give the company at least two chances to rectify.
If they've already had two shots, you can call in anyone,
pay them and charge the cost to the supplying company
('contra', it's called).

Double glazing – escape dangers
I was horrified recently to read about a couple trapped in their
bedroom by a house fire. The couple had to open a tiny window
and drop their baby into the arms of a rescuer. They themselves

were unable to break the double glazing and were only rescued after receiving dreadful burns.

My husband has always insisted that any house we have lived in has had at least one, fully opening, 'escape' window in each room. We are mystified as to why the Building Regulations allow a house to have all its windows replaced by double-glazed units, with only one or two small opening sections.

Apparently UPVC windows are cheaper in the non-opening version, but would appear to pose a danger to safety. The ones with 'leaded' features must be even more difficult to break in an emergency. People may assume that non-openers are more burglarproof, or safer in preventing small children from falling out, but a lock with nearby key covers this. (A determined burglar will simply remove an entire UPVC window frame anyway, not an option during an emergency!)

Please could you comment on this – how is it possible that lack of an escape route is not covered by some sort of regulation?

I agree this is an unheralded danger, and yet another disadvantage of double glazing. The trouble is, the Building Regulations do not cover replacement windows, nor most other refurbishment work. There have been several attempts to change this, including private members' bills in the Commons, but all to no avail.

(The new 'Part L' introduced in 2002 will cover replacement windows for the first time, but for the purpose of thermal insulation performance.)

WOODWORM AND
WOOD ROT

Regular news reports about the health problems suffered by Gulf War and Balkans War veterans are timely reminders of the dangers posed by exposure to toxic chemicals. Years after the events, there is disagreement over the causes of ill health suffered by returning troops, but the finger of suspicion points at the many chemicals encountered in the course of modern warfare. Unfortunately, some of those chemicals are used by the building trade as well.

Worryingly, chemicals in the house can pose risks even greater than when they are encountered on the battlefield. For one thing, their effects can be longer-lasting because they are trapped within the building, and for another, occupants can be exposed to them for longer periods. Young children and retired older people especially can be at high risk, as they often spend eighteen hours or more per day indoors.

But perhaps the most significant finding of the research into so-called Gulf War syndrome is the fact that combinations of two or more chemicals can be more damaging to health than the sum of each individual substance. For example, one researcher fed chickens with 'safe' doses of the insecticide permethrin (used to de-louse Iraqi prisoners) and the common insect repellent DEET (diethyl toluamide), and found that they became ill and died. Each chemical on its own had no significant impact; it was the cocktail effect that did the damage.

These findings deserve wider publicity, because permethrin has been sprayed in millions of British homes as a woodworm treatment, and it is also present in new clothes, carpets and soft furnishings, to prevent moth damage. Meanwhile, DEET is the active ingredient in insect repellents sold over-the-counter in pharmacists. So anyone using an insect repellent and living in a house sprayed with permethrin timber treatment could be exposing themselves to the same chemical combination as the Gulf War veterans. Not to mention those unfortunate chickens.

The timber treatment industry has put much effort into persuading the public that its products are risk-free. It defended its use of the deadly organochlorines DDT and dieldrin until they were finally banned in the 1980s, and then continued to spray homes with the organochlorine lindane until it, too, was withdrawn from use. It then put its weight behind permethrin, and I was even told on an industry training course in 1994 that it was quite safe to drink a pint glass of this stuff. Strange, then, if it is so safe, that the industry is now moving away from permethrin and switching to boron, the latest 'safe' pesticide.

But like its predecessors, boron is a poison. If it wasn't, then it would not be used to kill insects and fungi. And, like its predecessors, boron has never been tested for the effects it has on health when it is combined with other chemicals. So if you buy a house which has been previously sprayed with permethrin, and your surveyor advises you to have the empty woodworm holes sprayed again with boron, what effects will this chemical combination have on your health? Nobody knows, because the research has never been done.

In any case, most woodworm holes are the harmless relics of insects who departed many years ago, and spraying them is unnecessary. But when separate scientific research has suggested that Parkinson's disease may be linked to a cocktail of two readily available gardening pesticides, isn't it time for some serious research on the combination effects of all these common chemicals?

Woodworm and wood rot

I am an antique dealer and a customer recently brought back a set of chairs I sold her four years ago, which had developed woodworm holes in the seats, although I had treated them at the time. Is it necessary to treat woodworm on a regular annual basis?

Certainly not. Chemical wood treatments are usually guaranteed for twenty-five or thirty years, and you could be doubling the health risks if you apply one kind of chemical on top of another. The chairs must have been stored in damp conditions, and the woodworm eggs or larvae would have been in the timber before you treated it. Surface-applied insecticides do not penetrate deep enough to kill woodworm that are already active. Their life cycle is commonly three to five years, and the flight holes indicate their escape route, showing that they have now departed. If the chairs are kept in a normal dry, ventilated home, they should now be too dry to support any fresh infestation.

Woodworm in old furniture

Ten days ago I noticed that a chair from the 1860s, which I bought a few years ago, had new woodworm holes – i.e. the sawdust sort of dust coming out of new-looking holes. The holes are in the legs, which are made of beech. I treated the whole chair with an anti-woodworm treatment. Now I am wondering whether I need to treat the house timber (house built in 1880s) and the other furniture (mainly oak). I would hate to do that, partly because of the pollution, partly because I am asthmatic and just doing the one chair affected my breathing for a few days. On the other hand, everyone tells me that eventually the worms will eat half my house! I take great comfort from what you say about the worms preferring sap-wood, but do wonder why they invaded the chair in the first place – it is definitely not a new chair. I note that I live in an area where there are lots of garden trees, and the window is often open, so any beetle wanting sapwood would have no trouble finding it. What do I do, please?

Woodworm is not infectious, and there is no reason why it would spread from one piece of furniture to another or to house timbers. Each infestation results from the female adult beetle laying eggs in an environment that she thinks will be suitable for her offspring – i.e. moist nutritious wood. If you have moist nutritious wood anywhere in your house then adult female beetles – which are flying around everywhere between April and July – will lay eggs in it. If the wood is dry, as it will be if you live in a normal heated ventilated house, then they won't. The infestation in the beech chair probably happened five years ago when it was stored in damp conditions. Three to five years is the life cycle of the insects. Once this generation has hatched out and flown then that will probably be the end of it – regardless of how many chemicals you spray around the place.

Rot in furniture

I recently purchased a cradle c.1800. It has some dry rot. I cleaned the piece with Murphy's Oil Soap. The cradle will never be exposed to moisture. Should I worry about the spread of dry rot? I have been told that you can purchase a product to spray on which will harden the area which is soft.

It cannot possibly be dry rot. Maybe a few old woodworm holes? Whatever caused the damage, it wasn't dry rot. And whatever it was will not spread to the rest of the house. If I were you, I'd ask advice from a specialist antique furniture expert before doing anything. You don't want to risk doing anything that would spoil it.

Dry rot?

I have recently discovered that I have dry rot in my house, and I have found your information to be very useful. I am now wiser and ready to invite someone into my house to give me a quote for sorting/fixing this problem – but who? Where do I start – carpenter, plasterer, general builder, dry rot specialist – who would you suggest as the best starting place?

The first step is to ensure that the diagnosis of dry rot is accurate. There is nothing 'dry' about dry rot. This is a fungus which will only live on very wet wood, and in very humid conditions. If you have come across some decayed timber which is now dry, then it was probably left by a previous case of wet rot, caused by a water leak that has now been repaired. If you really have dry rot in the house, then it must be caused by a rainwater or plumbing leak, and the correct course of action is to locate the leak and have it repaired, by a builder or plumber as appropriate. A 'dry rot specialist' will be a commission-paid representative of a company that sells chemical timber treatments – and he will automatically try to sell you chemical remedies. If you feel that you still need independent, non-chemical, advice see USEFUL CONTACTS, Dampness and Timber Surveyors.

We have a three-storey Victorian house and we have dry rot in one ground-floor room, and there is evidence of woodworm throughout the ground floor, which I do not believe is active. I have been advised that the walls and floors need treating, and I am reluctant to do this because a ninety-year-old lady lives on the ground floor. Are there any chemicals that are safe to use with her living in the building, or is there another remedy that would stop the spread of infestation, so that treatment could be carried out at a later date?

I follow the advice given by the Health and Safety Executive and the Building Research Establishment that timber infestation should be dealt with by correct building practices – i.e. repairing sources of moisture ingress and drying timber out by normal heating and ventilation. Fungi and insects only attack damp wood. My personal view is that there is no such thing as a 'safe' pesticide, especially in cases involving the very young or the very old (see also HAZARDS, Timber Treatment Chemicals).

Dry rot 1

I have what a few builders call 'a serious problem, mate'. The problem is I have dry rot on one of my walls (outside wall with a gully). The rot has eaten away my stairs and strands appear to be coming from between the brickwork (I hacked off all the old plaster and mortar) over a certain area. I have taken away all the wood that is contaminated and believe that I have found where the damp is coming from, but after reading your article I wonder now will it really 'cost a packet' to fix. My problem now is what to do with the wall; should I plasterboard it up or get it rendered and plastered?

The key things are to stop the source of moisture ingress – which you appear to have done – and allow the affected area to dry out and 'breathe'. To this end cement-and-sand renders are usually a bad idea, especially if the house is old and the original plaster was lime-and-sand. Similarly, plasterboarding the area would be a bad idea, as any future problems would be hidden from view. The ideal would be lime plaster to match the original, but if you can't find anyone to do traditional lime-and-sand plastering then something like Tilcon's Limelite is a good second choice. Avoid gypsum finishing plasters as they do not perform well in damp conditions.

Dry rot 2

We have what look like roots growing up the living-room walls from the skirting boards, coming from under the floor. It is in the plaster as well and we have had two quotes, one for £600 and the other for £2,715 for the treatment of what they said was dry rot. There is no way we can afford this sort of money, but we need it sorting as we have a small child with asthma. Is there any way of treating this ourselves?

Yes. Locate and rectify the source of the incoming water, and improve ventilation. It sounds as though the problem is coming from below a suspended timber ground floor, and the usual problem in this case is raised outside ground levels, leaking rainwater downpipes and/or blocked soakaways, and blocked sub-floor ventilation. Fix these, and there will be no need for expensive chemical treatment or replastering – just making good damaged areas of timber and plaster.

Regarding the asthma, I would say the dry rot is probably a lot less of a risk than the toxic chemicals that the treatment companies undoubtedly want to use.

Senseless diagnoses

Your views on timber treatment and damp-proofing are very sound. This racket is fuelled by the mortgage companies more than anyone else. I've just bought a 400-year-old property. The mortgage was partly dependent on timber treatment to ground, first floor and loft space. Cost, £425 plus VAT. Now, the house has been standing for four hundred years, there's no evidence of rot or infestation. Doesn't make much sense to me.

The only sense comes in the form of the commission for the timber treatment 'surveyors' (i.e. salesmen) who tell people that this unnecessary and dangerous chemical treatment is required.

Death-watch beetle?

I have found that my 100-year-old Victorian terraced house has death-watch beetle, judging from the ticking coming from different locations in its pitch-pine timberwork. I'd greatly value your advice

Death-watch beetle prefer hardwoods, especially oak, so it would be unusual to find them in pitch pine. Are you sure it couldn't be expansion/contraction noises you are hearing?

Woodworm holes

I live in a converted barn and have just discovered live (fresh powder on the pointing) woodworm in one piece of timber. This single timber sits over a stone fireplace and was placed there about eight years ago. There is no other wood within 20ft (6m) and the timber is surrounded by stone. I believe the timber was placed over the top of the stone fireplace principally for decorative effect and possibly as a lintel for the fireplace itself. Can woodworm spread without contact with other wood?

If so, can I treat this single piece (DIY) by buying a product to spray or paint on to the surface? Unfortunately the timber cannot be removed from the fireplace without damaging surrounding brickwork.

If you have damp sapwood in the barn, then sooner or later wood-boring insects may decide to live in it. I guess your barn is probably in a country area, so the adult beetles will be able to fly in through the window and lay their eggs. The larvae that are in the fireplace lintel will be happy where they are, and have no reason to migrate to another piece of wood. If the lintel was made from a new piece of timber, then it is likely that the eggs were laid in it while it was still green and fresh, and provided the barn is heated and ventilated to normal standards, then it will probably be drying down to a level at which it will not support further infestations. In making your decision whether to go for chemical treatment, you should remember that the insect damage is probably only in the sapwood near the surface, and is very unlikely to damage the timber to the extent that it weakens it.

If you do decide that you must use an insecticide, then, apart from the health dangers, you should also appreciate that surface-applied pesticides only penetrate 1 or 2mm into the wood, and any recently laid eggs or existing larvae will be unaffected. So adult insects could continue to emerge for several years after treatment. There is also some evidence that emerging adult beetles are able to mate and lay their eggs down existing flight holes, thus starting off a new life cycle unaffected by the chemical treatment. This is probably why buildings that have been sprayed continue to have active infestations. So, since pesticide treatment is not even certain to be effective, there is really no alternative to making sure that the timbers are dried out and kept dry.

If it was my house then I would put up with the holes. They won't do you any harm, whereas the chemical treatments might.

Timber treatment – safe in kitchen?

I need woodworm treatment for a kitchen. Can you suggest a treatment that is safe to use in a kitchen environment? I have been told that certain products are not allowed where there is food preparation. Could you advise?

In my opinion no insecticide could be regarded as 'safe'. There is a borate product which is advertised as being completely benign, and suitable for kitchen areas, but if that is the case then how does it kill insects? If you really have active woodworm in your kitchen (and not just old flight holes in the floorboards), then the way to get rid of it is by normal heating and ventilation. If wood is dry then nothing can live in it. An additional measure is to use an ultraviolet 'insectocutor' to kill any adult beetles which emerge in the spring. This is a useful device to have in a kitchen anyway.

Woodworm – self treated

I would be grateful if you could advise me on our woodworm problem, although I can probably guess what your reply would be to my question. Also, after giving myself a headache for a month after painting some woodwork with Cuprinol woodworm solution in our last house, maybe I should just forget about the problem. We have recently moved into a new house, and are in the process of ripping out an old shower room and refurbishing. Over a two-day period last week I spotted five furniture beetles, three in the new shower tray and two on the wall of the adjoining bathroom. Quite frankly I didn't know if

I should panic and call in the pest control people, or relax because they were probably just visiting. Though what they are doing flying around in November is a mystery to me. In the process of refurbishing we have had many of the floorboards up on the first floor, and the joists/floorboards that we have seen looked sound. I have checked the timbers in the roof and the cellars and there was no sign of woodworm there. We live in a wooded area, so I guess they could have been blown in during the bad weather. I just have this niggling doubt that because there were so many beetles seen at the same time in such a small area, the little blighters must be nibbling away in some hidden spot. Any suggestions?

More likely to be Lyctus powderpost beetle, which has a longer adult season than furniture beetle. Dry out the timber in the old shower room and nothing will eat it. Save yourself another headache.

Dry rot

Can you advise me on how to treat dry rot in the roof of an old house, without using 'specialists'. The roof has been repaired and there is no more ingress of water.

It would be unusual to find dry rot in a roof space, since it needs a large amount of water and high humidity in unventilated conditions. Roof spaces are usually too warm and draughty for it. If the leaks have been fixed, and there is good ventilation, then nothing further should need to be done, apart from repairing any badly damaged timbers.

White mould

I have a house built c.1815 and one timber between the main trusses has become saturated with water leaking through the roof and has a white mould growth. The leaking roof has now been repaired and there should be no further ingress of water. What course of action do you recommend?

You shouldn't have to do anything else. Maybe brush off the mould growth and keep an eye on things to make sure it does not return.

Dodgy diagnosis

Are there any tradesmen you would recommend in the south Yorkshire area, who share your views about woodworm and rising damp? We are in the process of buying an old property, and after a survey by what we thought were reputable traders, we have been presented with an estimate for £3,000, for work that we believe has already been done. The estimate for damp was based on meter readings. Throughout the estimate comments regarding woodworm say it may be from old infestation and yet they still advise the treatment, but we understand the property was treated fifteen years ago.

You don't need a tradesman. You need a survey by an independent expert, who will not try to sell you anything (see USEFUL CONTACTS, Dampness and Timber Surveyors).

Health dangers

Can you suggest any woodworm fluid for an attic which has worm holes, that may have woodworm in? My mother is about to move out of the house and we shall have four weeks for modernizing, fixing etc. We would be concerned for our children's health particularly. We have installed modern Velux windows and need to protect these from any live woodworm. What would you suggest?

I cannot recommend any woodworm fluids. They are all

nerve poisons (see HAZARDS). Your 'worm holes' are probably a hundred years old. They are actually 'flight holes' of the adult beetles *leaving* the wood. There is no justification for using insecticides unless you have definitive evidence that there is a continuing active infestation, and that this cannot be dealt with by normal construction methods, i.e. central heating and ventilation. There is no way that your new Velux windows are going to be attacked by wood-boring insects – the timber in them is kiln-dried and sealed with a water-based varnish.

USEFUL CONTACTS

The following is a list of the various bodies and organizations mentioned in the book. Their inclusion does not mean that I endorse or recommend them, but they may be worth contacting for advice, or as a starting point in your investigation of a particular topic or problem.

Architects and Surveyors

Readers who have read my grumbles about surveyors and architects are sometimes confused when I then recommend that you engage one to plan and supervise your building work. But the fact is that, while there are many ignorant and incompetent building professionals, there are also some very good ones. The problem is sorting the wheat from the chaff. A good first point of contact is to call the Architecture and Surveying Institute and ask for a list of members in your area from their practice register.

Architecture and Surveying Institute 01249 444505
www.asi.org.uk

Building Organizatons
Chartered Institute of Building (Chartered Building Company Scheme) 01344 630700

National Federation of Builders 020 76085150
www.builders.org.uk

Building Societies

Ecology Building Society 0845 6745566
www.ecology.co.uk

Conservation

Society for the Protection of Ancient Buildings (SPAB)
020 73771644
www.spab.org.uk

Construction Literature

Building Research Establishment publications can be
ordered online from www.brebookshop.com or by phone
from CRC Ltd 020 75056622

Construction Industry Publications 0121 7228200
(supply the JCT Contract for the homeowner/occupier for
£10.99 including p+p).

Dampness

Cavity trays
Cavity Trays 01935 474769
www.cavitytrays.com

Manthorpe Building Products 01773 743555
www.manthorpe.co.uk

Drained membrane systems
Platon from Triton Chemicals Ltd 020 83103929

Newlath from John Newton & Co 020 72371217

Dampness and Timber Surveyors

Abbey Independent Surveys 01664 840673
abbeyis@talk21.com

Dampness Diagnosis Consultancy 020 86573750,
david.hewett@btinternet.com

Hutton and Rostron 01483 203221
www.handr.co.uk

Electrics

Honda generators 0845 2008000 or www.honda.co.uk,
through which you can contact a local supplier.

NICEIC 020 75642323
www.niceic.org.uk

Extractor Fans

Ferrob (Sensortronic humidity-switched fan) 01635 299266
www.ferrob.co.uk

Fireplaces and Chimneys

Chimney Balloon Company 01252 319325

A good (American) source of advice on fireplace problems
is Hearth News – www.hearth.com

Gas

CORGI 08705 168111
www.corgi-gas.com/index.asp

Hazards

National Federation of Master Steeplejacks and Lightning
Conductor Engineers 0115 9558818

Radon gas protection
Proctor Group Ltd 01250 872261

Household Pests/Animals

Bat Conservation Trust 020 76272629
www.bats.org.uk
(send SAE to 15 Cloisters House, 8 Battersea Park Road,
London SW8 4BG)

Bird repellers/flyscreens
Woodland Properties 01344 886459

Pest control
Merlin Pest Control Services 01491 652111
e-mail merlins@mail.com
www.merlinpestservices.co.uk

Loft Conversions

The Loft Shop 0870 6040404
www.loftshop.co.uk

Painting and Decorating

British Coatings Federation (lead paint advice) 01372
360660

Dulux Self Decorator Service 0840 7697668
www.duluxdecorator.co.uk

Paint removal: Stonehealth 01672 511515
www.stonehealth.com

Paving

Grass paving blocks
Hauraton 01923 285601

Hoofmark Ltd 0191 5845566

Pesticides Victim Support

Pesticides Action Network
Alison Craig 020 72748895
www.gn.apc.org

Plastering

British Gypsum 0990 456123
www.british-gypsum.bpb.co.uk

Lime Mortars and Plasters
The Building Limes Forum, School House, Rocks Road,
Charlestown, Fife KY11 3EN. Send SAE for a list of
suppliers, enthusiasts and tradesmen.

Plumbing and Heating

Betz Dearborn 0151 4209595
www.betzdearborn.com

Brannan pipe thermometers 01946 816600
sales@brannan.co.uk
www.brannan.co.uk

British Water publish ten free fact sheets on all aspects of
domestic water treatment on www.britishwater.org or call
020 79574554

Dualstream water-pressurized storage systems
01394 386699

Electroheat electric flow boilers 01256 363417

Fernox Helpline 01799 550811
www.fernox.com

Hudevad Radiators 01932 237714

The Institute of Plumbing 01708 472791
www.plumbers.org.uk

Plumbworld (online discount plumbing and heating
supplies)
www.plumbworld.co.uk

Renubath 01285 656624
www.renubath.co.uk

RS Components 01536 444222
www1.rswww.com

Thermecon oil boilers 01394 386699
www.thermecon.co.uk/thermecon

Rainwater Collection/Recycling

Aquarius Water Engineering 01704 878786
www.aquarius-uk.com

Tank Exchange 01226 206157

Roofers

Flat Roofing Alliance 01444 440027
www.fra.org.uk/home.html

National Council of Master Thatchers' Associations 0700 0781909

National Federation of Roofing Contractors 020 74360387 info@nfrc.co.uk

Self-Build

The Housebuilder's Bible by Mark Brinkley
Direct from 01223 290230, or e-mail
mark@brinkley.demon.co.uk

National Self-Build Homes Show 020 78378727

Soundproofing

Soundproofing leaflet available from BRE website
www.bre.co.uk/acoustics/soundins_homes.pdf

Timber Floors

Enfield Timber Company 020 88041800

Victorian Wood Works 020 85341000
www.victorianwoodworks.co.uk

Timber Repairs

Nickerson Chemicals ('Timbabuild' timber repair system)
01636 636369

Trees

The Tree Care Company 01234 376254 Michael Brightman
treecare88@hotmail.com

Windows and Glazing

Crittall Windows 01376 324106
www.crittall-windows.co.uk

Glazpart (window vents) 01295 264533

James Hetley (leaded light repairs) 020 77802344

Jay Webb (Fenestration Associates, window surveyors)
01676 523583
www.fenestrationassociates.com

Renson (window vents) 01622 685658

Steel Windows Association 020 7637 3571

INDEX